THE NEW ART OF AUTOBIOGRAPHY

THE NEW ART OF AUTOBIOGRAPHY

An Essay on the *Life of Giambattista Vico Written by Himself*

DONALD PHILLIP VERENE

CLARENDON PRESS · OXFORD
1991

Oxford University Press, Walton Street, Oxford OX2 6DP
Oxford New York Toronto
Delhi Bombay Calcutta Madras Karachi
Petaling Jaya Singapore Hong Kong Tokyo
Nairobi Dar es Salaam Cape Town
Melbourne Auckland
and associated companies in
Berlin Ibadan

Oxford is a trade mark of Oxford University Press

Published in the United States
by Oxford University Press, New York

British Library Cataloguing in Publication Data
Data Available
ISBN 0–19–823900–9

Library of Congress Cataloging in Publication Data
Verene, Donald Phillip, 1937–
The new art of autobiography : an essay on the Life of
Giambattista Vico, written by himself / Donald Phillip Verene.
p. cm.
Includes bibliographical references (p.   ) and index.
1. Vico, Giambattista, 1668–1744. Autobiografia.
2. Philosophers—Italy—Biography.   3. Vico, Giambattista,
1668–1744—Contributions in concept of autobiography.
4. Autobiography.   I. Title.
B3583.V53A33 1991 195—dc20 90–27567
ISBN 0–19–823900–9

Typeset by Cambridge Composing (UK) Ltd
Printed and bound in
Great Britain by Bookcraft (Bath) Ltd,
Midsomer Norton, Avon

To Molly
        a flower of the mountain
                                Ulysses
and Christopher
        what the heart is and what it feels
        A Portrait of the Artist as a Young Man

Preface

Vico published his autobiography somewhat unwillingly in Venice in 1728. He had been invited to write it by some of the leaders of Venetian and Italian intellectual life, and it was to be part of an original and important volume of lives of some of the most outstanding thinkers of Italy written by themselves. This volume of lives did not materialize, and Vico's manuscript instead appeared in the first issue of a new journal, among articles on the birth of vipers and a history of the city of Prato. The promoters of the volume published Vico's text in this journal in the hope it might encourage others to respond to their invitation and provide a model to follow.

Three years later, in 1731, just after he had published the second edition of the *New Science*, Vico wrote a continuation of his auto-biography. This was in response to a second invitation, this time for the preparation of a volume of lives of the members of one of Italy's most distinguished academies—the Academy of the Assorditi of Urbino. This volume too failed to appear and Vico's manuscript remained unpublished until the early part of the nineteenth century. The work that appeared in article form in Venice, together with his continuation, has come to be called Vico's *Autobiography*.

When I wrote *Vico's Science of Imagination* (1981), I employed Vico's *Autobiography* as other commentators have, as an auxiliary text, citing passages to verify and enlarge my interpretation of Vico's *New Science* and other philosophical works. I understood the *Autobiography* as just that, the story of Vico's life written by himself, requiring according to its various modern editors some corrections of dates, sequence, and occasionally fact. In the past ten years, since beginning to write the earlier work, I have come to realize that the *Autobiography* is Vico's most undervalued work. No one has written a book-length commentary on it in any language. No interpretation of it as a philosophical work exists.

There are scholarly studies of Vico's life and writings such as H. P. Adams's *The Life and Writings of Giambattista Vico* (1935) and Angela Maria Jacobelli Isoldi's *G. B. Vico: La vita e le opere* (1960) that are based on the *Autobiography* and the research on

Vico's career. Adams regards Vico's *Autobiography* as 'certainly one of the great autobiographies of the world'. There is also a fictionalized portrait of Vico's life: Anna Vittoria Arace d'Amàro, *L'adamantina rocca di G. B. Vico* (1986).

The great independent research into the details of Vico's life and career was done by Croce and Nicolini, who also established the definitive 'Laterza' edition of the *Autobiografia* (2nd edn., 1929). There are various essays of Croce, which appeared in volumes of *La Critica* and elsewhere, and there is his essay on Vico's life and character in the appendix to his *Philosophy of Giambattista Vico*, translated into English by R. G. Collingwood in 1913. There are Nicolini's many precise and far-reaching researches into the facts of Vico's life, notably his *La giovinezza di Giambattista Vico* (1932) and his many notes to the *Autobiography*, most fully elaborated in his one-volume edition of Vico's *Opere* (1953). It is unlikely anyone will ever equal Nicolini's great learning in this area, yet these studies and notes are not commentaries except in the historical sense of supplying the context of Vico's views and references and adding details to the text.

Attention has been given to the rhetorical principles employed in the *Autobiography* and to the history of its publication. Mario Fubini's *Stile e umanità di Giambattista Vico* (2nd edn., 1965) is relevant to reading the *Autobiography*, as is his introduction to his much reprinted edition of it. Andrea Battistini's *La degnità della retorica* (1975) contains a long essay on the *Autobiography* as a rhetorical text. Gustavo Costa's article on the *Autobiography* in the *Italian Quarterly* (1980) explains its origin and character within the tension between Italian and French letters of the period. The contributors to C. De Michelis and G. Pizzamiglio, eds., *Vico e Venezia* (1982), the volume of selected proceedings from the international conference held in 1978 to mark the 250th anniversary of the publication of the *Autobiography* in Venice, offer up-to-date accounts of the historical details of the publication of the *Autobiography*.

Despite the high quality of this scholarship, there is not a great quantity of work on Vico's *Autobiography*. Relative to other areas of Vico studies, the *Autobiography* is Vico's forgotten work: read by every Vico scholar, interpreted by few, and analysed as a part of his philosophy by none. Vico's *Autobiography* has not been misinterpreted: it has hardly been interpreted at all. The details of its publication, the facts of Vico's life independent of his narration of them, and the rhetorical elements of the composition of the work have all been soundly explored. But what of its philosophical meaning?

Vico produced the two portions of his *Autobiography* while writing his first and second versions of the *New Science*. Is the *Autobiography* an application of the principles of the *New Science* to the life of its author, or is it simply the story of his life? Is the life-narrative of the philosopher part of his philosophy itself, a form of its verification? Beyond its role in his philosophy, does Vico's unique work have implications for understanding the art of autobiography itself? These and related questions are the subject of this book.

I have called this book an 'essay' in its subtitle because my intention is to open up a discussion on a new topic, not to close one off with a treatise. What follows is intended as an invitation to the reader to form his own reading. If this essay is helpful to readers of Vico to see aspects of the *Autobiography* they might otherwise miss, then it has served its purpose. To this end the reader will soon note that I have employed a method of repetition. Throughout this interpretation I have repeated and reconnected points and quotations from Vico's *Autobiography* with other parts of his thought and the historical material generally. I have done this because I find that the details of Vico's career, although clear in themselves, are often quite elusive and easily forgotten from one place to the next. For some readers this may prove more repetition than is necessary, but for others less familiar with Vico, I hope it may be a welcome procedure.

There is no question but that Vico is the founder of a new art of autobiography. He is the first original thinker to apply the genetic method to comprehend the development of his own thought and writings. Vico is traditionally regarded as the founder of the philosophy of history. He is also, as Cassirer calls him in the *Problem of Knowledge* (1950), the 'real discoverer of the myth', the founder of modern philosophy of mythology. To these should be added his role as the originator of a form of autobiography. Vico's *Autobiography* is not just one work in the history of the writing of autobiography; it holds a special place in this history that has been only vaguely recognized by work in this area.

That all philosophies are in some sense autobiographical has been a topic since the nineteenth century. It is a topic in which there is a renewed interest of late that is to some extent connected to the study of the history of philosophy and the interest in theories of the reading of literary and philosophical texts. The broader aim of this book, beyond a contribution to Vico literature, is to raise some systematic questions about autobiography and philosophy, at least indirectly. Others have approached this topic as such; I wish to do so through a particular example, the first instance of philosophical autobiography in its modern form.

As I enter into the specific exposition of Vico's text and its background, larger issues of the bearing of these details on ethical, epistemological, and metaphysical issues are not far from my mind. My primary concern is always to interpret Vico's text, but as a part of this activity my aim is also to keep before the reader and myself the question of the philosophical significance and truth of Vico's work. In fact, I do not see how in writing about the meaning of a philosophical work these two dimensions can ever be divided.

Throughout this essay I have followed the general tradition in Vico studies of referring to Vico's work as his *Autobiography*. Vico's own title for his work was the *Life of Giambattista Vico Written by Himself*, the term 'autobiography' not yet having come into use in Italian or other modern languages. References throughout are to the Fisch and Bergin English translation and to Fubini's Italian edition. The Fisch and Bergin translation, the only English translation, is to be recommended for its accuracy and also for Fisch's incomparable introduction, the most informative short work on Vico in any language. Their translation of the *Autobiography* is a companion piece to their translation of Vico's *New Science*, both of which were originally published in the 1940s.

I have used Fubini's Italian edition of the *Autobiografia* instead of the older Laterza edition upon which it is based simply because of its greater availability as a single-volume edition of the work. The Laterza edition must be consulted for its annotations, many but not all of which are reflected in the footnotes of the Fisch and Bergin translation. In quoting passages from the *Autobiography* I have often modified them to my own translation to convey a further meaning or nuance of the original important to my particular point. When my modification differs fairly strongly from that of Fisch and Bergin, or where I disagree, I have noted it.

This work was written while on a sabbatical year spent, among

Preface

other places, in Italy and Oxford in 1988–9. Part of this leave was supported by a grant from the Emory University Research Committee. I thank the Committee and Emory College for their support of my project. I thank the Graduate School of Arts and Sciences and the Emory administration for their strong, continuing support of the Institute for Vico Studies.

I wish to thank Pembroke College, Oxford, for their generosity in appointing me Visiting Fellow for Michaelmas Term 1988 and in particular to extend my thanks to Z. A. Pelczynski for so kindly acting as my host.

Many persons have been of help and encouragement in my pursuit of Vico studies and Vichian themes over a long period of time. Primary among these are Giorgio Tagliacozzo and Ernesto Grassi, to whom I offer heartfelt thanks. I wish to thank my colleagues at Emory and other universities who generously read the manuscript and offered helpful comments and reactions: Richard Bellamy, James Gouinlock, Bruce Haddock, Ann Hartle, Ben Kleindorfer, Donald Livingston, David Lovekin, James Martin, Carl Page, Donald Rutherford, and Stefano Tani.

Finally, I express my thanks to Molly Black Verene who has been the constant witness and auditor to the odyssey and autobiography of this work. Not Jove, but Thalia is the source of whatever wisdom is spoken here.

D.P.V.
Atlanta 1990

Contents

Note

Citations of Vico's autobiography are from *The Autobiography of Giambattista Vico*, trans. M. H. Fisch and T. G. Bergin (Ithaca, NY: Cornell University Press, 1983) and *Autobiografia, seguita da una scelta di lettere, orazioni e rime*, ed. M. Fubini (Turin: Einaudi, 1970). Page numbers of these two editions are given throughout the text, with those of the English translation first and those of the Italian edition second, e.g. (111/3).

Citations of Vico's *New Science* are from *The New Science of Giambattista Vico*, trans. T. G. Bergin and M. H. Fisch (Ithaca, NY: Cornell University Press, 1984) and *La scienza nuova seconda*, ed. F. Nicolini, *Opere di G. B. Vico*, vol. iv (Bari: Laterza, 1942). The paragraph enumerations common to the Laterza and Cornell editions are given throughout the text, e.g. (348–9).

For a righteous man falls seven times and rises again; but the wicked are overthrown by calamity.

Proverbs 24: 16

1

Introduction: Vico's Life

In 1731 in his continuation of his autobiography, reflecting on the original version written and published several years earlier, Vico wrote: 'And, as may be seen, he wrote it as a philosopher, meditating the causes, natural and moral, and the occasions of fortune.' He says, referring to himself in the third person, that this text of the first portion of his life, that runs from his childhood and early education to his discovery of the *New Science*, confirms that his *vita letteraria*, his life of letters, 'had to be such as it was and not otherwise' (182/71).[1] Vico conceived his life as having a providential structure. The 'occasions of fortune' were never results of blind chance, like the motions of Epicurus' atoms, nor were they governed by a Stoic deaf necessity, an inexorable chain of causes and effects.

In his *New Science* (1730), discussing the method by which the truth of its principles of human history can be established, Vico invites the reader to consider whether the causes of the life of nations in their rise, maturity, and fall are fewer than or different from those he has given. This meditation, Vico says, will produce in the reader's mortal body a divine pleasure and provide a proper and continual proof of this science. This new science of the common nature of nations, Vico says, must be a demonstration of what 'providence has wrought in history' (342–5).[2] Vico's life of nations and Vico's own life of letters share the principle that what they each describe had to be such and not otherwise; the events narrated in both are products of neither chance nor fate. How the events of nations are governed constitutes a 'rational civil theology of divine providence', as Vico puts it in the *New Science* (342), an

---

[1] *The Autobiography of Giambattista Vico*, trans. M. H. Fisch and T. G. Bergin (Ithaca, NY: Cornell University Press, 1983); *Autobiografia, seguita da una scelta di lettere, orazioni e rime*, ed. M. Fubini (Turin: Einaudi, 1970).
[2] *The New Science of Giambattista Vico*, trans. T. G. Bergin and M. H. Fisch (Ithaca, NY: Cornell University Press, 1984); *La scienza nuova seconda*, ed. F. Nicolini, *Opere di G. B. Vico*, vol. iv (Bari: Laterza, 1942).

idea that falls naturally to a humanist reader of Plato, who, as Vico says in the *Autobiography,* is one of the authors he proposed always to have before him.

Vico's conception of his own life as a provident, ordered course suggests that to the philosophical conception of a rational civil theology of collective historical life there exists an implicit analogue at the level of Vico's conception of his individual life, allowing him to write it, as he says, 'as a philosopher'.

Vico does not call his work an autobiography because the word does not come into the Italian dictionaries until the 1820s, one hundred years after the writing of Vico's work.[3] The term has no general use in Italian, English, or other modern languages until the nineteenth century. The fact of autobiography, the writing of one's life or part of one's life in one form or another for one purpose or another, has existed from the time of the ancients. In the history of the writing of autobiography, and specifically the modern task of intellectual autobiography, Vico's *Life of Giambattista Vico Written by Himself* occupies a unique place. It is, as Fisch says, 'the first application of the genetic method by an original thinker to his own writings'.[4]

St Augustine's *Confessions,* the classic work of philosophical autobiography that immediately comes to mind, describes Augustine's childhood, education in his native Tagaste and Carthage, involvement with the Manichees, and career as a teacher of rhetoric in Carthage and Rome that leads to his conversion to Christianity and baptism by St Ambrose at Milan. But these life-events act as a grid upon which Augustine places his presentation of the truth of the Christian religion which exists externally as a whole, waiting to enter his life. There is a sense of spiritual development and intellectual turning-points, but there is no genetic method of causes at work. Augustine's life is an instrument used by him to verify God's grace.

Rousseau's *Confessions,* which was written in the later 1760s,

---

[3] See my discussion of the origin of the term 'autobiography' in Chapter 2, esp. n. 27.

[4] Preface to *Autobiography,* p. v. Fisch does not define 'genetic method'. I take the term in its broad sense to refer to the fact that Vico's purpose is to understand his life as an intellectual development that moves from step to step and which has an overall coherence. As will be shown, in Vico's case this coherent pattern of development is tied to his conceptions of 'ideal eternal history' and 'providence'.

about forty years after Vico's *Autobiography*, has more of a genetic sense of causes. But Rousseau is concerned to bare his heart, to confess, or appear to confess, the events shaping his inner self and sensibilities.[5] Vico confesses nothing. Vico's *Autobiography* is not like Dante's *Vita nuova*, nor Cellini's *Life*, Guicciardini's *Ricordi*, Petrarch's *Epistle to Posterity*, St Teresa's *Life of Herself*, Abelard's *Historia Calamitatum*, the *Bios* of Josephus, the *Letters* of the younger Pliny, nor other ancient, Renaissance, or early modern lives or memoirs. In Vico's work there is a new and distinctive art of autobiography that is based on his perception of himself as a philosophical historian who can narrate in proper order the causes of his intellectual development.

Vico's *Autobiography* is the story of a great intellectual break-through—his discovery of the new science, based on the principles of humanity, showing the common history of all nations within the 'great city of the human race'. The only model that Vico explicitly claims to have before him in writing his life is Descartes's *Discourse* (1637), and he regards this not as an example to be followed but as a text to write against. In the *Discourse* Descartes presents his own great intellectual breakthrough—the discovery of the method 'for rightly conducting one's reason, and seeking truth in the sciences', specifically metaphysics and the mathematical sciences, excluding, as Vico strongly notes, the human sciences of erudition.

The *Discourse* is presented by Descartes as if it were an intellectual autobiography, but he pins this largely on a single life-scene— the famous *poêle*, the stove-heated chamber where in solitary fashion he 'discoursed with himself about his thoughts', and on a constant repetition of the personal pronoun *I*. He gives no account of the specific causes or 'occasions of fortune' that actually led him to his striking discovery. His own *I* as an autobiographical reality remains as devoid of historical life as his clear and distinct idea of the *cogito*. Descartes does not call his *Discourse*, published about ninety years earlier than Vico's *Autobiography*, a 'life', but Vico takes its autobiographical dimension as important to Descartes's case and as a device that accounts for a great deal of the force and attraction of the text. It is in Vico's view an example of a 'feigned' life-narrative to which he opposes his own (113/5).

Vico's *Autobiography* was written in two parts, the first in

---

[5] See my discussion of Vico and Rousseau in Chapter 2.

1725–8, the second, a continuation of the first, in 1731. The first part is Vico's original conception of the whole *Autobiography*. He probably wrote most of this in May and the early part of June 1725 and sent this manuscript to Count Porcìa in Venice, at whose invitation he had written it and who was to supervise its publication there. In December of 1725 he drafted a few more pages to add to it describing the publication of his first edition of the *New Science*, which had appeared in October. In March 1728 he sent to Count Porcìa a revised and corrected version of the total manuscript, which was published as *Vita di Giambattista Vico scritta da se medesimo* the same year. Vico's work is nearly the same size as Descartes's *Discourse*, which in its modern editions is approximately fifty pages. The *Autobiography* in its original form, in which Vico places his attack on the false autobiographical character of Descartes's work, is about ten pages longer than the *Discourse*, suggesting perhaps that an 'unfeigned' or truly historical narrative need not require a work of substantially different size than Descartes's compact presentation of his method.

In 1731 at the urging of his friend Muratori, who was collecting material on the lives of the members of the Academy of the Assorditi of Urbino, to which Vico had been recently elected, Vico wrote out a corrected copy of the published *Autobiography*, presumably correcting the many printer's errors that he remarks on as existing in the original Venice publication (187/75). This corrected text has been lost, but the manuscript of the continuation of 1731 was published by Villarosa in his edition of Vico's works in the early nineteenth century. Vico's continuation adds about another thirty pages to the original, making the complete text of the *Autobiography* a work of about ninety pages in its modern Italian and English editions.

The first two-thirds of Vico's *Autobiography*, the original text published in Venice in 1728, contains Vico's account of his intellectual development from his early education to the greatest failure of his career—his loss of the concourse to obtain a university chair in 1723 at the age of 55—and the greatest achievement of his life—his publication of the first edition of the *New Science* two years later in 1725. Vico's 1731 continuation of the *Autobiography*, the last third of the modern text, is partially a reflection on some events not discussed in the earlier portion, including the invitation to write this original version and a relation of the details and publication of the second edition of the *New Science*, which appeared in 1730. The continuation goes through the first months of Vico's sixty-third year. In his edition Villarosa added a few pages of his own account of Vico's final years. This is frequently reprinted in modern editions of the *Autobiography*. Although Villarosa's account is inaccurate in some details and tends toward gossip, it offers at least a partial portrait of Vico's last years, if read in connection with Nicolini's notes. Vico lived a little more than a decade beyond the period of his career described in his continuation of the *Autobiography*. He died in the night of 22–3 January 1744, while seeing a third edition of the *New Science* through the press.

In his one-volume anthology of Vico's *Opere* (1953), Nicolini has organized the *Autobiography* into eight chapters.[6] In fact, the whole anthology is organized so as to give a picture of Vico's career; Nicolini says that with it he hopes to present a kind of *breviario vichiano* ('Vichian breviary').[7] Nicolini's chapters are useful to recall the basic story-line of the *Autobiography*.[8] I wish to recount this story-line here so the reader may, if he does not already, have the basic structure and some of the details of Vico's life in mind. There is no perfect, objective way to summarize such a text and thus I must highlight some things and leave out others. What I say here is meant only as a general aid to the reader in approaching my later interpretation. I invite the reader here and elsewhere always to go to the text itself.

1. *First years 1668–86* (Vico's birth to his defence of his father's court case—birth to 18 years of age) (111–18/3–10).

Vico begins his *Autobiography* with his birth-date, which he gives as 1670, two years later than his actual date of birth, 23 June 1668. He gives no description of his father or his mother beyond saying that his father had a cheerful disposition and his mother was melancholy. He makes no mention of brothers or sisters and offers no description of family life except to say that his parents were of good reputation. This is consistent with his method throughout the work. He reports no facts of his personal life, not even the date of his marriage or births of his children.

[6] Giambattista Vico, *Opere*, ed. F. Nicolini (Milan: Ricciardi, 1953).
[7] Ibid. xi.
[8] See also the 'Chronological Table' in *Autobiography*, 224–30.

From Nicolini's research into his early years and *vita domestica* the facts of Vico's personal life are known.[9] Vico had seven brothers and sisters; one of these, who was born seven years earlier but died in infancy, had the same name, Giambattista, which was also the name of his maternal grandfather. Vico was born in a room above his father's bookshop in Naples in via San Biagio dei Librai (*libraio*, 'bookseller, bookshop'), which is one of a system of several streets commonly called *Spaccanapoli* because they split the ancient centre of Naples in two. The plaque, placed at the instigation of Croce in 1941, that now marks this as Vico's birthplace refers to the room in which Vico was born as a *cameretta* (a small bedroom or bed chamber), which today stands above a shop selling commercialized religious articles. Nicolini refers to the room of Vico's birth in a less dignified, and probably more accurate, way as a *bugigattolo* (a cubby-hole of a room, a dark recess).[10] The whole family lived in this room which, according to Nicolini, measured six metres by three metres. Meals were cooked in accordance with the custom of the day on a portable stove in the street.

Vico's father, Antonio de Vico of Maddaloni (*c*.1636–1708), was a farmer's son who came to Naples from the country about 1656. He worked first as an apprentice in a print shop and then opened a bookstore which was among the least of about forty bookstores in the street of San Biagio. But to have a bookshop at all was a remarkable feat for someone of his origins. In addition to demonstrating his enterprising spirit, it meant that he could read and write, even if imperfectly. The family from which he came was illiterate, but they did own the small amount of land they farmed. Vico's mother was Candida Masullo of Naples (1633–*c*.1695). She

---

[9] F. Nicolini, *La giovinezza di Giambattista Vico 1668–1700: Saggio biografico* (2nd rev. edn., Bari: Laterza, 1932) and 'Il Vico nella vita domestica', in *Opere*, 94–106. See also Nicolini's various interpretive essays such as 'Di un'asserita crisi religiosa giovanile del Vico', in *La religiosità di Giambattista Vico: Quattro saggi* (Bari: Laterza, 1949), 17–63, and his studies of Vico's friends and associates, 'Di alcuni amici e conoscenti di Giambattista Vico', in *Atti della reale accademia pontaniana di scienze morali e politiche* (Naples, 1941), and of the period, *Uomini di spada, di chiesa, di toga, di studio ai tempi di Giambattista Vico* (Milan: Hoepli, 1942). Nicolini's notes to the *Autobiografia* in his one-volume *Opere* add to those of the earlier Laterza edition. The notes in the Fisch and Bergin translation are largely derived from the Laterza edition.

[10] *Opere*, ed. Nicolini, 99. In *La giovinezza* Nicolini refers to this room as *topaia* (27).

was the daughter of a carriage-maker, Giambattista Masullo, and was Antonio's second wife. Vico was the sixth of their eight children. Other than Vico and his older brother, Giuseppe, who had a minor position as a notary, there is no record of any profession or distinction achieved by their children. Nicolini says the care with which Vico writes his manuscripts and the clarity of his handwriting may have their origin in imitation of his older brother.

These details make it clear that although Vico was of an upright family, his origins were humble and undistinguished in a society that was hierarchically ordered and in which to rise in academic, civil, or political life, name and family connections, if not also a certain wealth, usually meant everything. For Vico to have become well educated and have a career at all is remarkable and perhaps represents an absorption of the enterprising spirit of his father. Vico lived all his life in Naples, never travelling to another city except for nine years spent as tutor at the Rocca family's castle at Vatolla in the Cilento, a mountainous region down the coast from Naples, below the Gulf of Salerno, a three-day journey by carriage from Naples. In confining his life to one place, not even visiting, for example, Rome, Vico reminds one of Kant, the sage of Königsberg; he was completely unlike contemporaries such as Leibniz or the Enlightenment figures who moved freely and constantly about Europe.

In Naples Vico lived his entire life essentially within one quarter, occupying several different addresses. In 1699, the year he began as professor of rhetoric at the university, he took a small residence in the vicolo dei Giganti, an accident of address a Joycean mind could appreciate, given Vico's conception in the *New Science* of giants forming the beginning of humanity, professing to the world their bodily rhetoric of *topica sensibile* ('sensible topics') (495). There is a Joycean juxtaposition and sad irony in the fact that Vico, born in the street of Saint Blasius (San Biagio), the saint known for cures of the throat, in his later years suffered from a 'gangrenous ulcer of the throat' (188/76) and from 'a strange disease devouring all the tissues between the palate and the lower bone of the head' which was apparently with him until his death (198/85).

The first event of his life that Vico describes in the *Autobiography* is a fall head-first from a ladder (Fisch suggests from a ladder in his father's bookshop) at the age of 7. He fractured his skull and was unconscious for five hours. The physician thought that he would either die or grow up mentally retarded. He survived but required a good three years of convalescence, and as a result of this fall, Vico claims he acquired a melancholy temperament, the classic humour of the thinker. He kept up and in fact advanced in his studies by working at home during these years of convalescence and, on his return to the grammar school he had been attending before his fall, he requested to be passed to the class above. To prepare for this, he claims his teacher beheld him, the pupil, acting as his own teacher. Vico regarded himself as an 'autodidact' (a term by which, he says, Epicurus was called) (136/27). He fore-shadows this image of the self-teacher in his description of this early incident.

However, Vico, left this teacher and moved to a second school where he formally competed to be promoted from the second to the third class. But in the competition a favourite pupil was promoted over him and, discouraged and insulted, he withdrew from the school to master Alvarez's *De institutione grammatica* on his own. This is the first of a series of enrolments, dissatisfactions with the level or method of teaching, and withdrawals from formal instruction to study on his own that occurred throughout Vico's early years. This grammar school experience is also the first of many injustices and perceived injustices suffered by Vico at the hands of academic institutions and colleagues throughout his career. The promotion of a favourite, and presumably less-talented, pupil over him foreshadows his loss of the concourse for a university chair in his mature career.

Vico passed from grammar to the study of logic, at which time he began to study all night, such that his mother, he says, would awake and ask him to go to bed, but would find him at his desk in the morning. He says that this all-night study was a sign that he would strongly maintain his reputation as a man of letters. Encouraged by one of his Jesuit teachers who was a nominalist philosopher, he began to try to master scholastic summulae, but despaired because his mind was too young for such topics, and he strayed from his studies, he reports, for a year and a half. He uses himself here as an example of the thesis of his later university oration, *On the Study Methods of Our Time*, that it is dangerous to introduce students to logic and metaphysics before their memories and imaginations have been properly cultivated by poetry and rhetoric. Recovering from this period of despair Vico returned to study more philosophy, which included some Platonic philosophy. He reports he discovered Suárez and again left school, this time to spend a year at home studying Suárez. This was followed by study largely on his own of the institutes of both civil and canon law, which he mastered to the extent that at the age of 18 (having petitioned for admission to the Bar) he was able successfully to defend his father in a minor suit brought against him by another bookseller (in June 1686 by Bartolomeo Moreschi). In accord with the birth-date of two years later given in the first line of the *Autobiography*, Vico states his age at the time of this case as 16.

2. *Stay at Vatolla and independent study 1686–95* (tutor for nine years at the Rocca family's castle and use of the convent library—18 to 27 years of age) (118–32/10–23).

Following his defence of his father's court case, Vico met Monsignor Rocca, whom he describes as a distinguished jurist (who published a large work on jurisprudence). They met in a bookstore and, after a conversation on Vico's views on the right method of teaching jurisprudence, the Monsignor urged him to take a position as tutor to his nephews at the family's castle at Vatolla. Vico reports that at this time his health was endangered by consumption and the good climate and fresh air would restore him.

Vico served in this post as tutor for nine years. He says nothing of his pupils, teaching duties, or methods, nor does he give his personal impressions of what must have been extraordinary for him, living in a place and at a social level beyond his experience. There were four Rocca children, the eldest of whom was 14. He says that on taking the position he was assured that he would be treated as a 'son of the family' and that this proved true. He remarks that he found the Monsignor's brother, Don Domenico Rocca, most kind and someone who shared his taste in poetry, and Vico dedicated his first published poem, 'Affetti di un disperato', to him. He had access to a good library in the Franciscan convent of Santa Maria della Pietà (three hundred volumes of which were found still to exist by Nicolini on a visit to Vatolla, although much the worse from years of infestation by mice). Vico describes in some detail the course of his self-directed study. He says that at this time he was wedded to a corrupt form of modern poetry, but was saved from this by being seized by a desire to read the Latin poets. He devised a method of reading the ancients against the Tuscan classics, pairing Cicero with Boccaccio, Virgil with Dante, and Horace with Petrarch. He studied Aristotle's metaphysics but became dissatisfied with it as an aid for understanding moral philosophy. But he became attracted to Plato's *Republic* and the physics of the *Timaeus*.

Here Vico inserts a rather long digression from one of his annual university lectures, discussing the proper order of studies for the young. The lecture from which these remarks are taken is lost and Vico does not identify its date of origin. He apparently inserts it here because of its connection with his own pattern of studies, to show how his theory of studies was based on his own self-education. He says that he read the work of Richardus (Étienne Deschamps, 1637–1701), who he claims had shown by a 'geometrical method' how the doctrine of St Augustine is midway between the extremes of Calvin and Pelagius. This he says enabled him later to meditate a principle of the natural law of nations. Vico also says that in this period of study he discovered 'the whole secret of the geometric method', and he is most proud of the fact that in a review of his later work on universal law Jean Le Clerc says it 'is composed by a strict mathematical method'. Vico also studied Lucretius, and was at this period more involved with the views of Epicureanism than he indicates. Although he does not mention it, it was during these years that his friends were condemned by the Inquisition and he was beset by strong religious doubts. He briefly looked into the experimental physics of Robert Boyle, but abandoned it, he says, because it contributed nothing to the understanding of man. He studied the *Natural Philosophy* of Henri Du Roy and claims thus to have grasped the basis of Cartesian physics. His mind was now apparently mature enough to master the physics and metaphysics of Descartes, which he criticizes as inconsistent with each other.

I have not attempted to mention all of the works Vico cites nor all the turns of his thinking that he reports during his years of early education and later self-directed study at Vatolla. These are among the most densely packed pages of his work.

3. *Return to Naples—the first form of Vichian philosophy 1695–1707* (resumes residence at Naples, professor of rhetoric, first six orations—27 to 39 years of age) (132–45/23–36).

Vico returned to Naples, where he claims he was 'a stranger in his own land' because in his absence the physics of Descartes had become renowned and that of Aristotle had become a 'laughing-stock'. Metaphysics and the learning of the ancients which had flourished in the Renaissance had fallen into disrepute, as had scholastic logic and Euclid's *Elements*. Nicolini and Fisch both claim that Vico greatly exaggerates his isolation from Naples in this period because the Rocca family divided the year between its residences in Vatolla, Portici (very near Naples), and Naples, and presumably Vico was never completely out of touch with the intellectual climate of Naples.[11] For example, Vico never mentions that he was enrolled for several years in the University of Naples during his Vatolla period. Fisch further claims that Vico was a Cartesian until about the age of 40, and thus in his description of this period Vico is reading his later position into his earlier.[12]

Vico says he felt fortunate that he had sworn no allegiance to a particular teacher and thus was free from fashions of thought and could be guided by his own good genius. At this point he reports that he decided to abandon Greek and Tuscan, that he never wished to learn French (although this claim about French is probably exaggerated), and that he would concentrate only on Latin. Of course Vico's later works such as the *Autobiography* and the *New Science* are written in Tuscan, the language of Dante, which has become the basis of modern standard Italian. Rather than be a polyglot of several languages, half-learned, Vico decided to master Latin completely, which he later says he could write as his own native language (154/45).

Vico claims that his education and views were so much against the grain that he 'lived in his native city not only a stranger but quite unknown'. It was at this time that Father Don Gaetano d'Andrea, a Theatine, while in conversation with Vico in a book-store on the history of the collections of canons, offered Vico the possibility of entering the clergy, an offer which Vico managed graciously to avoid. In 1698, at the age of 30, at the urging of friends, Vico entered and won the competition for a chair of rhetoric at the university, presenting a lecture on Quintilian, specifically on the etymology of the term *status*. Vico was reluctant

---

[11] Fisch, Introduction to *Autobiography*, 35–6; Nicolini, *Opere*, 25 n. 1.
[12] Fisch, Introduction to *Autobiography*, 36.

to enter the competition since a year earlier he had been unsuccessful in seeking the position of 'town clerk' (*segretario della città*), a position previously held by other men of letters. Vico's lecture for the university position was on 28 October 1698. The vote of the examining commission, held on 3 January 1699, was twelve favourable and ten against. The closeness of the vote is a fact Vico does not report.

Vico assumed his university position in the autumn of 1699, married Teresa Caterina Destito that December, and moved into the residence in vicolo dei Giganti, a proper house having several rooms, a terrace, and a garden. He later moved to the Largo dei Gerolamini, where there is now a plaque. Vico maintained a private studio in his home and supplemented the income from his poorly paid chair by giving private lessons and by earnings from poems, inscriptions, and other commissioned literary works. In total Vico occupied about a half dozen addresses during his lifetime. His wife was the daughter of a neighbouring family which he had known all his life; at their marriage he was 31 and she was 21. Teresa Caterina Destito was illiterate. As Adams puts it, she 'was unable to sign her name and was obliged to put a cross to the record of their marriage'.[13] They had eight children, three of whom died in infancy.

The first of the surviving children, Luisa, was born one year after their marriage in 1700 and was, in Nicolini's view, by far the most intelligent among the children. She had ability in singing and music; Vico himself taught her in the liberal arts; and she achieved some minor success in writing poetry. Vico used the honorarium he was paid for writing the biography of Antonio Carafa for the dowry of Luisa, who, in fact, married well. Ignazio, born in 1706, was apparently a petty criminal who, Villarosa dramatically reports, was on one occasion turned in to the police by Vico himself. However, at his death in 1736 (several years before Vico's own death) Ignazio was serving as an official in the Naples customs office. Angela Teresa was born in 1709, Gennaro in 1715, and Filippo in 1720. Angela Teresa did not have good health. It is not

---

[13] H. P. Adams, *The Life and Writings of Giambattista Vico* (London: Allen and Unwin, 1935), 68. A. M. Jacobelli Isoldi, *G. B. Vico: La vita e le opere* (Bologna: Capelli, 1960), says Vico's wife was 'probabilmente analfabeta' and certainly had no ability to comprehend Vico's work (118). Nicolini, *Autobiografia di Giambattista Vico* (Milan: Bompiani, 1947) refers to her as 'illetterata' (282).

known what profession Filippo ultimately followed. Gennaro succeeded Vico in his professorship at the university. Vico, who had been appointed Royal Historiographer in 1735 by Charles of Bourbon, the year after he had conquered the Kingdom of Naples, petitioned Charles to allow Gennaro to assume his duties at the university without a qualifying concourse. This was approved, and Gennaro began to assume some of Vico's duties in 1736, when Vico was 68, which was also the year of Ignazio's death. Gennaro, who had a long and undistinguished career, died at the age of 91 in 1806.[14] Vico's wife, Teresa Caterina, died fifteen years after her husband and was buried in the church of Gerolamini on 3 June 1759.

At the time of his competition for the chair of rhetoric, Vico met Paolo Mattia Doria (1662–1746),[15] one of the brightest philosophical minds of Vico's day and the first, Vico says, with whom he could discuss metaphysics, and to whom Vico was later to dedicate his own first work of metaphysics in 1710. At this point Vico reports his attraction to the first two of what he calls his 'four authors'—Plato and Tacitus. Plato represents the universal wisdom and Tacitus the practical wisdom of human affairs in their clashes of malice and fortune. Plato and Tacitus parallel Vico's distinction between philosophy and philology developed in the *New Science*. To these Vico says he wishes to add Bacon. Plato has a *sapienza riposta* (esoteric wisdom) and Tacitus a *sapienza volgare* (common wisdom). Bacon, Vico says, combines both in one career. What impresses Vico would seem to be not the Bacon of later philosophical textbooks, the empiricist founder of inductive thinking. What interests him is the Bacon of the *De augmentis scientiarum*, his ability as a single mind to project a total arrangement of the fields of human knowledge. In his oration of 1708 (published in 1709), *On the Study Methods of Our Time*, Vico says that 'the whole is the flower of wisdom'.[16] It is this sense of the development of

---

[14] See Nicolini's comments on Gennaro Vico in *Opere*, 96. For a more positive account, see G. Gentile, 'Il figlio di G. B. Vico e gl'inizi dell'insegnamento di letteratura italiana nella Università di Napoli', in *Studi vichiani* (2nd rev. edn., Florence: Le Monnier, 1927), 195–372.

[15] For some of Doria's writings, see P. M. Doria, *Manoscritti napoletani di Paolo Mattia Doria* (5 vols., Galatina: Congedo, 1981–2). See also H. Stone, 'Vico and Doria: The Beginnings of Their Friendship', *New Vico Studies*, 2 (1984), 83–91.

[16] *On the Study Methods of Our Time* , trans. E. Gianturco, reissued with a preface by D. P. Verene (Ithaca, NY: Cornell University Press, 1990; orig. pub. 1965), sect. 14.

knowledge as a whole that, among other things, attracts Vico to Bacon as his third author.

Part of the duties of Vico's professorship was to present an oration at the opening of each academic year. These were held each year on 18 October, the day of Saint Luke. Nicolini regards the first six of these orations (delivered between 1699 and 1706, when Vico was in his thirties) as the first form of the Vichian philosophy. No oration was delivered in 1701 because the death of the Spanish king in 1700 had initiated the War of Spanish Succession (about which Vico was later to write a history) and had thrown the political situation in Naples into confusion. Vico saw the orations not simply as ceremonial occasions, but as the opportunity to present his views on human education and scholarship. In the *Autobiography* Vico presents the themes of these orations as a system of ideas, although the texts themselves are not quite as interlocking nor as non-Cartesian in their viewpoints as he presents them.

Vico says that the first three of the orations treat the ends suitable to human nature. The first of these concerns the idea of self-knowledge as the motive for studying all branches of knowledge. The second argues that man should by nature be dedicated to truth and goodness. The third, Vico says, is intended as a kind of practical appendix to the two preceding orations, urging that the republic of letters must avoid false learning and deceit.

The fourth and fifth orations, he says, treat of political ends and the sixth of the Christian end of learning. The fourth argues that scholars should be dedicated to the good of the community and not simply to their own fame. The fifth argues that states have been most politically and militarily strong when they have supported letters. The sixth holds that man should attempt to perfect his corrupt nature through the complete study of the arts and sciences. Vico ends the sixth oration with a sketch of the order of studies that should exist for human education, which is a kind of introduction to the presentation of his own original position in the seventh oration.

As Vico presents the overall pattern of these orations, then, the first three concern the internal, self-directed order of the republic of letters—the motivations scholars and students should have as such. The final three relate to 'external' ends—the scholar's relation to the community, the state's self-interest in learning, and the value of studies in relation to the Christian conception of man.

4. *The second form of the Vichian philosophy 1708–16* (the seventh oration on *Study Methods* and publication of the *Ancient Wisdom*—40 to 48 years of age) (145–55/36–46).

The inauguration of the university year in 1708 was planned as a special event dedicated to Carl of Habsburg, whose armies had conquered the Kingdom of Naples the year before, and whose viceroy, Cardinal Grimani, would be present at the ceremonies. The oration Vico would present was planned to be published. It appeared the next year, in 1709, under the title of *De nostri temporis studiorum ratione (On the Study Methods of Our Time).*[17] This is Vico's first published philosophical work and is traditionally taken in Vico literature to be the first statement of his original position. It is a theory of human education that balances the ancients against the moderns. It is certainly an attack on Descartes and the Cartesian conception of the order of studies, although it is not as explicit as in Vico's subsequent work, in which he attacks Descartes by name. Vico compares the glory of his oration to Bacon's '*New Organ of the Sciences.*' Certainly what Vico says in this seventh oration is more original than his views in the previous orations, but his own view that these lead up to the seventh must also be taken seriously. The seventh is not a complete break with many of the themes of the previous orations.

Vico says that Bacon's *De sapientia veterum* (On the wisdom of the ancients) and Plato's *Cratylus* suggested to him the means to his two successive works. He decided to search out the origins of Latin words in a manner independent of the etymologies of the grammarians, which he found unsatisfactory. This led him by formulating connections between the original meanings of words such as *coelum, ingenium, anima, animus,* and *mens* to the conception of a physics of the motion of bodies entitled *De aequilibro corporis animantis* (On the equilibrium of living bodies). This was posthumously published toward the end of the eighteenth century in the Neapolitan periodical *Scelta miscellanea* and was read by the Neapolitan political historian and Vichian, Vincenzo Cuoco, but no copies of the issue of the *Scelta* in which it was

---

[17] See my discussion of the translation of *studiorum ratione* in the title of the *Study Methods* in Chapter 4 below.

printed are known to exist. These investigations also led him to his treatise, *De antiquissima Italorum sapientia ex linguae latinae originibus eruenda* (*On the Most Ancient Wisdom of the Italians Unearthed from the Origins of the Latin Language*), which he published in 1710. This treatise was reviewed in the *Giornale de' letterati d'Italia* which led to Vico's two replies that are known as the *Risposte*, 1711 and 1712. Uncharacteristically in relation to criticism of his work, Vico says in the *Autobiography* that this dispute was carried on with good grace.[18] But, then, unlike the later Leipzig 'review' of the *First New Science* and Vico's *Vindiciae*, this was a genuine intellectual exchange.

This book was planned in three parts: book 1, Metaphysics; book 2, Physics; and book 3, Morals. Only the first book was completed (sometimes referred to just as *Liber metaphysicus* in Vico literature), which is presented as a direct attack on Descartes's metaphysics of the *cogito*, which Vico criticizes as the production of a principle of certainty but not a principle of the true. In the first chapter is to be found Vico's now famous assertion *verum esse ipsum factum*, that the true is the same as the made or that what is true is convertible with what is made (*verum et factum convertuntur*). Vico's general thesis is that at the root of Latin words can be found certain original insights from the ancient Ionian philosophers and insights into the nature of the sacred from the Etruscans, who were expert in divination. These meanings have entered into Latin in its earliest form. Vico's approach may seem strange until it is seen that he has devised a confrontation between Descartes's abstract manner of arriving at metaphysical principles and his own method of arriving at them from the oldest insights of Western culture.

At this time Vico discovered the fourth of his 'four authors', as a result of his commission to write a biography of the military figure, Antonio Carafa (1646–93), *De rebus gestis Antonii Caraphaei* (1716). In preparation for writing this work Vico read Hugo Grotius, *De iure belli ac pacis* (*On the Law of War and Peace*) (1625). Grotius's work is the first major exposition of the conception of a system of international and natural law. Vico saw Bacon as joining common and esoteric wisdom in a single career but

---

[18] *On the Most Ancient Wisdom of the Italians Unearthed from the Origins of the Latin Language*, trans. L. M. Palmer (Ithaca, NY: Cornell University Press, 1988), 113–87.

Bacon does not have, as Grotius does, a conception of laws that encompass 'the universe of cities and the course of all times, or the extent of all nations' (155/45). Vico began to write a set of notes on Grotius's work but abandoned it, he says, because he realized it was not fitting for a man of Catholic faith to adorn the work of a heretical author. Fisch points out that 'Vico says nothing of the Inquisition in his autobiography, but his writings are not fully intelligible to one who does not bear in mind that it was active in Naples throughout his lifetime'.[19] Many of Vico's statements about how what he is claiming accords with the truth of Christian religion, that run throughout his works, read like a self-induced oath Vico is declaring, perhaps to avoid being asked formally to do so. Vico often appears more like the virtuous pagans he so admires than a glossator of Christian doctrine.

5. *The definitive form of the Vichian philosophy and the concourse of 1723; 1717–23 (Vico's work on Universal Law and his defeat for the chair of civil law—49 to 55 years of age)* (155–65/ 46–55).

In 1717 the 'first morning chair of law' became vacant because of the promotion of Nicola Capasso to the first 'afternoon' chair. This opened the possibility for Vico to obtain a position in the university that would pay him an appropriate salary. He was now 49 and had held his present, poorly paid position since he was 31. On the title-page of *On the Most Ancient Wisdom of the Italians* he gives his title as 'Royal Professor of Eloquence', the university being under the king ('eloquence' specifically implying 'Latin eloquence' or generally implying simply 'rhetoric'). The chief function of Vico's position was to prepare students for admission to the law course.[20] Vico's earnings were sufficiently little that according to Villarosa (201/89) he was obliged to supplement his income with private lessons in Latin rhetoric and literature, although Croce and Nicolini in their annotations to the Laterza edition hold that Vico was 'no richer, but rather less poor' than Villarosa says.[21] But Vico lived without pretence, within his

---

[19] Fisch, Introduction to *Autobiography*, 34.

[20] Regarding Vico's teaching see Nicolini's appendix, 'Il Vico maestro di scuola', in *Opere*, 957–69.

[21] *L'autobiografia, il carteggio e le poesie varie*, ed. B. Croce and F. Nicolini, 2nd rev. edn., in *Opere di G. B. Vico*, vol. v (Bari: Laterza, 1929), 129. Given the traditional view of Vico's poverty, the reader is surprised to learn that at his death,

income; as he once remarked to his pupil, the political economist Genovesi, 'there are too many whose carriages are drawn by their own guts'.

To show qualification for this chair Vico conceived of a multi-part work on universal law that would extend the ideas of his *Study Methods* and *Ancient Wisdom* into a new theory of jurisprudence. Vico announced this project in his inaugural oration of 1719 on universal law, the text of which is lost but the basic ideas of which are clear. He based this oration on the Augustinian tripartization of *nosse*, *velle*, and *posse*, proposing the argument, as he says, that 'All divine and human learning has three elements: knowledge, will and power, whose single principle is the mind, the eye of which is reason, to which God brings the light of eternal truth' (156/46). Vico makes clear that he wished to bring the major ideas of his four authors (two of whom are pagan, and two heretical) together in a single system for the glory of the Christian faith (perhaps thinking again of the Inquisition).

Although written in Latin, Vico called this multi-part work by the Italian title *Il diritto universale* (Universal law). In 1720 he published *De uno universi iuris principio et fine uno* (On the one principle and the one end of universal law). He followed this in 1721 with *De constantia iurisprudentis* (On the constancy of the jurisprudent), which is divided into two parts: *De constantia philosophiae* (On the constancy of philosophy) and *De constantia philologiae* (On the constancy of philology). In this latter part there is a chapter entitled 'Nova scientia tentatur' (A new science is essayed) in which, Vico says, he began to reduce philology to scientific principles and with which he says some readers were displeased. It is Vico's first sketch of his idea of a 'new science'.

Copies of these works were sent to the theologian and biblical scholar Jean Le Clerc, in Amsterdam, who was editor of the *Bibliothèque ancienne et moderne* (29 vols., 1714–26). Le Clerc wrote Vico a very favourable reply, which Vico quotes in full,

---

in addition to debts and household goods, Vico left a collection of about 100 paintings of the 16th, 17th, and 18th cents. This collection included the original of Solimena's portrait of Vico and portraits of his wife and of Ignazio, probably also done by Solimena. These were inherited by Gennaro who left them as part of his estate, but all were destroyed by fire about 1819, including the portrait of Vico, a copy of which had been made at Villarosa's insistence for the Academy of Arcadia and which is the one surviving likeness of Vico (ibid. 132).

saying that he would review both books and that it 'will give me occasion to show our northern scholars that acumen and erudition are to be found among the Italians no less than among themselves'. His review of them appeared the same year as his letter to Vico, 1722. This was the only explicit positive recognition Vico would ever get from the world of northern Europe, which he so much desired. Although they were generous reviews, as Fisch points out, 'they betrayed no real understanding' of what Vico had done,[22] and being by a Protestant author they would do Vico no special good in Naples. When Vico had finished and sent off for review the copies of the first two books, he proceeded to write a third book, which, among other things, applied the principles of philology and mythology he had formulated in the first two books to a reading of Homer's *Iliad* and *Odyssey*. He published this in 1722 as *Notae in duos libros*, appended to the first two books of his theory of universal law. A copy of this was also sent to Le Clerc, but Vico received no reply. This appendix (*Dissertationes*) is a precursor to Vico's 'search for the true Homer' in the *New Science*.

Vico says that a short time after the appearance of his *Universal Law*, the 'morning' chair in law became vacant, but in fact it had become vacant (as mentioned above) in 1717, six years before the announcement of the concourse to fill it in January 1723. Vico had been writing his work on universal law in anticipation of this concourse. This chair was in fact one of eight vacancies that then existed in the law faculty. Vico had also carefully circulated in Naples copies of Le Clerc's review. Vico announced his intention to compete for the chair. He prepared his concourse lecture, working until five in the morning amid, he says, the 'conversation of his friends and the cries of his children, as his custom was, whether reading, writing, or thinking'. The topic of his lecture, by the rules selected the day before the concourse, was on a fragment from the *Digestum vetus*, and according to Vico's account all went well. He felt assured of receiving the position, but he was advised that the decision was already determined through academic politics, so he withdrew his name from competition. This loss of the concourse, he says, 'made him despair of ever holding a worthier position in his native city' (164/54). Although Vico does not report it, the position was in fact given to a Domenico Gentile of Bari, a

---

[22] Fisch, Introduction to *Autobiography*, 10.

seducer of servant-girls (*grande insectator puellarum*) who committed suicide over one of them in 1739, and whose only book was withdrawn from the press for plagiarism.[23]

Vico's text to this point, ending with his description of the loss of the concourse and the publication of Le Clerc's review, is designated as part A in the Fisch and Bergin translation. Vico completed it in 1725 and sent it to Porcìa for his opinion in June of that year.

6. *The First New Science 1723–5* (publication of the first edition of the *New Science—55* to 57 years of age) (165–73/55–62).

Having lost the concourse for the chair of civil law, Vico composed by the end of 1724 the major part of what he later called his 'new science in negative form'. When he sent the foregoing part of the *Autobiography* to Porcìa (through Porcìa's agent in Rome, Abbé Esperti, who in fact sent it on to Porcìa on Vico's birthday, 23 June 1725), Vico anticipated that this manuscript of his new science would soon appear in print. It was to be financially underwritten by Cardinal Corsini, to whom it was dedicated, and the text received its imprimatur on 15 July 1725. But on 20 July Vico received a letter from the Cardinal saying that because of unusual expenses incurred on a visit to his diocese of Frascati, he was unable to support printing costs.

Vico could not afford the printing costs of such a large manuscript himself, but he says he felt honour bound to publish his work. He thus recast the work during August and part of September in a positive form, greatly reducing its size, and to finance the printing costs he sold a ring 'set with a five-grain diamond of the purest water'. He graciously retained the dedication to Cardinal Corsini and included an inscription addressing it to the universities of Europe. The manuscript of the new science in negative form is now lost but apparently it was a presentation of Vico's views through the critical analysis of the errors and inconsistencies of other views, principally those of the seventeenth-century natural law theorists. Vico's recasting of the work in positive form became a concise statement of his own theories and interpretations of the materials of human society, with a minimum of criticism of other views. Corsini's retraction of his promise became a providential turn that made the first *New Science* what it is.

---

[23] *L'autobiografia*, ed. Croce and Nicolini, 118.

In October 1725 Vico published the first edition of the *New Science* or what he later called the *Scienza nuova prima,* with the title *Princìpi di una scienza nuova intorno alla natura delle nazioni, per la quale si ritruovano i princìpi di altro sistema del diritto naturale delle genti* (Principles of a new science concerning the nature of the nations, by which are found the principles of another system of the natural law of the gentes). In December following the October publication of this work Vico drafted the final pages of the original text of his *Autobiography,* which he would correct and revise two years later and send to Porcìa for publication in Venice in 1728. These final pages (part B in the Fisch and Bergin translation) are essentially a summary statement of the thesis of the *New Science,* emphasizing to some extent that this new science makes its discoveries by a 'new critical art' (*nuova arte critica*) of examining and discovering the universal truths within the details of the civil world of nations. He closes with the statement that this is all for the glory of the Catholic religion and quotes words of praise from Cardinal Corsini. In a letter to his friend Father Bernardo Maria Giacco of 25 October 1725, sent with a copy of the *New Science,* Vico says that with this work he feels himself 'a new man' and 'filled with a certain heroic spirit'.[24] Besides its own merits this publication certainly offered him some vindication in the injustice present in his loss of the concourse. He felt a sense of freedom to write for himself and not the burden to write for his career. He now began to write his works in Italian rather than Latin.

According to Nicolini's divisions within Vico's career, which I am following here, the Vichian philosophy takes three forms before reaching the *New Science.* The first is that of his six orations inaugurating the university year delivered by Vico from his early to late thirties. As Vico relates them in the *Autobiography* they present a series of interlocking theses on the nature of learning and purposes of human knowledge that lead up to the published seventh oration, *On the Study Methods of Our Time,* in which he attacks the modern, Port-Royalist, Cartesian conception of studies. The traditional interpretation of these orations does not accept

---

[24] Fisch, Introduction to *Autobiography,* 15; 'Al Padre Giacco', in *Autobiografia,* ed. Fubini, 107.

Vico's own presentation of his progressive transition from the views of the first six to the seventh oration. It regards the first six as more Cartesian in tone and ideas, the seventh as a rather strong break with these earlier views, and Vico's own account as influenced by hindsight from the *New Science*. But the truth may lie somewhere between this view and Vico's own.

The second form of the Vichian philosophy, formulated by Vico in his early forties, is his *Study Methods* and *Ancient Wisdom* (of which, as mentioned above, he wrote only the first book, the metaphysics, of a planned three-part treatise), and his lost work on the motions of living bodies. The *Study Methods* attempts to balance the ancients against the moderns and ask what is good about each; this may, in fact, go back to what Vico was trying to decide in his own patterns of reading and study in his years at Vatolla. The *Study Methods* is a short treatise on human education concerning the order of studies as they relate to the natural growth of the faculties of the mind, based on a conception of knowledge as a whole and the relation of knowledge or wisdom to eloquence. In effect it challenges the Cartesian exclusion of human erudition (poetic and rhetorical training in the arts of memory and imagination, and Vico includes geometry because of its use of figure) from knowledge by showing that these non-Cartesian arts are required for the education of the young in order that they can later make progress in logic, metaphysics, and criticism. Formulation of arguments requires as its starting-points the mind's memorial powers of finding topics or commonplaces and its imaginative powers of metaphor. These are natural to young minds, but if not cultivated then they are absent when older, and the mind cannot reach underpinnings or content for its abstractions. Vico uses a theory of education to challenge the validity of the modern conception of knowledge.

Vico's plan for the three books of the *Ancient Wisdom*—metaphysics, physics, and morals—appears as a direct challenge to the *arbor scientiae* Descartes describes in the 'Author's Letter' to the *Principles*. Vico challenges the Cartesian metaphysics directly, and in effect all modern philosophy, with its 'quest for certainty', by disrupting the equation of certainty and truth. He replaces this with the notion of 'making', the divine making of the world and the human making of intellectual truth or 'intelligibilities'. The truths or intelligibilities of mathematics are true because we make them in accordance with the human mind, not because we discover them as principles of an independent order of reality. There can be no science (*scientia*) of 'certainties' or the certain (*certum*), what is merely determined as clear and distinct and whose truth is not made by us. The knower can only have a kind of 'consciousness' (*conscientia*) that witnesses with definition and certainty what is there. What is truly intelligible to the knower (*verum*) must be made by him; only then is its form or 'cause' fully grasped by the knower and not simply 'recognized' by the knower in a special way. Descartes's *cogito*, Vico claims, is a certainty, but not being made by the thinking agent, it is without ultimate intelligibility and cannot be the basis of any science of metaphysics.

The positive doctrine of Vico's metaphysics in the *Ancient Wisdom* is parallel to the *Study Methods*. The *Study Methods* shows that the modern conception of knowledge as based on the study of the rules of logical and abstract thinking does not fit the first sensibilities and natural development of the mind. The *Ancient Wisdom*, by being based on philosophically discovered etymologies of the Latin language, advances a conception of metaphysics based on the discovery of the original forms of knowledge of things human and divine (from the Ionian philosophers and the Etruscans) that are at the basis of Western culture. Thus the humanistic arts of erudition which Descartes explicitly excludes from his method of right reasoning are exactly what are required to discover these beginning points. Etymology is the science upon which a science of metaphysics can be based; it cannot be successfully based on the science of logic. The truths of logic are always rooted in the human world, not the reverse, and metaphysics must account for the principles of the generation of this human reality that allows for logical intelligibilities to be intelligible at all. The traditional view of the *Ancient Wisdom* is that Vico chose a rather long and odd route to make his point by casting his work as research into the origins of the Latin language, doing this perhaps partially out of the motivation of it being appropriate to his position as professor of Latin eloquence. But the above comments suggest more fully the actual strength of his case; it is this interest in etymology and philology generally that is the basis of his future work.

The third and 'definitive' form of the Vichian philosophy is contained in the books of Vico's work on *Universal Law*, written in Vico's early fifties. It is 'definitive' in the sense that in this work

Vico arrives at the conception of a new science combining philosophical and philological modes of understanding that will in some way reveal the order of the human world. Vico describes the purpose of this work in this way in the *Autobiography*. His attempt to understand the Latin language as it relates to law and the basis of law leads Vico to the *New Science*, the title of which, as mentioned above, he employs for the first time as a chapter in the second book (*De constantia*) of the *Universal Law*.

A view that is frequently encountered and often stated very superficially is that Vico's principle of *verum ipsum factum* of the *Ancient Wisdom* leads him into the idea of the new science. Holders of this view often cite the famous 'night of thick darkness' passage in the *Second New Science* which says that 'the world of civil society has certainly been made by men' (331). In fact it is more likely that in his own intellectual development Vico came to the *New Science* through interest in the connection of the certain (*certum*) and the true (*verum*), the idea of *certum est pars veri* (the certain is part of the true) that he uses as a term in the first book (*De uno*, ch. 82) of the *Universal Law*.[25] The sense that a law is always something definite and particular to time and place in its meaning and interpretation, yet is 'law'—its force and validity rests ultimately on the fact that it is part of the human sense of 'right'—may have led Vico to his perception of the philological and the philosophical as the two factors necessary for the understanding of anything in the civil world. Vico overtly employs the conceptions of the true (*il vero*) and the certain (*il certo*) in the *New Science*, organizing his axioms around them and discussing the importance of joining philosophy as the impetus toward the universal with philology as the apprehension of the particular custom, deed, or word. He only indirectly refers to the principle that the true is the made in the *New Science* (331, 349, 374), but he presupposes it throughout the work. Although *verum ipsum factum* is the metaphysical principle behind Vico's 'new science of the common nature of nations', the philosophical grasp of Roman law and the actual interlocking of the universal and particular in law is what Vico requires to get to his science.

In outline, the *Autobiography* as it was published in Venice in

---

[25] G. Fassò, 'The Problem of Law and the Historical Origin of the *New Science*', in G. Tagliacozzo and D. P. Verene, eds., *Giambattista Vico's Science of Humanity* (Baltimore: Johns Hopkins University Press, 1976), 3–14.

1728, when Vico was 60, describes Vico's education from his earliest years (Secs. 1 and 2 above) and the development of his philosophy from its first form in his early years as professor of rhetoric to his publication of the first edition of the *New Science* in 1725, when he was 57 (Secs. 3–6 above). His education falls into two periods: a first period of his on and off formal education in grammar school through the 'higher studies' of philosophy and logic and his study of law up to the age of 18, and a second period of his nine years of self-directed study while at Vatolla (although during this period he officially matriculated in the school of law and at some point received an LL D from the University of Naples).[26] His philosophy took three forms prior to his discovery of the new science: remarks on the purposes and value of education; a conception of human learning, knowledge, and metaphysics based on non-Cartesian forms of thinking; and a comprehensive theory of universal law worked out through a conception of human society. It is a story of success but also a story of despair, from the Lucretian mood of Vico's first published work, his poem, 'Affetti di un disperato' ('Feelings of one in despair'), which appeared while he was at Vatolla (1692) but which he does not mention in his *Autobiography*,[27] to his statement following his loss of the concourse, that he 'despaired' (*disperò*) of ever having a worthier position in his native city.

7. *Various minor writings 1702–27* (Vico's continuation of his autobiography in 1731, recapitulating earlier writings through the publication of the earlier portion of the *Autobiography*—34 to 59 years of age) (173–82/63–71).

Three years after the publication in Venice of the *Autobiography*, Vico drafted a continuation which, as mentioned above, was not published until Villarosa's nineteenth-century edition of Vico's *Opuscoli* (1818). As also mentioned above, the occasion for writing this continuation was a volume planned, but never published, of the lives of the members of the Academy of the Assorditi of Urbino, to which Vico had been elected in 1730. This volume would potentially have reprinted a corrected version of the original

---

[26] See my discussion of Vico's university studies in Chapter 5.
[27] Fisch, Introduction to *Autobiography*, 36. See also Nicolini, *La religiosità di Giambattista Vico.*

autobiography that Vico made, but which is now lost, along with the continuation he left in manuscript form.

Vico begins this continuation with a description of his attempt to send a copy of the 1725 edition of the *New Science* (*Scienza nuova prima*) to Le Clerc, but as with his earlier sending of the third part of the *Universal Law*, he had no reply. Vico suggests that this might be because Le Clerc was dead or because of age had given up such literary correspondence. The latter was probably the case; Le Clerc died in 1736. Vico also sent a copy of the *New Science* to Newton, which may have reached him about a year before he died in 1727.[28]

Vico now goes back to many of the years covered by the earlier portion of the *Autobiography* and relates details of occasional and minor works from these years, beginning with his 'Panegyric to Philip V' of 1702, and entering into a kind of annotated list of commissioned inscriptions, odes, and funeral orations, ending with that on the death of Angela Cimini in 1727. Vico says that 'adverse fortune dealt a blow to his scholarly repute' (176/65). He was commanded by the viceroy of Naples, Cardinal Wolfgang von Schrottenbach, to compose the inscriptions for the royal chapel for the funeral rites of Empress Eleanor of Neuburg, but those of another were put up instead. Vico claims he actually triumphed in this adversity because he received the honour of an apology from a representative of the viceroy. Vico nevertheless reproduces the inscriptions here in full.

These and the other ceremonial and occasional items Vico enumerates cover the period from his third inaugural oration, given when he was 34, to just beyond his writing of his autobiography and publication of the first edition of the *New Science*, when he was 57. In each case Vico emphasizes how important these minor works were, how well they were received by the Neapolitan aristocrats and political figures who commissioned them, and even describes the details of some of the luxurious editions in which these rather shallow works were ceremoniously printed and circulated. Vico closes this section with a significant paragraph describing the details of the publication of the original *Autobiography* in

---

[28] Fisch, Introduction to *Autobiography*, 82. See the note of Croce and Nicolini to Vico's reproduction of the letter from Attias in *L'autobiografia*, 55 n. 3.

Venice and expressing his dissatisfactions with it and reservations about it, including the errors in its printing.

8. *The 'Vindiciae' and the Second New Science 1728–31* (Vico's reply to the Leipzig book notice of the *First New Science* and details of the publication of the *Second New Science*—60 to 63 years of age) (182–200/71–87).

Vico describes how he was in touch with Father Carlo Lodoli, censor of publications in Venice and someone with a genuine interest in Vico's work. Lodoli was a central figure of Venetian intellectual life, and introduced some of Vico's ideas into architectural theory. Vico reprints Lodoli's letter to him of 15 January 1728 urging Vico to publish an edition of the *New Science* in Venice, at that time one of the great centres of book printing for Europe. He invites Vico to include any corrections or additions he might wish to make. Vico then found in the post office other letters supporting this idea, from Abbé Antonio Conti, whom Vico describes as a 'Venetian nobleman and great metaphysician and mathematician', and from Porcìa, whose letter of 14 December 1727 had been lying in the post office for about a year. Vico points out the obvious—that he was not in the habit of visiting the post office. But this point has the rhetorical power of underlining his theme of his isolation.

While Vico was making additions and corrections to the first edition of the *New Science* (1725) with a view to accepting the offer to have a new edition published in Venice, there appeared in the book notices of the Leipzig *Acta Eruditorum* for August 1727 a misleading and in fact malicious announcement of the publication in 1725 of Vico's *New Science*. Among other things it said that, on the authority of 'an Italian friend', the author is an 'abbé' of the Vico family, and it went on to distort the subject-matter of the work. As Vico points out, he is hardly an abbé but a father and even a grandfather. The review notice is anonymous. Vico was strongly offended by this misrepresentation, if not mockery, before the northern scholars whose approval he always desired, and he published a reply that is generally referred to by the title *Vici vindiciae*, in which Vico in legalistic fashion challenges the truth of the book notice word by word (*vindiciae* is, in law, a laying claim to a thing before the praetor by both contending parties). Vico pleads his civil case before the praetor of the intellectual public, initiating in a sense a *vindicatio* against the anonymous person who has made false claims about his work and publicly asserting his title to it as its true owner. Vico addresses the anonymous author of this book notice as 'unknown vagabond' (*Ignotus erro*), saying he is the sort of person who treats friends worse than enemies and gives false information about his own nation to foreigners; Vico finally recommends that this person 'take his departure from the world of men and go live with the wild beasts in the African desert'. Some commentators have seen a relationship between this and Descartes's comment at the end of the third part of the *Discourse* that he had 'been able to live a life as solitary and retired as though I were in the most remote deserts'.

The source of this malicious notice was most probably Vico's colleague, Nicola Capasso (1671–1745), who in collaboration with other colleagues in Naples sent it to the Leipzig *Acta*.[29] Vico himself may have believed that the source of the book notice was the Neapolitan historian Pietro Giannone (1678–1748) who was then in exile in Vienna, hence the term 'unknown vagabond'. Giannone, Vico's long-standing adversary, in a letter of 13 June 1728 claimed that he was 'flabbergasted' that the *Acta* would even take notice of Vico's work. In a later letter of 29 July 1729 Giannone (who wrote his own life, *Vita scritta da lui medesimo*) said that Vico's autobiography was 'both the most insipid [*sciapita*] and most braggadocian [*trasonica*] thing one could ever read'.

Capasso was throughout Vico's career his *tormentatore*. It was Capasso, who was a versifier in dialect and a writer of macaronic poetry, who gave Vico the cruel nickname of 'mastro Tisicuzzo' (*tisico* means 'tubercular'), an antique slur, but one that perhaps captured Vico's gaunt, skin-and-bones appearance.[30] Vico, by his own account in the *Autobiography*, was threatened by tuberculosis at the point when he went to Vatolla. At the time of the Leipzig book notice he was suffering from and under treatment for the gangrenous ulcer of his throat. His student and disciple, Nicola Solla, who wrote a brief biography of Vico, describes him as being 'of medium height, his body tended to be adust [*adusto*], aquiline

---

[29] *Opere*, ed. Nicolini, 82 n. 3; *L'autobiografia*, ed. Croce and Nicolini, 125.

[30] *L'autobiografia*, ed. Croce and Nicolini, 116. For the lines from one of Capasso's macaronic verses where he refers to Vico as 'Master Tisicuzzus', see A. Altamura, 'Giambattista Vico, "Homo Neapolitanus"', *Forum Italicum*, 2 (1968), 498.

nose, and lively penetrating eyes'.[31] Indeed this is close to the impression one has from the portrait of Vico done about 1730, when he was in his early sixties (or possibly a decade later, between 1742 and 1743), by Francesco Solimena, the painter of the great frescoes in the Gesù Nuovo church in Naples. The original of Vico's portrait was destroyed by fire in 1819, but Villarosa had had a copy made which remains the only portrait of Vico.

Vico had agreed to have the *New Science* reprinted in a new edition in Venice, the manuscript for which had now become quite large, with all his annotations and additions. He sent it to Lodoli in October 1729. But the printer began to treat Vico in a way that he says displeased him, and he asked that the manuscript be returned; he received it six months later. In the meantime Vico had begun arrangements for its publication in Naples. He could not find a publisher there or elsewhere for a work of its size. He then, under this necessity, hit upon a plan to recast the work as a single text, incorporating the notes and revisions and bringing it into publishable size. He began writing this version on Christmas morning 1729 and finished it, he reports, at nine o'clock on Easter Sunday evening, 9 April 1730 (a period of 106 days). Although smaller, it is still a work of nearly five hundred pages, which was published by Felice Mosca, the publisher of the first edition of the *New Science* and almost all of Vico's works. He had planned that this edition would begin by printing all the letters he had exchanged with Father Lodoli on the printing of the work in Venice. But after half the volume had been printed in Naples, he received, as he says, 'a final communication from Venice', which was probably a conciliatory letter from Lodoli.

Thus he suddenly had to replace this *Novella letteraria* with which the volume was to begin with something else. Under this new necessity Vico commissioned the prominent sculptor, architect, and painter Domenico Antonio Vaccaro (1681–1750) to do an emblematic engraving to serve as frontispiece of the work, the actual engraving of which was done by the prominent engraver Antonio Baldi (1692–c.1773), and Vico wrote to order an explanation of the significance of its elements to stand in place of the more than eighty missing pages and serve as introduction to the work. Although this was done as a result of these accidental circumstances, while the volume was in press in Naples, the work most certainly benefited from the disappearance of the *Novella letteraria*, and what Vico wrote in its place are some of the most illuminating passages of the *New Science*. In this 1730 edition he did include a short preface recounting the circumstances of its publication titled 'Occasione di meditarsi quest' opera'.

There is a sense of *déjà vu* in the conditions of the publication of this *Second New Science* in relation to the publication of the *First New Science*. The first had to be written in a short period in positive form in order to reduce its size to an affordable printing cost, in that instance due to the withdrawal of financial support by Cardinal Corsini, and Vico, feeling honour bound to publish it, paid the costs himself by selling the ring. The second, also dedicated to Corsini, who had since become Pope Clement XII, had to be recast in a short time as an integrated and shortened text to save printing costs. This time Vico also felt it necessary to go ahead with publication, because the new edition had been announced twice as forthcoming (in the catalogue appended to the 1728 autobiography and in his remarks in the *Vici vindiciae*, 1729). But this time the publisher bore the cost. Vico immediately began to write annotations, corrections, and additions to the second edition and produced three sets in 1730 and 1731, saying that these could be incorporated 'when a third edition is printed'. A fourth set was written in 1733 or 1734, incorporating parts of the third, and became the basis of a revision of the entire work in 1735 or 1736, which was what Vico was seeing through the press at the time of his death in 1744.[32]

Vico ends his continuation of his autobiography with a comment on his dedication to teaching, saying that he always endeavoured to practice what he had held in the *Study Methods*. He says that he never discussed matters of eloquence (i.e. rhetoric) apart from wisdom, and that he regards eloquence as nothing but 'wisdom speaking' (*la sapienza che parla*). He says, a little sadly, that he lectured every day with elegance and profundity, 'as if famous men of letters had come from abroad to attend his classes and to hear him' (199/86). His lectures were in fact well attended, but no one of such stature was present.

Vico says that his temperament was 'choleric to a fault' and that

---

[32] *Autobiography*, trans. Fisch and Bergin, 221 n. 200.

he often responded too strongly and publicly to his rivals. He says that 'among the caitiff semi-learned or pseudo-learned, the more shameless called him a fool [*pazzo*], or in somewhat more courteous terms they said that he was obscure or eccentric and had odd ideas' (199–200/87). Although Vico does not report what was actually said about him, he has not simply invented this. Amongst surviving examples from the 'caitiff semi-learned [*cattivi dotti*]' is Finetti's tale (1768) of having heard from a Neapolitan of noble birth who had been a student and follower of Vico for many years that 'until a certain time Vico was regarded by the Neapolitans as a truly learned man, but later because of his extravagant opinions he was generally held to be a fool [*pazzo*]'. When Finetti then asked him what was thought of the *New Science*, he replied: 'Oh! by then he had become completely mad [*pazzo*].'[33] Another concerns Capasso, who read the *New Science* but understood nothing of it, and is said to have run to Nicola Cirillo (a noted physician and one of the eight scholars from Naples whom Porcìa invited to write their own lives when he invited Vico)[34] to have his pulse taken, fearing, he said farcically, that he had suffered a stroke that had taken all exercise of reason from him. Vico on being told of this replied that he had not written it *pei poetuzzi* (for petty little poets).[35] Vico says that all the adversities he suffered were for him so many occasions to withdraw to his desk as to a 'high impregnable citadel' to meditate and write further.

He ends his autobiography with the claim that through these responses to these adversities and detractors he had finally been led to the discovery of the *New Science*. He concludes the *Autobiography* with a quotation from 'Socrates to His Friends', from the *Fabulae* of Phaedrus (*c*.15 BC–*c*. AD 50): 'If I were consigned his fame, I would not shun to die as he, and because I would be acquitted when I became ashes, I would endure the inequity of the sentence' (*Fabulae* III. ix. 3–4). Vico must have chosen this final quotation very carefully. He says that having discovered the new science he felt himself more fortunate than Socrates, of whom Phaedrus 'made this magnanimous wish' (*fece quel magnanimo voto*), the force of which is not quite so clear in the rendering of

[33] *L'autobiografia*, ed. Croce and Nicolini, 129.
[34] *Opere*, ed. Nicolini, 75 n. 3.
[35] *L'autobiografia*, ed. Croce and Nicolini, 129.

the Fisch and Bergin translation. Vico, writing this in his early
sixties, is taking his readers ahead to his own death. He feels, as he
says in his description of the *Second New Science* in these pages,
that he has succeeded in placing in one book all of his thought. He
says that the *First New Science* and the *Universal Law* should be
consulted only for several passages; these remain important for
their statements of particular discoveries (three chapters of the
former concerning Vico's idea of the possibility of a common
mental language for all nations and his discussions of the Law of
the Twelve Tables and of Tribonian's fable of the 'Royal Law' in
the latter). The *Second New Science*, then, is a whole thought, a
book of wisdom, 'wisdom speaking'.

Because Vico is so forceful in his judgement that the *Second New
Science* replaces the *First*, Vico scholars have generally believed
him and developed their scholarship around the *Second* practically
to the exclusion of the *First*. It is curious that Vico did not just
incorporate the passages he mentions into the text of the *Second
New Science* because these are not long. His judgement of their
importance must leave the reader puzzled. The *First New Science*
is quite an eloquent speech in itself and is in many ways a more
rewarding statement of the essentials of Vico's position than the
Second. Because Nicolini merged Vico's revisions with what can be
called his *Third New Science* (1744) with his *Second* (1730), calling
them both the *Scienza nuova seconda*, scholars have treated them
as one text, as I do here, but for some purposes they would be
better kept apart, even though the *Third* is not extensively different
from the *Second*.

The context of the full fable of 'Socrates to His Friends' should
not be missed. The lines Vico quotes are present in it as an aside,
parenthetically stated. Phaedrus' fables have themes like those of
Aesop; the theme of this fable is friendship, that 'the name of a
friend is common; but fidelity is rarely found'. Socrates is come
upon having laid a foundation for a small house and is asked why
someone as famous as himself is building such a small house. He
replies: 'I *only* wish that I could fill it with real friends.' Only if this
is understood is it clear why Vico compares himself to Socrates.
His comparison is with the Socrates of the fable and is a continuation of his foregoing remarks on his status and treatment in his
native city. Phaedrus frequently retorts to his own detractors in his
fables, and resignation or pessimism is traditionally ascribed to

his personality. The melancholic temper that Vico says he acquired as his nature from his fall at the age of 7 makes a complete circle to the end.

As mentioned above, Villarosa appended to his edition of 1818 several pages of his own account of Vico's last years. His account is flawed, overly dramatic, and even romantic at points. It is best read with Croce and Nicolini's corrections,[36] but it contains worthwhile elements. Certainly Villarosa's description of the problems of Vico's burial justifies the existence of the whole short piece. Villarosa's comments on Vico's loss of memory, failure to recognize his own children, etc., may derive as exaggerations from Solla's biography. At the time of his death Vico certainly was not in the state of physical and mental incompetence that Villarosa describes. Vico was correcting proofs of the third edition of the *New Science*, wrote out instructions for the frontispiece portrait of himself (to be placed opposite the engraving or *dipintura*), and just twelve or thirteen days before his death drafted the dedication to Cardinal Troiano d'Acquaviva, with whom he was in correspondence.[37] Villarosa may be incorrect in his claim that Vico's wife, Caterina, was wanting in talents 'required even in a mediocre wife and mother' and that Vico had personally to take care of the household matters and even clothes for the children. Nicolini finds no evidence for this and holds the opinion that in this respect her character may have been mistaken for that of Ignazio's wife, also named Caterina, who lived for a period in the same household.[38] But where the truth may lie is not clear.

The most vivid part of Villarosa's remarks is his fascinating sketch of Vico's burial, the basic facts of which are not disputed, and which has the character of something Vico himself would have expected. According to Villarosa Vico did in a way anticipate it. He reports that Vico said to friends that 'misfortune would pursue him even after his death' (204/91). At his death Vico's body was carried down into the courtyard from the house. The professors of the university gathered there, as did the members of the Confraternity of Santa Sofia, of which Vico was a member (the custom was to

---

[36] *L'autobiografia*, ed. Croce and Nicolini, 129–34.
[37] *Autobiography*, trans. Fisch and Bergin, 221–2 n. 210.
[38] Nicolini, 'Il Vico nella vita domestica', in *Opere*, 94–106, esp. 95.

pay dues during one's life to a confraternity which was responsible for the funeral and burial of its members). A dispute ensued over which group had the right to act as pallbearers. The confraternity departed, leaving the delegation of professors from the university, who had no power to conduct a burial. The result of this 'misfortune' was that the corpse had to be carried back into the house and kept overnight, and the next day it was necessary for Gennaro to request and pay for the cathedral chapter of Vico's church to conduct the burial. The years of membership in the confraternity were in vain, but the professors did return to be present for the burial in the church Vico attended, Gerolamini.

Where Vico's remains lie is not known; that is, there is no proper tomb in the church. According to Villarosa, in 1789, about forty-five years after Vico's death, Gennaro placed an inscription in a corner of the church, which Villarosa reprints. As Villarosa records it, but without comment, ironically misfortune followed Vico even into the wording of this inscription by his son. The end of it reads: 'He died 19 January, 1744 / He lived seventy-four years [VIXIT ANNOS LXXIV] / Placed by his grieving son / Gennaro.' Vico in fact died in the night between 22 and 23 January 1744, at the age of 75. He would have turned 76 on his birthday, the following 23 June. Villarosa, a few pages earlier, despite his verbatim reprinting of the dates of Gennaro's inscription, states that Vico died peacefully on 20 January 1744, 'having passed the seventy-sixth year of his age'. The difficulty of attributing correct dates to Vico appears parallel to his own seeming failure to give the precise date. If, however, Vico's own incorrect birth-date of 1670 (instead of 1668) that he gives in the first line of the *Autobiography* is taken as correct, Gennaro's inscription makes sense, or nearly makes sense.

This concludes the story-line of Vico's autobiography which I have formulated from the standpoint of the reader of the modern Italian and English editions. I have attempted to convey three things in its telling: the basic drift of what Vico himself says in the text; what the reader would bring to this through looking at notes and annotations in the modern editions of the text; and a number of observations that can be made to keep the text in perspective, drawn from a general knowledge of Vico's works, the Italian language, and some of the figures and works to which Vico refers. I hope this summary may serve the reader as a reference point for my researched interpretations, as the general development of Vico's thought is not as easy to hold in mind as it may appear on just reading the *Autobiography*.

In the *Autobiography* Vico gives little information on the intellectual, political, and religious climate in which he wrote. It is important for the modern reader to keep some of the leading features of this climate in mind. Principal among these features are Vico's relationship to Doria and the various academies of Naples, particularly as these reflect differences between the ancients and the moderns; the shift from Spanish to Austrian rule of Naples, and the beginning of the rule of the Bourbons; and the presence of the Roman Inquisition.[39]

In the years of Vico's and Doria's youth Naples was the most free-thinking society in Italy. The revival of Epicureanism in the writings of Gassendi, the rationalism of Descartes and Hobbes, and the experimentalism of Galileo, Bacon, and Boyle were topics of constant discussion. The discussion of these new ideas took place not in the university but in the various academies, which met in the houses of their influential patrons, who also provided some buffer against the suspicions of the clergy. The members of these academies came in and out of existence and were in some cases revivals of earlier academies. They were united in their opposition to scholastic philosophy, to Aristotle, and to Galen.

Vico and Doria met perhaps as early as 1695[40] and both attended sessions, several years later, of the Accademia Medinaceli. This Royal Academy was founded on 20 March 1698 by the viceroy of

---

[39] My brief remarks on these themes cannot do justice to the complexities of Vico's times. On the academies much can be learned from M. H. Fisch, 'The Academy of the Investigators', in E. Ashworth Underwood, ed., *Science, Medicine and History: Essays on the Evolution of Scientific Thought and Medical Practice Written in Honour of Charles Singer* (2 vols., London: Oxford University Press, 1953), i. 521–63, and from D. Carpanetto and G. Ricuperati, *Italy in the Age of Reason 1685–1789*, trans. C. Higgitt (New York: Longman, 1987), ch. 7. The best general account is N. Badaloni, 'La cultura', in *Storia d'Italia*, vol. iii, *Dal primo Settecento all'Unità* (Milan: Einaudi, 1973), 699–984. Concerning the political and religious climate see V. Ferrone, *Scienza natura religione: Mondo newtoniano e cultura italiana nel primo Settecento* (Naples: Jovene, 1983), G. Giarizzo, *Vico, la politica e la storia* (Naples: Guida, 1981), and G. Bedani, *Vico Revisited: Orthodoxy, Naturalism and Science in the 'Scienza Nuova'* (Oxford: Berg; New York: St Martin's Press, 1989). Also of considerable value is Nicolini, *Vico storico*, ed. F. Tessitore (Naples: Morano, 1967), esp. Nicolini's discussion of Vico's life of Carafa.

[40] Stone, 'Vico and Doria', 85.

Naples, the Duke of Medinaceli, who had come to Naples with instructions to bring together the leading minds of the city and conciliate matters, especially in regard to the Inquisition. The mother of the Duke had died in 1697 and Vico, as he reports in his autobiography, had contributed a Latin oration to the volume of her funeral rites, which was published the same year (136/27). Thus Vico, at the beginning of his career, found himself a member of this prestigious Academy. In the Academy were Vico's young friends Cristofaro, Galizia, and Giannelli, who, in 1692, were stigmatized by the Inquisition, and later imprisoned. Also present were his older, more established friends, Valletta and Caravita.

Giuseppe Valletta (1636–1714) owned the best philosophical library in the city, for which Vico did the appraisal when it was purchased by the Fathers of the Oratory, in 1726. When the Accademia Medinaceli was founded it was actually a continuation under royal patronage of meetings which had been taking place in the house of Nicola Caravita (1647–1717). Both Valletta and Caravita were leaders in resistance to the Inquisition (which for a long time had not been popular in Naples), and both were Cartesians. The Accademia Medinaceli met twice a month in the royal palace, to discuss 'matters physical, astronomical, geographical and historical'.[41] It was to this Academy, and presumably in relation to this last category, that Vico presented his lecture 'Delle cene suntuose de' Romani' (On the sumptuous dinners of the Romans) in 1699. The Academy continued until 1702.

Vico's friendship with Doria became the principal friendship of his later life. Doria was a Cartesian; yet Vico found that he was also a Platonist and that they could talk profitably together during these early years and throughout Vico's career. If Vico was indeed closely involved with Cartesian ideas until his criticism of this position in his oration on *Study Methods* of 1708–9, then certainly he and Doria would have had no strong intellectual conflict during the sessions of the Royal Academy. Later Vico and Doria became part of the reaction against the moderns and the Cartesianism associated with the *moderni*, endorsing the importance of humane letters as the basis of human education. Doria came to the attention of the European public through his *La vita civile*, which appeared in 1709 and in another edition in 1710, the same year that Vico

---

[41] Fisch, 'Academy of the Investigators', 547.

dedicated to Doria his attack on Descartes, *De antiquissima Italorum sapientia.*[42]

La vita civile in its very title indicates a humanist point of view, reflecting a work of more than three centuries earlier, with the same title, by Matteo Palmieri. Doria's work is essentially republican in its sentiments and it sought to reopen discussion of politics and its relation to society where Machiavelli and the Humanists had left off. Doria's work had the great success with the northern European thinkers which Vico always sought for his own works, but never achieved. Doria's own critique of Cartesian philosophy, *Discorsi critici filosofici intorno alla filosofia degl'antichi e dei moderni*, was written in 1724, and this was followed by his attack on Locke and the moderns in his *Difesa della metafisica degli antichi contro il signor Giovanni Locke* (2 vols., 1732–3). In effect what Doria accomplished in his various works was the creation of one of the first and most important lines of argument against Enlightenment thought, by criticizing not only its economic and political models but also its views of scientific philosophy, using the perspectives of the ancients and the humanists as a base.

Vico and Doria are leaders in the great quarrel in Italy between the ancients and the moderns that stretched from the sixteenth century until the end of the first half of the eighteenth. The ancients were largely in control of the universities and they used both civil and ecclesiastical censorship and, in some instances, the Inquisition as their weapons. In Naples the moderns are most fully identified with the tradition of the Academy of the Investigators, which was organized in 1649 by Tommaso Cornelio, Lionardo di Capua, and Francesco d'Andrea, and which went through several periods of decline and revival until its termination in 1737. Following the death of Di Capua in 1695 there was an interval of about forty years during which the Academy of the Investigators was replaced by others, including the Accademia Medinaceli.

In 1732 Celestino Galiani, Prefect of the University of Naples, founded the Academy of the Sciences. It was modelled on the Paris

---

[42] On Doria see R. Ajello, 'La critica del regime in Doria, Intieri, Broggia', in *Arcana Juris: Diritto e politica nel Settecento italiana* (Naples: Jovene, 1976), 391–420, and D. Lachterman, 'Vico, Doria e la geometria sintetica', *Bollettino del Centro di Studi Vichiani* 10 (1980), 10–35. See Badaloni, 'La cultura', 808–12.

Academy of the Sciences; it conducted various physical and chemical experiments and gathered various types of scientific information. Galiani was a friend of Vico and supported Vico's son Gennaro in becoming Vico's successor at the university. Galiani was in charge of the reform of the university in 1735 under the rule of Charles of Bourbon. In founding the Academy of the Sciences three years earlier Galiani had had the help of Giannone in Vienna, with Charles VI of Austria, to obtain an imperial diploma for the establishment of the Academy. Giannone was no friend of Vico and there is no evidence that Vico was ever a member of this Academy which in fact ceased to exist in 1744, the year Vico died. When it was revived in 1780 Gennaro was made one of its fellows.

Vico and Doria were representatives of the *veteres* against the *moderni*, a fact which is symbolized in their association with the Academy of Oziosi, which began in 1733 and ceased five years later, in 1738. The year before its close Vico delivered his address on the relation between philosophy and eloquence, in which he criticizes the separation of the modern conception of knowledge from eloquence.[43] The Academy of the Investigators was revived for a brief period between 1735 and 1737, and Vico was a member. The opening address in 1737, by G. G. Carulli, was published with a dedication to Vico's old friend Doria.

Although it is clear that Vico and Doria are leading exponents of the *veteres* against the *moderni* and that by the middle of the eighteenth century the moderns had won control of the universities, it is also clear that Vico moves freely throughout his career among these academies. He is always the 'insider-outsider'. His final concern is with the ancients as the fountain-head of human wisdom, but he moves freely among the moderns and makes few enemies on either side of the quarrel. He is one of the leaders of the *veteres* of the Academy of Oziosi but he is a friend of the founder of the opposing Academy of the Sciences. Toward the end of his career he is one of the *Investiganti* in the revival of the Academy of the Investigators in 1735 by Stefano di Stefano, as he

---

[43] 'The Academies and the Relation between Philosophy and Eloquence', trans. D. P. Verene, in *On the Study Methods of Our Time*, 85–90. See *Opere di G. B. Vico*, vol. vii (Bari: Laterza, 1940), 36–7.

was a member of one of its earlier versions, the Accademia Medinaceli, but he is no longer in any sense a Cartesian.

The mid-eighteenth century can claim to be the most splendid period in Neapolitan history, but this phase of rejuvenation did not take place until the end of the long period of domination of Naples by the succession of Spanish and Austrian viceroys and the establishment of Naples as an independent kingdom under a Bourbon king. In fact, Naples was not in this position until just ten years before Vico's death, when the city was conquered by Charles of Bourbon in 1734. Thus for most of Vico's life Naples was not in its flourishing period. It was ruled by Spanish viceroys from 1509 to 1707, and by Austrian viceroys from 1707 to 1734. Vico dealt with these shifts of power much as he appears to have dealt with the presence of the Roman Inquisition—he was a conservative who stood on the side of authority. He was not incapable of creating the opportune moment, such as writing the 'In morte di Antonio Carafa' on the death of Marshal Carafa in 1693, which certainly encouraged the Marshal's nephew, a pupil of Vico, to offer him a commission in 1714 to write the life of Carafa.

As stated earlier, Vico did not deliver the customary inaugural oration for the university year in 1701 because of the confusion into which Naples had been thrown by the death of the Spanish king in 1700. The king's death provoked the War of Spanish Succession (1700–13), a war Vico regarded as the modern counterpart to that between Rome and Carthage. There was a failed attempt to assassinate Medinaceli. Soon after, Medinaceli was recalled and replaced by the last of the Spanish viceroys, the Duke of Escalona. The so-called conspiracy of Macchia took place in September 1701 and its leaders, Capece and Sangro, were put to death. Any remains of the conspiracy were definitely dispersed by February 1702, and that spring Philip V visited Naples (17 April– 2 June). Vico was appointed as one of two writers to write the official history of the disturbances, which he did, as *De Parthenopea conjuratione*, but it was not accepted, perhaps because of its impartiality. It was not published in his lifetime.[44]

As Vico reports in his autobiography on the visit of Philip V, the Duke of Escalona commanded Vico to write a panegyric. In his oration Vico tells Philip, King of the Spaniards, that he is the

---

[44] On Vico's *Coniuratio* see Nicolini, *Vico storico*, 424–8.

greatest being on earth and that he in his body is more beautiful than the most beautiful of all women. Yet in the next paragraph of his autobiography Vico blithely reports that at a later time (1707), when the Austrians had taken charge of Naples, he responded to a request by Count von Daun, the new viceroy, to draft funeral inscriptions to honour Capece and Sangro as martyrs. He reprints the entire text of von Daun's letter. Yesterday's enemies of the state, who had sought to keep the greatest being on earth from becoming ruler of Naples, became today's martyrs. Vico has no problem in mentioning these two tasks in the same breath; of course, he is writing about them in retrospect.

At the end of Austrian rule and the conquest of the Kingdom of Naples in 1734, Vico served as head of the university delegation to greet Charles Bourbon. Vico soon took advantage of the change in political order to request, the following year, that he be appointed Royal Historian, which was quickly granted, at an annual stipend of 100 ducats. That same year he dedicated his *De aequilibrio* to Charles. The following year he was successful, with the help of Galiani, in gaining royal permission for his son Gennaro to succeed him in his university chair without any public competition.

Croce claims of Vico that 'political life rolled past his head, like the sky and its stars' and that both political and religious controversy were so completely out of his sphere that 'he was indeed a non-political person'.[45] Such a judgement is too much to accept. There is certainly a sense in which Vico was outside politics. He was never publicly opposed to present authority and the real power that such authority implied. It might be argued that Vico, like Hobbes, had a good sense of how absolute and yet how changing real political power could be, and kept his distance. With certain of the ancients Vico had learned the lesson that philosophy is not politics, a lesson that Plato took longer to learn than Aristotle, and that true philosophy is not the instrument for immediate political change. Vico was able to write and publish ideas that could have been seen as highly controversial in both political and religious spheres without anyone making a successful attempt to censor him or place the authorities against him. The myth that his ideas could not really be understood

---

[45] B. Croce, *The Philosophy of Giambattista Vico*, trans. R. G. Collingwood (New York: Russell and Russell, 1964; orig. pub. 1913), 250.

and that he was even an odd and pedantic thinker certainly did no harm in this respect.

Vico in fact had little personally to fear from the governments of the Spanish and Austrian viceroys who ruled through his youth and most productive years. He submitted every word he wrote to both civil and ecclesiastical censorship as well as to various friends and advisers. Vico, unlike his contemporary Giannone, was never perceived as a threat. Giannone's *Civil History of the Kingdom of Naples* was published in 1723 and was the first modern masterpiece of constitutional history. It was also a polemic against the papacy. By his use of historical analysis, Giannone showed how the Church had come to have a dominance over civil government. Giannone represented 'jurisdictionalism' and the notion of a national kingdom as opposed to the jurists who were for local autonomy and local interests. The storm of controversy over Giannone's work caused him both ten years of imprisonment and lifelong exile from Naples.

Vico never mentions Giannone in his *Autobiography* and a strong animosity certainly existed between them, at least on Giannone's side. The cause of this bad feeling may have been a treatise against Giannone's *Civil History*, written by Vico's friend Giulio Nicola Torno (1672–1756), who was the ecclesiastical censor of most of Vico's books. Vico's ideas of the feral state of the first men and his ideas of law and the life of the nation are much more radical in their challenge of Church doctrine and political authority than are those of Giannone, but they are also less immediate. Vico's *New Science*, defended and used by figures such as Duni and Cuoco, was passed on later to Italian nationalists such as Foscolo, Prati, and Mazzini, and it became the book of the Risorgimento.[46]

The Inquisition functioned throughout Vico's career, and its activity is particularly important for understanding Vico's early years because of Vico's probable early attachment to Cartesianism, Epicureanism, and the atomism of Gassendi. The period of 1668 to 1693 was one of intensified activity by the Roman Inquisition in Naples. The Church was intent on eliminating Epicureanism and atomism, which were equated with atheism and associated with

---

[46] On *il vichismo* see Badaloni, 'La cultura', 875–81; on Foscolo, see ibid. 904–8.

the views that there were men before Adam and that the soul
dissipated with the body at death. These doctrines were thought to
have been spread by the general interest in and discussion of the
ideas of the new philosophy by Cornelio and Di Capua. In 1693,
the same year that Cristofaro, Galizia, and Gianelli were condemned by the Inquisition, Di Capua's *Parere,* which had been
published in 1681, was placed on the Index. Di Capua's work,
which advocates a modern empirically based conception of medicine, was the most important production of the *Investiganti.*

The Spanish Inquisition had withdrawn from Naples before
Vico's birth, after a century of strife with the Roman Inquisition
and protests from the populace. Valletta and Caravita were the
chief protectors of Cristofaro, Galizia, and Gianelli, and they were
also Vico's patrons. Thus Vico may have been very close to the
situation. After the arrests Valletta sent protests to the Pope.
Valletta's protests were not isolated acts but were reflections of a
history of unrest and general dissatisfaction in Naples concerning
the power of Inquisitorial proceedings. Despite its unpopularity,
the Roman Inquisition persisted even after the arrival of Charles of
Bourbon in 1734.

In the *Autobiography* Vico passes very lightly over the doctrines
of Gassendi, saying 'this is a philosophy to satisfy the circumscribed
minds of children and the weak minds of silly women' (126/18).
But these lines, written in 1725 to describe his investigation at
Vatolla of atomism and the doctrines of Lucretius, seem very
strong. He probably had a crisis of religious doubt, and may have
come very close to involvement in the difficulties of his condemned
friends. In 1720 in a letter to Father Giacco, Vico writes that errors
of his early years are remembered in Naples and used against him,
but he does not say precisely what these errors were. In 1720 Vico
began to bring out his theory of universal law, a topic that could
have opened him to religious criticism. As mentioned above, he
says that he began to write a commentary on Grotius's work on
universal law but desisted because 'it was not fitting for a man of
Catholic faith to adorn with notes the work of a heretical author'
(155/46).

Vico answered any criticism that suggested impiety in his works
by pointing out his associations with the clergy and pointing to
facts of his exemplary personal conduct. This is the tack he takes,
for example, to answer his critics in the *Giornale de' letterati.* In

this exchange concerning his views in the *De antiquissima*, Vico refuses to enter into any dispute involving religious feeling or argument and holds only to objective metaphysical points.

The presence of the Inquisition never stemmed the flow of ideas that took place within the various academies throughout Vico's lifetime, especially in the activity of the *Investiganti*. Throughout Vico's career it was widely known that there was a constant coming and going of clerics at Vico's house, and Vico was known for his personal piety. His claim to piety was really his response to the ever-present possibility that his ideas would come under ecclesiastical scrutiny. It seems likely that in the 1690s Vico concluded that this was the course to follow, and it was one that generally fitted with his political conservatism.

Croce claims that 'all Vico's writings show the Catholic religion established in his heart, grave, solid and immovable as a pillar of adamant'.[47] Opposite this view is another, one that regards Vico's constant reminders in his *Autobiography, New Science,* and elsewhere that what he is saying is for the greater glory of the Catholic religion, as 'protesting too much'. In this view, Vico knew that if many of his ideas about history and natural law were ever really understood they would be more dangerously offensive to conventional religion and the established political order than atomism, republicanism, and the new philosophy ever were.

In the *New Science* Vico quotes from the *Fables* of Phaedrus, that the art of fable first arose as a means for slaves to express their thoughts and feelings without affronting their masters (425). As discussed above, Vico ends the 1731 continuation of his autobiography with a citation of Phaedrus. Vico may use his constant profession of piety to distract the suspicious or conventional reader and at other times say controversial things obliquely or incompletely.[48] In *Giunone in danza* (Juno in dance) (1721), for example, which Vico wrote for a marriage of the Rocca family, he put in fable form all the elements of his theory of universal law. Certainly

---

[47] Croce, *The Philosophy of Giambattista Vico*, 248.

[48] The interpretation which most systematically deals with this feature of Vico's thought is F. Vaughan, *The Political Philosophy of Giambattista Vico: An Introduction to 'La Scienza Nuova'* (The Hague: Nijhoff, 1972). See also the remarks by Bedani, *Vico Revisited*, 31–2, and by Nicolini, 'Il Vico e il suo censore ecclesiastico', in *Saggi vichiani* (Naples: Giannini, 1955), 281–95.

the technique of the fable and of special ways of expressing ideas were never far from Vico's mind.

I do not mean that Vico was not himself pious and probably religious. It is not reasonable to regard him as carrying on a lifetime masquerade of faith because of an early fright at the scene of his friends being imprisoned by the Inquisition. But Vico was certainly an advocate of civic religion and, in an age such as I have tried briefly to describe, his best protection for the communication of his ideas and the survival of his great discoveries for the future was to surround himself with religious authority, which included interspersing his works with the kind of professions of faith desired and understood by the conventional religion of his day.

Croce has remarked that Vico's *Autobiography* is 'the application of the *New Science* to the life of the author, to the history of his own individual life; and the method of it is as much original as it is just and true' (L'Autobiografia *del Vico è insomma, l'estensione della* Scienza nuova *alla biografia dell'autore, alla storia della propria vita individuale; e il metodo ne è, quanto originale, altrettanto giusto e vero*).[49] Croce does not say more than this; that is, he does not pursue this idea in terms of what the specific relationships between these two works may be to produce an interpretation of the philosophical character of the *Autobiography*. My interpretations which follow begin from this suggestive statement, although my own interpretation of Vico's philosophy is very different from and, certainly in respect to the role of imagination and the importance of the 'imaginative universal', opposite to Croce's.

Fubini, in the preface to his edition of the *Autobiografia*, says that from Nicolini's researches we can see that in relating the story of his life 'Vico has given us a story indeed, but a mythical story, almost the myth of himself' (*il Vico ci abbia dato una storia sí ma una storia mitica, quasi il mito di se stesso*).[50] Enrico De Mas and Donald Kelley have made similar remarks. De Mas writes, 'From the very first pages, the reader of Vico's *Autobiography* cannot fail to be struck powerfully by the mythical and prophetic tone that

---

[49] Croce, *La filosofia di Giambattista Vico* (Bari: Laterza, 1962; orig. pub. 1911), 276.
[50] Fubini, Preface to *Autobiografia*, p. xiii.

animates the narrative.'[51] Kelley, commenting on Vico's statement in the *Universal Law* that 'history does not yet have its principles', says, 'Vico's lament about the disorder of history applies also to his own career, for his biography likewise lacks its "principles", in his sense of the term, though his *Autobiography* certainly provides materials for such a project.'[52] Edward Said, in his remarks on Vico at the end of *Beginnings*, claims that in understanding Vico, 'What needs emphasis, however, is Vico's passionate concern with the fundamentally severe and economical operations of the autodidactic humanistic mind. This concern, then, condones, even requires, the application of *The New Science* to the *Autobiography* and vice versa.'[53]

Vico claimed in the *New Science* that the 'master key' to this science was the discovery that the first language of gentile humanity took the form of 'poetic characters' or 'imaginative universals,' a discovery, he says, that took him a good twenty years to make (presumably the period from his oration on the *Study Methods* (1708/9) and his researches into the origins of Latin in the *Ancient Wisdom* of 1710 to the *First New Science* in 1730) (34). Does Vico intend the story of his life, at one level, to be a fable of himself? To what extent should the reader take Vico's distortions such as his claim that on returning to Naples he arrived as a 'stranger in his own land' as simple transgressions of fact, or as being part of a deliberate underlying fabulous structure of his narration?

Croce's and Fubini's remarks, as well as those of De Mas, Kelley, and Said, call for a full reading of Vico's *Autobiography*. The rewards for such a reading may be twofold: light may be thrown on his *Autobiography* as an essential part of Vico's philosophical system; some light may be thrown on the nature of philosophical autobiography itself. The questions I wish to address in what follows may be put into three groups.

[51] E. De Mas, 'Vico's Four Authors', in G. Tagliacozzo and H. V. White, eds., *Giambattista Vico: An International Symposium* (Baltimore: Johns Hopkins University Press, 1969), 3. De Mas, 'On the New Method of a New Science: A Study of Giambattista Vico', *Journal of the History of Ideas*, 32 (1971), 86, speaks of Vico's 'allusive and symbolic discourse' in his autobiography and claims that Vico wrote it 'as if he were treating the life of a great commander or a messianic redeemer'.

[52] D. R. Kelley, 'Vico's Road: From Philology to Jurisprudence and Back', in Tagliacozzo and Verene, eds., *Vico's Science of Humanity*, 15.

[53] E. W. Said, *Beginnings: Intention and Method* (New York: Basic Books, 1975), 363.

1. What in detail can be said about the observation that the *Autobiography* is an application or extension of the *New Science*? What principles of the *New Science* may be present in Vico's structuring of his own life as a text? Does Vico employ the 'new critical art' that he speaks of in the *New Science* in the creation of this text? Is his life constructed as an analogue to his concept of an 'ideal eternal history', in some sense having three ages analogous to his three ages of a nation governed by a principle of providence? Does his conception of *fantasia* as the primary mode of understanding anything in the world guide him in some way to construct a 'poetic character' of himself as the 'heroic' or first modern philosopher set upon by his detractors, who cannot comprehend his science? In other words, in what way does Vico perhaps make the story of his life a particular locus of the main principles of his philosophy, a particular point on which they converge?

2. If the *Autobiography* may be a point of application of the *New Science* in which the principles of the life of nations are tranferred or carried over to principles of a particular life, does the *Autobiography* in turn provide a verification of these principles? What is the ground of the metaphysical idea of 'ideal eternal history', that is, that all nations pass through stages of gods, heroes, and human society, a cycle of origin, rise, maturation, decline, and fall? We are never told this in the *New Science*. 'Ideal eternal history' (*storia ideale eterna*) is not presented as one of the axioms of the new science, but is employed to order and illuminate their operation (e.g. 239–45; 349). Is this metaphysical idea of an eternal cycle that illuminates the workings of history grounded in the phenomenon of human life, that is, a life that has a natural narrative of beginning, middle, and end? Is the fact that we can make a philosophical narrative of ourselves, that is, understand our particular lives as a total order of causes, the reason we can make philosophical sense of history? Is Vico, in taking the occasion to write his life story, doing only that, or can he be seen to be doing more than that (perhaps not wholly consciously), to add a needed dimension for the understanding of his philosophy?

3. An autobiography is not simply a chronological account of events, although Vico's, as most autobiographies, holds to a general chronological sequence. An autobiography, at least a philosophical autobiography, one that seeks causal order, is not memory in its ordinary psychological sense. To tell one's life is to enter a theatre

of memory that is both inside oneself and also tied to the external order of past events through which one has lived. The self has no more than momentary reality without a narrative of itself which constantly lives below the surface of our actions. To produce this narrative in explicit form is to enter into the depths of the animus and produce its persona. This act must in some way be tied to the first human act of narration—the *mythos,* which Vico says is always *vera narratio* or 'true speech'. He claims *mythos* to be the source of the Latin *mutus,* 'mute' (401), which is the original life-speech of signs that is transformed into narrative. Behind Vico's autobiography is this understanding of the origin and nature of narrative.

If we consider his conception of narrative and original speech as related to his own act of narrative, what might this suggest for the art of autobiography generally? What kind of true speech is narrative? What kind of truth is autobiographical truth? Vico is not like other modern writers of autobiography, Gibbon, for example, or Franklin; he writes his autobiography as the possessor of an original philosophical understanding of the origin and nature of narrative itself. In the writing of his life has Vico discovered a new literary art, that still largely remains to be discovered from him, that parallels his discovery of a new science? Should the term 'new' be in some way applied to his *Autobiography,* as it is attached to the title of the *New Science,* not just in the sense that his autobiography is the first work in the history of autobiography to apply a genetic method to his own writings, but because it is done by a thinker whose own narrative is tied to a philosophy that is based on a new science of narration? In other words, in addition to what the *Autobiography* may mean in its internal connection to the *New Science,* does it also hold unexplored clues to what autobiography as a process is and what narrative is, that have yet to be found elsewhere?

The first of these sets of questions concerns the application, the second the verification of the *New Science;* both fairly closely remain within the sphere of Vico scholarship. The third points to implications for the nature and art of philosophical autobiography.

2

The Idea of Autobiography

If we think of philosophical autobiographies written since the eighteenth century, conceived in the conventional sense of the philosopher giving the history of his own life, Vico's *Autobiography* is the first of a series of works that includes Rousseau's *Confessions*, Hume's *Life of Himself*, Mill's *Autobiography*, Spencer's *An Autobiography*, Nietzsche's *Ecce Homo*, Kierkegaard's *Journals*, the autobiographies of Croce and Collingwood, Berdyaev's *Dream and Reality*, Santayana's *Persons and Places*, Sartre's *Les Mots*, Russell's *My Philosophical Development* and his three-volume narration of his life, the autobiographical sketches that are part of the 'Library of Living Philosophers' series, including ones by such figures as Dewey and Whitehead, Ayer's *Part* and *More of My Life*, Quine's *The Time of My Life*, J. N. Findlay's 'My Life: 1903–1973', and Richard Popkin's 'Intellectual Autobiography: Warts and All'.

Sometimes a distinction is made between formal and informal autobiography, formal being when the author has deliberately attempted to tell the story of his life as a whole or to relate some part of it in a holistic manner, informal being what is usually told in memoirs, letters, diaries, and journals. Memoirs, for example, differ generally from autobiography because they usually emphasize what is remembered rather than who is remembering; the author of the memoir is not so much recounting his life as a narrative whole as making a record of certain events of which he was a part. But these are not firm categories.

I would like to consider the idea of autobiography in two ways. I wish first to make a number of general, essentially informative remarks concerning the study of autobiography and the extent to which Vico has and has not figured in it, including the particular idea that led to the publication of Vico's autobiography itself. I wish then to discuss the idea of autobiography in philosophical terms, specifically showing how the Vichian conception of autobiography is derived from the ancient problem of self-knowledge.

The idea of autobiography as an explicitly stated philosophical idea derives not from Vico but from Wilhelm Dilthey (1833–1911). In 'Entwürfe zur Kritik der historischen Vernunft', published in *Der Aufbau der geschichtlichen Welt in den Geisteswissenschaften* (Formation of the historical world in the human studies) (1910), Dilthey briefly but importantly applies some of the central concepts of his philosophy to the idea of autobiography. In sketching out his conception of a critique of historical reason Dilthey entitles the opening section 'Das Erleben und die Selbstbiographie' ('Lived experience and autobiography').[1] Dilthey uses the older term *Selbstbiographie*, which derives from Herder, rather than *Autobiographie*. Dilthey says that 'Autobiography [*Selbstbiographie*] is the highest and most instructive form in which the understanding of life confronts us'.[2] In Dilthey's view *Selbstbiographie* as a form of literary expression requires *Selbstbesinnung* (self-reflection). Self-reflection on the course of one's life is present in various degrees in every individual and expresses itself in ever new forms. Dilthey says that *Selbstbesinnung* is present in the verses of Solon, the Stoic philosophers, meditations of the saints, and modern *Lebensphilosophie*. He says only *Selbstbesinnung* 'makes historical insight possible'.[3]

Rudolf Makkreel, in his study of Dilthey's philosophy, explains Dilthey's conception of *Besinnung über das Leben* (reflection about life) as 'concerned with those aspects of life that cannot be assigned a definite historical meaning, but nonetheless are not to be reduced or elevated, as the case may be, to having a transcendent significance only'.[4] Life is the total framework to which everything has a relation. Life, as a whole that encompasses everything, cannot in Dilthey's terms have a meaning (since meaning would require interpretation of the relationship the parts have to a whole), but life can make sense. As Makkreel puts it, '*Besinnung* (reflection) produces a *Sinn des Lebens* (sense of life) rather than a *Bedeutung des Lebens* (meaning of life).'[5]

---

[1] W. Dilthey, *Gesammelte Schriften*, vol. vii (Stuttgart: Teubner; Göttingen: Vandenhoeck and Ruprecht, 1979), 191–204.   [2] Ibid. 199.   [3] Ibid. 201.

[4] R. A. Makkreel, *Dilthey: Philosopher of the Human Studies* (Princeton, NJ: Princeton University Press, 1975), 376–7.

[5] Ibid. 377. See also W. Dilthey, *Selected Works*, vol. v: *Poetry and Experience*, ed. R. A. Makkreel and F. Rodi (Princeton, NJ: Princeton University Press, 1985), 230 and 274–5.

Makkreel says, 'Autobiography [for Dilthey] is the literary expression of an individual's self-reflection. It illustrates how reflection attains an evaluative sense of life before definition of its historical meaning in biography.'[6] In biography there is a life history that is complete and can be given determinate meaning, but in autobiography the life history of the individual is always incomplete and must appeal to reflection to hold together the diverse elements of life. Life, in Dilthey's view, has in fact already worked out much of what comes into the autobiographer's framework because his memory has allowed only certain events and patterns to remain for the basis of his reflection.

The central principle of Dilthey's interest in autobiography, which takes him very close to Vico, is that 'the one who understands the course of life is the same as the one who produced it'.[7] This is very like Vico's principle of *verum ipsum factum*, that the true is the same as or convertible with the made, although Dilthey does not derive it from Vico. Makkreel, in an essay comparing certain features of Vico's and Dilthey's thought, points out that 'In moving from the understanding of nature to the understanding of history, Dilthey stresses the element of making or *poiesis*'.[8] In relation to the *Geisteswissenschaften* Dilthey says that 'The subject of knowing is here one with its object, and this is the same on all levels of its objectification of itself'.[9] The historical world is built up in connection with the development of the *Geisteswissenschaften*.[10] Our world becomes historical for us because we are able to understand it through the formation of historical judgements that themselves are part of its making and its truth.

A further aspect of Dilthey's philosophy that connects with Vico is his conception of *Sosein-Müssen* (having-to-be-thus), which he contrasts with the determinate idea of necessity (*Notwendigkeit*). Dilthey's example is the feeling of appropriateness we have when a musical composition has had the proper finish. It is the sense of the attainment of some value but not something as explicit as a specific

---

    [6] Makkreel, *Dilthey*, 379.
    [7] Dilthey, *Gesammelte Schriften*, vii. 200; Makkreel, *Dilthey*, 379.
    [8] R. A. Makkreel, 'Vico and Some Kantian Reflections on Historical Judgment', in G. Tagliacozzo, ed., *Vico: Past and Present* (2 vols. in 1, Atlantic Highlands, NJ: Humanities Press, 1981), ii, 28.
    [9] Dilthey, *Gesammelte Schriften*, vii. 191.
    [10] Makkreel, 'Vico and Some Kantian Reflections', 34.

meaning. This is frequently experienced in instrumental music and is also, as Makkreel puts it, 'most evident in the impression or sense of life connected with anthropological reflection. Thus the self-reflection of the autobiographer involves a feeling of rightness or appropriateness about the overall development of his life . . .'.[11] This sense of *Sosein-Müssen* can be viewed as the general phenomenon of consciousness underlying Vico's assertion in the *Autobiography* that his *vita letteraria* 'had to be such as it was and not otherwise' (182/71). Vico means something more rigorous by this than that his life has a sense of appropriateness. This sense of 'having-to-be-thus', that in Dilthey's terms is natural to autobiographical self-reflection, is what is transformed by Vico into his conception of the providential character of his life.

Georg Misch (1878–1965), Dilthey's disciple and literary executor, devoted his long life to writing his four-volume history of autobiography, *Geschichte der Autobiographie*.[12] Misch says that 'the purpose of this book is to relate the limitless variety of autobiographical writing to the history of the human mind, and to present it in a historical perspective'.[13] Although Misch does not discuss Dilthey's conception of autobiography at any length, his aim is to give historical content to Dilthey's view that autobiography is rooted in a natural drive toward *Selbstbewusstsein*.[14] He says, 'In a certain sense the history of autobiography is a history of human self-awareness [*Selbstbewusstsein*].'[15]

Misch takes the idea of autobiography in its broadest possible sense, such that any instance of self-awareness or self-portrait becomes part of his history. Any piece of writing that has an autobiographical cast to it can count as part of the genre, from the earliest fragments to the Renaissance writing of lives to the modern writing of autobiographies that begins in the eighteenth century, and including in between all passages and parts of ancient and medieval texts where the author recounts something of himself. Misch points out that this is largely a Western and even European

---

[11] Makkreel, *Dilthey*, 392–3.
[12] G. Misch, *Geschichte der Autobiographie*, vol. i. (3rd rev. edn., Bern: Francke, 1949–50; orig. pub. 1907); vols. ii–iv (Frankfurt-on-Main: Schulte-Bulmke, 1955–69).
[13] G. Misch, *A History of Autobiography in Antiquity*, trans. E. W. Dickes (2 vols., Cambridge, Mass.: Harvard University Press, 1951), i. 4.
[14] Misch, *Geschichte*, i. 10–11; *History*, i. 8.
[15] Misch, *History*, i. 8.

form of literature, rooted in the Western conception of the individual, and says that his work is intended to follow along lines
recommended by Goethe, to study 'the ways in which the individual's sense of personality has developed in the Western world'.[16]

Misch does not ask questions about which works may be truly
decisive for the idea of autobiography but focuses on the gradual
development and shifts in conceptions and forms. For example, he
says that in Dante autobiography fulfils for the first time the
function of exposing the relations between the life and work of an
author, and concludes, 'thus Dante is the predecessor of Vico and
Goethe' (thinking of Goethe's autobiography, *Dichtung und
Wahrheit*).[17]

Because any literary act of self-reflection can count as autobiography in Misch's view, he fails to recognize Max Fisch's point,
mentioned above, that 'Aside from the light it sheds on his other
works, and the interest it has in common with every other
intellectual autobiography, Vico's has the unique interest of being
the first application of the genetic method by an original thinker to
his own writings.'[18] Misch remarks on Vico as one of many figures
of 'literary' autobiography; that is, autobiography that presents the
author's career with attention to the 'subjective motive' behind it,
although in a more limited fashion than the intense analysis of
personality engaged in by the Renaissance thinker Cardano, which
is according to Misch the first autobiography of this type.[19] Misch
recognizes practically nothing of the uniqueness of Vico's work.

Misch presents Vico's autobiography as a first and typical
example of the idea of development present in Enlightenment
philosophy, offering a solution to the 'biographical task'.[20] Apart
from this assertion, the substance of Misch's discussion is a
summary of Vico's autobiography. The summary is basically
correct with regard to the contents of Vico's work, but the only
footnote reference to Vico's text is to '*Raccolta di vite e memorie
d'uomini illustri*, ed. G. Compagnoni (Milano, 1821)'.[21]

---

[16] Misch, *History*, i. 3.   [17] Misch, *Geschichte*, iv. 533.
[18] Fisch, Preface to *The Autobiography of Giambattista Vico*, trans. M. H. Fisch
and T. G. Bergin (Ithaca, NY: Cornell University Press, 1983), p. v.
[19] Misch, *Geschichte*, iv. 733–8.   [20] Ibid. iv. 803–9.
[21] Ibid. iv. 803 n. 17. See the description of this edition in 'Editions of Vico's
Autobiography'. Compagnoni is not the editor of this volume but the author of a
letter which the publisher and editor, Gian Battista Sonzogno, prints instead of a

Concerning Vico's conclusion of his 1731 continuation of his autobiography with his quotation about Socrates' death from Phaedrus' *Fabulae*, Misch comments that Socrates was selected as the symbol for the ideal of correct living and dying throughout eighteenth-century autobiography.[22] Although this is true it offers no interpretation of the possible meanings of Vico's specific use of his quotation from Phaedrus (see my comments in Chapter 1). As a short sketch of Vico's life Misch's discussion has some use, but there is no comparison between it and, for example, Michelet's sketch of Vico's life in the *Biographie universelle*.[23]

The term 'autobiography' is constructed from Greek by the combination of *graphē* 'writing' with *bios* 'life' (in the sense of the course or way of living, as opposed to *zōē*, 'animal or organic life'), prefixed by *auto-* 'of or by oneself' (from *autos*, 'self'). 'Autobiography', as used in all modern languages, whether French, German, English, or Italian, means 'the writing of one's own history; the story of one's life written by himself'.[24] The first use of 'autobiography' is traditionally ascribed to Robert Southey in the first issue of the *Quarterly Review* (1809), in describing a forgotten book by a Portuguese painter on his own life, and may have been coined by Southey or within his circle of literary friends. But there is an earlier use in the *Monthly Review* of 1797.[25] According to Larousse

---

preface. Vol. iv, prepared from Misch's *Nachlass*, was written in 1904, before the critical edition of Vico's *L'autobiografia* by Croce and Nicolini (1911). Misch must have used more than the edition he cites, since that edition reprints only Vico's Venice text of 1728 and Misch discusses the material of Vico's continuation of 1731. This would have been available in the then standard Ferrari edition of Vico's works of 1852–4.

[22] Misch, *Geschichte*, iv. 809.

[23] J. Michelet, 'Vico', entry in *Biographie universelle ancienne et moderne* (new edn., 45 vols., Paris: Desplaces and Brockhaus, 1854–65), xliii. 295–301.

[24] *The Oxford English Dictionary* (2nd edn., 20 vols. Oxford: Clarendon Press, 1989), i. 801.

[25] For the details of Southey's use see Misch's note in *History*, i. 5. Southey's use is what is reported in the entry for 'autobiography' in the OED prior to the second edition of 1989. *A Supplement to the OED, Vol. 1 (1972)* under 'autobiography' reports its mention in the *Monthly Review*, 2nd Series, 24 (1797), 375. A. Momigliano, *The Development of Greek Biography* (Cambridge, Mass.: Harvard University Press, 1971), mentions the Southey citation as the first use to be found in the OED and says: 'The facts known to me seem to point to an interesting origin' (14). He then relates details of the *Monthly Review* reference. The reference is to a reviewer's comment on a book by Isaac D'Israeli published in 1796, in which he uses the term 'self-biography'. The review doubts whether such a term is legitimate

(1866) it enters French from English.[26] In Italian it is first recorded in Marchi's *Dizionario tecnico-etimologico-filologico* (1828–9), but does not enter common usage until much later.[27]

The German *Selbstbiographie* derives from Herder's suggestion of *Selbstbiographieen berühmter Männer* (Self-biographies of famous men), compiled for publication by David Christian Seybold in 1796 and 1799.[28] Herder wished to distinguish between confessions, whether religious or humanistic, and the actual life-stories (*Lebensbeschreibungen*) of famous men. The more modern Anglicization, *Autobiographie*, and the original *Selbstbiographie* are now used interchangeably (e.g. in Misch's work).[29] Goethe, as Misch says, had the whole genre in view when he spoke of the 'so-called confessions' of all ages.[30]

'Autobiography' is a distinctively modern word, not used in the ancient world. This is not true of 'biography', the earliest known use of which is attributed to the Greek writer Damascius, born at the end of the fifth century AD, who wrote a life of his tutor Isidorus. The earliest known writers of biographies are Scylax of Caryanda and Xanthus of Lydia, who were older contemporaries of Herodotus and who are referred to as *logopoioi* ('tellers of tales'). *Biographia* was used in Latin but 'biography' is not used in English until a little more than a century before 'autobiography', the first use being attributed to Dryden's reference in 1683 to the literary work of Plutarch.

In relation to biography and also autobiography, the views of the little-known English thinker Roger North (1653–1734) deserve to be noted. North is not generally discussed in the literature on

and says (as quoted by the *Supp. OED* and Momigliano): 'yet autobiography would have seemed pedantic'. The *OED* (2nd edn., 1989) incorporates the *Monthly Review* reference of the earlier *Supp.*

[26] Larousse, *Grand Dictionnaire Universel du XIX Siècle*, i. 979: 'ce mot, quoique d'origine grecque, est de fabrique anglaise.'

[27] Marchi, *Dizionario tecnico-etimologico-filologico* (Milan, 1828–9). Later in the century N. Tommasèo, *Dizionario della lingua italiana* (4 vols., Turin, 1861–79), reports that *autobiografia* is not in common use, but that it has literary use that is increasing.

[28] See Misch's note in *History*, i. 5–6.

[29] *Grimms Deutsches Wörterbuch* (Leipzig, 1905), vol. x, pt. 1 gives only an entry for *Selbstbiographie*, defining it as the concept of *Selbstlebensbeschreibung*. *Autobiographie* is probably an Anglicization (as Larousse claims for the French, see n. 26 above).

[30] See Misch's note in *History*, i. 6.

autobiography (he is missing from Misch's work), but he wrote several distinguished biographies and an autobiography titled *Notes of Me*, and formulated a theory of what he called 'life-writing'. None of this material was published during his lifetime, and so it exerted little influence, and of course no influence on Vico, although his thinking on such subjects predates Vico.[31] He wrote a *General Preface* which he intended to affix to the biographies he wrote of his brothers, *Lives of the Norths*. This *General Preface* outlines a theory of biography which includes a conception of autobiography which North calls 'idiography' and in which he offers Cardano's *De vita propria liberu* as a leading example.[32]

The idea of modern autobiography is a product of the eighteenth century, with its roots in the great Renaissance 'lives', such as those of Montaigne, Cellini, and Cardano and in the archetypal text of Augustine's *Confessions*, which has influenced practically every work of intellectual autobiography in some way. Although the writing of lives, in the sense of biography, and 'autobiographies' (which often took the form of letters, such as Cicero's account of his consulship in his *Epistulae ad Atticum*) has existed since the ancients, autobiography as a subject of literary, historical, and philosophical investigation is a twentieth-century phenomenon. From the remarks of Dilthey and the history of autobiography begun by Misch in the first decade of the twentieth century, no sustained attention is given to autobiography as a subject of scholarly investigation until the 1960s. Then a body of critical literature develops and it develops very rapidly and intensely.

Elizabeth Bruss in *Autobiographical Acts* says: 'Living as we do at a time and in a literary community which recognizes autobiography as a distinct and deliberate undertaking, it is difficult for us to realize that it has not always existed.'[33] Because autobiography has become a popular form and self-introspection is an everyday affair as well as a literary art, we tend to think that autobiographies

---

[31] R. North, *General Preface and Life of Dr John North*, ed. P. Millard (Toronto: University of Toronto Press, 1984). There is a general lack of accurate and critical editions of North's work and much remains in manuscript.

[32] Ibid. 78. The OED does not give the term 'idiography'.

[33] E. W. Bruss, *Autobiographical Acts: The Changing Situation of a Literary Genre* (Baltimore: Johns Hopkins University Press, 1976), 6. Regarding the processes of memory involved in autobiographical consciousness see D. C. Rubin, ed., *Autobiographical Memory* (Cambridge: Cambridge University Press, 1986).

and critical studies on them are as old as literature.[34] James Olney, in his introduction to his useful collection of representative essays by various authors, *Autobiography: Essays Theoretical and Critical* (1980), dates the beginning of a body of critical literature from Georges Gusdorf's 1956 essay, 'Conditions et limites de l'autobiographie'; prior to this, in Olney's view, there are only a few scattered studies, which are not conceptually fundamental in their approach.[35] Gusdorf's essay derives from his *La Découverte de soi* (1948)[36] and Olney's from his own longer work on the nature of autobiography, *Metaphors of Self* (1972).[37]

The themes which dominate this recent development of a critical

[34] The idea of autobiography seems to have entered quickly into popular literature in the 19th and early 20th centuries. As can be seen from the following titles, it was used as a kind of podium for the odd or dispossessed point of view— for anthropomorphized objects, animals, soldiers, slaves, women, children, ministers, missionaries, executioners, working men, beggars, etc. There are autobiographies of a *Dissenting Minister* by W. P. Scargill (1834), perhaps the first use of autobiography in a title; an *Irish Traveller* (1835); a *Notorious Legal Functionary* by Jack Ketch, 'name' of the executioner of London (1836); a *Private Soldier, Showing the Danger of Rashly Enlisting* (1838); a *Reformed Drunkard* (1845); a *Working Man, by 'One Who Has Whistled at the Plough'* (1848); an *English Soldier in the United States Army* (1853); an *Indian Army Surgeon* (1854); a *Beggar Boy* (1855); a *Wesleyan Methodist Missionary, Formerly a Roman-Catholic, Containing an Account of His Conversion* (1856); a *Female Slave* (1857); a *Married Woman: No Girlhood* (1859); a *Cat; of the Cream of Cats, Too: Illustrating the Truth of the Proverbs Respecting Them* (1864); a *Small Boy* (1869); a *Rejected MS* (1870); a *Pint of Ale, etc.* (1871); a *Methodist Preacher's Daughter* (1872); a *Clay Pipe* (1873); a *Scotch Lad, Being Reminiscences of Three Score Years and Ten* (1887); a *Flea* (1887), the famous pornographic text, fictitiously dated as 1789; a *Missionary Box* (1896); a *Child* (1899); an *Ordinary Man* (1903); a *Super-Tramp* by W. H. Davies (1908); a *Woman Alone* (1911); a *Happy Woman* (1915); an *Androgyne* (1918); a *Winnebago Indian* (1920); a *Journalist* (1929); a *Rascal* (1935). These works represent a chapter in the use of the term 'autobiography' that I have not found discussed in the critical literature. Autobiography obviously develops in the 19th cent. not only as a literary genre, but also as a form of the common imagination and as a form of social consciousness. In the 20th cent. autobiography has expanded as far as a form of do-it-yourself literature and become part of popular 'how-to' paperbacks, e.g. L. Daniel, *How to Write Your Own Life Story: A Step by Step Guide for the Non-Professional Writer* (rev. edn., Chicago: Chicago Review Pub., 1985). Other works instruct the reader in how to make tape recordings and create oral autobiographies.

[35] J. Olney, ed., *Autobiography: Essays Theoretical and Critical* (Princeton, NJ: Princeton University Press, 1980), 7. Gusdorf's essay is translated in Olney's volume, see pp. 28–48.

[36] G. Gusdorf, *La Découverte de soi* (Paris: Presses Universitaires de France, 1948).

[37] J. Olney, *Metaphors of Self: The Meaning of Autobiography* (Princeton, NJ: Princeton University Press, 1972).

literature on autobiography principally concern the conception of truth that is most applicable to autobiography (correspondence to historical fact, internal coherence, or metaphorical);[38] the extent to which autobiography merges with the novel and whether it can be defined as having its own genre;[39] and whether certain conceptions of stylistics can reveal important features of autobiography, the primary exponent of this theme being Jean Starobinski.[40] Into these traditional approaches there has intruded the French attack on the author led by such thinkers as Foucault, Barthes, and Derrida.[41]

[38] The seminal work which raises this question is R. Pascal, *Design and Truth in Autobiography* (London: Routledge and Kegan Paul, 1960). Pascal takes the view that truth is dependent upon the coherence or design of the autobiography as a whole as opposed to the search for a literal truth of fact (see. esp. ch. 12). A very suggestive and sophisticated version of a coherence view is W. L. Howarth, 'Some Principles of Autobiography', in Olney, ed., *Autobiography*, which holds that 'an autobiography is a *self-portrait*' (85) which can be understood by analogy with the elements of Renaissance and early modern portraiture.

[39] The view that autobiography is like the novel derives from a comment by N. Frye in *Anatomy of Criticism: Four Essays* (Princeton, NJ: Princeton University Press, 1957): autobiography 'merges with the novel by a series of insensible gradations' (307). In relation to the question of autobiography as a genre, P. Lejeune's *Le Pacte autobiographique* (Paris: Éditions du Seuil, 1975) works from the standard definition of autobiography as the individual writing his own life to a generic definition of what can be understood as autobiography. Elizabeth Bruss, *Autobiographical Acts*, claims that 'autobiography is an act rather than a form' and thus autobiography cannot be said to exist until it could be distinguished from other illocutionary acts (6). P. J. Eakin, *Fictions in Autobiography: Studies in the Art of Self-Invention* (Princeton, NJ: Princeton University Press, 1985) connects Bruss's conception of the relationship of the self and language in autobiography with Searle's conception of speech acts (219 ff.).

[40] J. Starobinski, 'The Style of Autobiography', in S. Chatman, ed., *Literary Style: A Symposium* (London and New York: Oxford University Press, 1971). See also the treatment of 'autobiography in the third person' in P. Lejeune, *On Autobiography*, ed. P. J. Eakin and trans. K. Leary (Minneapolis: University of Minnesota Press, 1989), 31–51.

[41] Two of the most important essays on which this attack is based are M. Foucault, 'What is an Author?', trans. J. Venit, *Partisan Review*, 42 (1975), 603–14, and R. Barthes, 'To Write: an Intransitive Verb?', in Richard Macksey and Eugenio Donato, eds., *The Structuralist Controversy: The Languages of Criticism and the Sciences of Man* (Baltimore: Johns Hopkins University Press, 1972). For a general discussion of this French movement see M. Sprinker, 'Fictions of the Self: The End of Autobiography', in Olney, ed., *Autobiography*. As Sprinker points out, 'Roland Barthes, Jacques Derrida, and the *Tel Quel* group have produced a ceaseless torrent of writing in an effort to establish the primacy of what Jean Thibaudeau has called the "textual, non-subjective 'I' " as the creator/originator/producer of a discourse' (324). On a letter of Vico's that appeared in French translation in *Tel Quel* see M. Rak, 'Vico in "Tel Quel"', *Bollettino del Centro di Studi Vichiani*, 1 (1971), 53–7.

The gist of this attack has been the insistence that in the understanding of any work the text is the proper object of analysis; the author is inessential.[42] The absence of the author raises special issues for the interpretation of autobiography which have been prominently pursued by Derrida, especially in relation to Nietzsche.[43] However, this French approach has given no attention to Vico.

If I were to characterize my approach to Vico's autobiography in literary critical terms, I would think that my conception of Vico's fable of himself is closest to the conception of autobiography as metaphor as pioneered by Gusdorf and Olney, and my emphasis on the importance of Vico's third-person style is partially compatible with Starobinski's conception of autobiography as 'discourse-history'.[44]

In all the works published on the development and nature of autobiography in English, French, and German, Vico is either forgotten or was never known to their authors. Not only is Vico not discussed: he is not cited.[45] Two exceptions to this, besides

---

[42] Foucault puts the irrelevance of the author this way in *Les Mots et les choses: une archéologie des sciences humaines* (Paris: Gallimard, 1966): 'qui ne veulent pas penser sans penser aussitôt que c'est l'homme qui pense, à toutes ces formes de réflexion gauches et gauchies, on ne peut qu'opposer un rire philosophique—c'est-à-dire, pour une certaine part, silencieux' (354).

[43] J. Derrida, *Otobiographies, l'enseignement de Nietzsche et la politique du nom propre* (Paris: Gallilée, 1984). See also Derrida's remarks in 'Roundtable on Autobiography', in C. V. McDonald, ed., *The Ear of the Other: Otobiography, Transference, Translation* (New York: Shocken Books, 1985), 39–91. Derrida states: 'La signature de l'autobiographie s'écrit de ce pas. Elle reste un crédit ouvert sur l'éternité et ne renvoie à l'un des deux *je*, contractants sans nom, que selon l'anneau de l'éternel retour' (*Otobiographies*, 73). The signature on an autobiography is not possible; the circle of the writing and reading of the text can never be closed off.

[44] Starobinski, 'The Style of Autobiography', 288.

[45] Among works, other than those already cited above, which from their title and general purpose one might expect something on Vico's place and significance in relation to the concept of autobiography that they do not give, are: W. C. Spengemann, *The Forms of Autobiography: Episodes in the History of a Literary Genre* (New Haven, Conn.: Yale University Press, 1980); J. Pilling, *Autobiography and Imagination: Studies in Self-Scrutiny* (London: Routledge and Kegan Paul, 1981); G. May, *L'Autobiographie* (2nd edn., Paris: Presses Universitaires de France, 1984; orig. pub. 1979); B. Neumann, *Identität und Rollenzwang: Zur Theorie der Autobiographie* (Frankfurt-on-Main: Athenäum, 1970); R.-R. Wuthenow, *Das erinnerte Ich: Europäische Autobiographie und Selbstdarstellung im 18. Jahrhundert* (Munich: Beck, 1974). Given that this last work is directed to studies in 18th-cent. autobiography, one might expect discussion of Vico; Vico is mentioned once and associated with Gibbon on pp. 39–40.

Misch's history, are Karl Joachim Weintraub's *The Value of the Individual: Self and Circumstance in Autobiography* (1978) which contains a chapter comparing Vico's and Gibbon's autobiographies,[46] and a study comparing Vico and Giannone by Hans-Jürgen Daus, *Selbstverständnis und Menschenbild in den Selbstdarstellungen Giambattista Vicos and Pietro Giannones* (1962).[47] I am in basic agreement with the views stated in both of these works,[48] but neither explores the claim as fully as I wish to do in what follows of the uniqueness of Vico's text or its interconnections with the rest of his philosophy.

Most writers on autobiography who give any attention to the history of autobiography take at face value Rousseau's claim with which he begins his *Confessions,* that he is the first modern autobiographer: 'I have resolved on an enterprise which has no precedent, and which, once complete, will have no imitator. My purpose is to display to my kind a portrait in every way true to nature, and the man I shall portray will be myself.'[49] Rousseau took the title of his work (completed in 1765 and first published in 1781) from Augustine and must presume that the reader will read his work against Augustine's.[50] Rousseau's are secular confessions, confessions of the heart, the body, and the sensibilities that have

---

[46] K. J. Weintraub, *The Value of the Individual: Self and Circumstance in Autobiography* (Chicago: University of Chicago Press, 1978), ch. 11. See G. Costa's review, 'La posizione di Vico nella storia dell'autobiografismo europeo', *Bollettino del Centro di Studi Vichiani,* 10 (1980), 143–6.

[47] H.-J. Daus, *Selbstverständnis und Menschenbild in den Selbstdarstellungen Giambattista Vicos und Pietro Giannones: Ein Beitrag zur Geschichte der italienischen Autobiographie* (Geneva: Droz, 1962). This work is the publication of a doctoral dissertation at the University of Cologne. It raises a number of issues about Vico's text, principally discords between Vico's own claims about his development and the independent facts of his career. See also A. Forti-Lewis, *Italia autobiografica* (Rome: Bulzoni, 1986), 70–3. In her brief discussion Forti-Lewis regards Vico as an instance of the discovery of the narrative of *autocoscienza* among Italian thinkers.

[48] In 'Autobiography and Historical Consciousness', *Critical Inquiry,* 1 (1975), 821–48, Weintraub states, of Vico's autobiography: 'The *Vita* is an impressive work. It is, in a way, a prototype for certain autobiographies, and it illustrates some fundamental problems in such historical forms as the history of thought or ideas' (831).

[49] J.-J. Rousseau, *The Confessions,* trans. J. M. Cohen (London: Penguin Books, 1988), 17. Among the contributors to Olney, ed., *Autobiography,* only Sprinker, 'Fictions of the Self', raises the question whether Vico instead of Rousseau should be considered the 'father of autobiography' (326).

[50] A. Hartle, *The Modern Self in Rousseau's Confessions: A Reply to St. Augustine* (South Bend, Ind.: University of Notre Dame Press, 1983).

certain parallels to Augustine's divinely inspired confessions of his early sins and ignorances. But Rousseau does not stand outside his narrative in the way that Augustine does, who has already been converted and is relating the tale of a form of his selfhood that is over (that which Augustine presents in the first nine books of his work). Rousseau proclaims himself to be fully within his work and does in fact tell the history of what has happened to him in the first fifty-three years of his life.

Rousseau's work is in the great French tradition of the introspective *I* from Montaigne, to Descartes, to the romantic conception of self-discourse and *Bildungsroman*. Although Vico has nothing to confess and reveals nothing of his feelings or motives, writing in the third person, which in principle excludes introspection, Rousseau's work has more in common with Vico's than with the abstract autobiography of Descartes's *Discourse*, for both Vico and Rousseau in their own ways narrate their respective curricula vitae. But Rousseau's *Confessions*, unlike Vico's *Autobiography*, is not a systematic narrative applying the genetic method to the causes of his own writings. Rousseau's work is indeed the story of the modern philosophical self, but his narrative is much broader and his manner of relation and exploits might remind the reader of parts of such works as Goldoni's *Mémoires*, Carlo Gozzi's *Memorie inutili*, and Casanova's *Histoire de ma vie jusqu'à l'an 1797*.

Ann Hartle in *The Modern Self in Rousseau's Confessions* points out that Rousseau writes his work as such a readable narrative, almost a novel at times, that it is easily regarded simply as the story of his life, as simply 'autobiography'. Hartle states: 'Thus, before we can have access to the philosophical significance of Rousseau's *Confessions*, a way must be cleared: it must be shown that *The Confessions* is *not* essentially autobiography.'[51] In the sense that she intends 'autobiography' here I believe Hartle is right. Both Rousseau's and Vico's autobiographies are essentially philosophical works, not simply life stories.

It is worth considering whether Rousseau's writing of his life was influenced by Vico. Rousseau's *Confessions* does not appear to be overtly influenced by Vico's autobiography, although Fisch and Garin hold that there is a line of influence between their conceptions of language. Fisch thinks it possible that Rousseau

---

[51] Hartle, *Modern Self*, 9.

bought a copy of Vico's 1744 *New Science* while he was secretary to the French ambassador in Venice in 1743–4, since Venice was one of the great book centres of Europe and Conti, Porcìa, and Lodoli had made Venice the chief centre of interest in Vico's work.[52] Rousseau in the first six chapters of his *Essay on the Origin of Languages* repeats the main points of Vico's views of language.[53] Garin points out that even if Rousseau did not in fact study Vico's work directly, he may have heard discussions of the Vichian theses.[54] It seems likely that such discussions took place, but if so, Rousseau records nothing of them in his *Confessions* for this period, reporting only on his duties and on the amusements of Venice, principally music and secondly the fabled Venetian women.[55]

Since Conti (1677–1749), Porcìa (1682–1743), and Lodoli (1690–1771) were involved in the publication of Vico's autobiography about fifteen years earlier, could views from their circle that Rousseau may have heard or that were reported to him have concerned the contents of the inaugural issue of the *Raccolta*? Would the news of Vico's death in January 1744 have reached Venice, causing his autobiography to be a topic of discussion before Rousseau's departure in August? From where did Rousseau get his idea to write his 'unprecedented' work? Perhaps he had heard of Vico's work on his own life or seen a copy of the *Raccolta*, but at present no evidence has come to light to demonstrate this. One conclusion can certainly be drawn: it is Vico, not Rousseau, who writes the first 'unprecedented' work of modern autobiography.

The source for the idea behind Vico's autobiography is a letter from Leibniz to Bourguet which he wrote from Vienna on 22 March 1714. He speaks of various matters and mentions he has found others who agree with Bourguet's positive opinion of Abbé

---

[52] Fisch, Introduction to *Autobiography*, 73.

[53] Ibid. Also, Nicolini, 'La teoria del linguaggio in Giambattista Vico e Giangiacomo Rousseau', *Revue de littérature comparée*, 10 (1930), 292–8; and A. Verri, 'Vico e Rousseau filosofi del linguaggio', *Bollettino del Centro di Studi Vichiani*, 4 (1974), 83–104.

[54] E. Garin, 'A proposito del rapporto fra Vico e Rousseau', *Bollettino del Centro di Studi Vichiani*, 2 (1972), 62. See also A. Verri, 'Vico, Rousseau e Venezia', in C. De Michelis and G. Pizzamiglio, eds., *Vico e Venezia* (Florence: Olschki, 1982), 322.

[55] Rousseau, *Confessions*, 278–313.

Conti, saying that Conti should be properly honoured as original if he one day produces something in his own right. Leibniz then writes: 'Monsieur Descartes would have us believe that he had hardly read anything. That was a little too much. However, it is good to study the discoveries of others in a manner that exposes to us the source of their inventions, and that renders them in a way our own. And I wish that authors would give us the history [*l'Histoire*] of their discoveries, and the progress by which they have arrived at them. When they fail to do this, it is necessary to try to divine it, in order better to profit from their works.'[56] Conti, although on an extended sojourn in France and England at the time of Leibniz's letter, was one of a group of Venetian scholars who had strong interest in Vico's work and who joined Lodoli and Porcìa in writing letters to Vico in 1727 and 1728, encouraging him to publish a new edition of the *New Science* in Venice.

As Fisch points out, Bourguet was in touch with other scholars in Venice and Padua, and we may be sure that Leibniz's opinion of Conti was conveyed to them and that Leibniz's letter became a matter of discussion.[57] In the *Autobiography*, in remarking on Conti, Vico says that on his travels Conti had 'won the high esteem of Leibniz' (183/72). What was to become a 'Proposal to the Scholars of Italy to Write Their Own Lives' by Count Gian Artico Porcìa was under discussion for several years by recognized scholars such as Vallisnieri, Muratori, Scipione Maffei, Apostolo Zeno, and Count Pier Jacopo Martello.[58] Gustavo Costa has ascribed the motivation for this project to the quarrel between French and Italian culture.[59] The proposal is an act of literary patriotism, in reaction to attacks against Italian letters by such French critics as Boileau and Bouhours. In this proposal Porcìa says that every cultivated person in Europe will come to know 'the name and the merit, and the good taste of our *Letterati*'.[60] This, at least, is part of the immediate context out of which the proposal was advanced.

Vico's autobiography was published in the first issue of *Raccolta*

[56] Leibniz, *Die philosophischen Schriften G. W. Leibniz*, vol. iii, ed. C. J. Gerhart (Hildesheim: Olms, 1960; orig. pub. 1887), 567–8. My trans.

[57] Fisch, *Autobiography*, 5.

[58] Ibid. 4.

[59] G. Costa, 'An Enduring Venetian Accomplishment: The Autobiography of G. B. Vico', *Italian Quarterly*, 21 (1980), 45–54.

[60] Count G. A. di Porcìa, 'Progetto ai letterati d'Italia per scrivere le loro Vite', *Raccolta d'opuscoli scientifici e filologici*, 1 (1728), 131.

d' opuscoli scientifici e filologici, edited by Don Angelo Calogerà, a young Camaldolite monk. The details of the publication of this are complicated. In his 1731 continuation of the *Autobiography*, Vico expresses his reluctance to have only his life, one of eight originally invited from Naples (others had been invited from Rome and Venice), appear in this form (182/70–1). The most recent account of this publication is an article by Gaspardo and Pizzamiglio.[61] This first issue of the *Raccolta* appeared in 1728 in Venice, as stated on its title-page, and not in 1729 as Nicolini suspected, for Vallisnieri received a copy on 20 October 1728.[62]

The two copies of this number of the *Raccolta* which I have seen in the Biblioteca Nazionale Marciana in Venice and the British Library, British Museum in London, are small bound volumes, about 9 × 15 cm., just over five hundred pages in length, including the preface by Calogerà and front matter.[63] The *Raccolta* endured for over half a century, publishing fifty-one numbers edited by Calogerà between 1728 and 1757, then entering a new series of forty issues, with the first fourteen edited by Calogerà, after which the editorship was assumed by Mandelli; it ceased publication in 1784. This first issue is true to the journal's title, 'Collection of Short Scientific and Philological Studies'. It opens with two scientific studies, the first being communications to Count Antonio Vallisnieri, who was Professor of Medicine at Padua and a member of the Royal Society of London, and his own remarks on the birth of vipers from the mouth of their mother, including some fold-out drawings of this event.[64] Following this there is a description of a *planisferologium* invented by a Bernardo Facino, a small device capable of showing all that goes on from moment to moment in

---

[61] P. G. Gaspardo and G. Pizzamiglio, 'La pubblicazione dell'autobiografia vichiana nella corrispondenza di Giovan Artico di Porcìa con il Muratori e il Vallisnieri', in De Michelis and Pizzamiglio, eds., *Vico e Venezia*, 107–30. In addition, in this volume, E. De Mas, 'Vico e la cultura veneta' (1–26), and C. De Michelis, 'L'autobiografia intellettuale e il "progetto" di Giovanartico di Porcìa' (91–106), expand the understanding of Vico's text in terms of Venetian culture and the details of Porcìa's proposal; see also M. Cottino-Jones, '*L'autobiografia* vichiana: Il rapporto vita-scrittura' (131–41), in the same volume.

[62] Gaspardo and Pizzamiglio, 'La pubblicazione', 124 n. 28.

[63] Costa mentions a copy in France deriving from the library of Camille Falconet; see 'Enduring Venetian Accomplishment', 47 and 52 n. 13.

[64] In the *Raccolta*, 2 (1729) there is an essay written as a letter to Abbé Carlo Girolami by Vallisnieri on 'Istoria di un mostro raniforme' (History of a monster in 'frog-form'), including fold-out drawings of a man with a head of frog-like features.

the *primum mobile*, that is, 'the courses of the brightest stars of the firmament, the sun, the moon, its epicycle and dragon's head; that is to say, the essentials of astronomy according to the most accurate ephemerides [astronomical almanacs]'.[65]

Following these scientific presentations is Porcìa's 'Progetto ai letterati d'Italia per scrivere le loro Vite', which is sixteen pages in length. As Gaspardo and Pizzamiglio show, the basic ideas of this were worked out and circulated between 1721 and 1723.[66] The invitation Vico received prior to 1725 would have contained the basic form of this printed proposal and would be in effect that to which Vico and others were responding. When Vico received this invitation he would have published his work on *Universal Law*, or part of it, but not the *First New Science*, which appeared in October of 1725. Porcìa's statement is essentially a filling out of Leibniz's original idea, coupled with what Costa has noted regarding its patriotic intent of the advancement of letters in Italy and demonstration to the world of the importance of Italian scholars, an aim which in itself would have appealed to Vico, given his life-long desire for recognition from the scholars of northern Europe.

The second feature that would have had deep appeal to Vico was the pedagogic intent of the project, which is also at the heart of Leibniz's idea. However, neither Porcìa nor Calogerà, in his prefatory remarks on the contents of the issue, refer to Leibniz. Rhetorically, at least, it would have dampened the spirit and originality of the project to have acknowledged its source as being outside Italy. In fact, considering the connection in his letter of his idea with his remark on Conti, Leibniz may have been reflecting something already in the air. In terms of Leibniz's own philosophy, the interest his letter expresses in knowing the history of discoveries is in keeping with his general methodological concerns—the practical value of not ourselves repeating the work that has been done by others, and the possibility of thus obtaining percepts for future enquiry.

Writers of their own lives are asked to give the date and place of their birth and the names of their parents, and honestly to relate all of the adventures of their life that render it most admirable and most curious that can be revealed to the world and to posterity

---

[65] Fisch, *Autobiography*, 2.
[66] Gaspardo and Pizzamiglio, 'La pubblicazione', 109.

without affecting the author's good name. The author is asked to give an account of all his studies, beginning with how he was taught grammar, whether by methods in common use or by novel ones. He is then to go through the whole course of his studies, evaluating how each subject was taught to him and saying how it should be taught if it was not taught well. He is finally to pass on to the field to which he has devoted himself and explain the authors he has followed, the works he has published and their fortunes at the hands of his critics, and his reactions. In this he is to confess candidly all errors and maintain a neutral viewpoint; that is, he is not simply to take this as an occasion for a defence but to offer a judicious self-account from which the reader may learn. It is finally emphasized that this proposal is addressed to genuine men of letters, not to those who have simply published slender works of poetry, legal books, or treatises on moral theology. Vico, of course, had in a sense done the first two of these and had seriously looked into the subject-matter of the third. But presumably it is meant to exclude those who had engaged in such activity in an unimaginative and unoriginal way, or who had done nothing else.

The proposal explains that Vico's account of his own life which follows is an admirable example of fulfilling the conditions of this proposal and thus both the concept and an instance of it are being offered to the reader and to potential contributors. Vico's text of just over a hundred pages ends with a catalogue of his works. Following Vico's entry is a history of the city of Prato, a biography of the sixteenth-century historian Gualdo, a review of an edition of the *Decameron*, and finally a discussion of the use of *voi* and formal modes of address in Italian. The invitations to write one's life were originally issued on the basis that they would appear in a volume of distinguished lives, which did not materialize, hence Vico's dissatisfaction with his work appearing in such a manner, despite the respectful comments on it by Porcìa. The one advantage, however, that cannot have escaped Vico is that its appearance in such a journal assured its circulation throughout Europe, perhaps much more than the originally planned volume would have achieved. In fact, Costa points out that the autobiography was 'constantly used by the compilers of German and Italian reference works which dedicated an entry to Vico'.[67]

---

[67] Costa, 'Enduring Venetian Accomplishment', 51.

There were two other known results of Porcìa's proposal. In the second number of the *Raccolta*, in 1729, there appears a very short 'Vita di Pier Jacopo Martello scritta da lui stesso fino l'anno 1718 e consegrata al signor Giovanartico Conte di Porcìa, secondo il di lui progetto'.[68] And Muratori sent his contribution to Porcìa on 10 November 1721, but it was not published until the latter part of the nineteenth century.[69] Both of these scholars were among the original supporters of the project of a volume of lives of distinguished Italians.

Calogerà, in his editorial preface to the first issue of the *Raccolta*, attributes the idea of such a text on one's own life to Lodoli, who coined from Greek the term *periautografia*, using *peri-* (around, what surrounds or encloses) rather than *bios* as the term to connect to *autos* and *graphē*. *Peri-* is a life-term, often used as a prefix to anatomical terms to characterize what surrounds a designated organ. Lodoli's term is remarkably ahead of its time and is in many ways a better term than autobiography for the presentation of one's intellectual life, because it conceives the subject as something that exists in a surrounding that affects what it is.

Costa holds that in additon to its relation to Descartes's *Discourse* Vico's autobiography imitates that of the poet Gabriello Chiabrera (1552–1638). Costa says, 'We can also safely assume that Vico imitated the style of the autobiography of Gabriello Chiabrera, a model of literary perfection according to Arcadian taste, and the *Vite degli Arcadi illustri*, published under the supervision of Giovan Mario Crescimbeni since 1708.'[70] It should be remembered that Vico was a member of the Arcadia of Rome (under the name of Laufilo Terio) and that after Vico's death, as Villarosa reports in his continuation of the *Autobiography*, the

---

[68] A. Battistini, *La degnità della retorica: Studi su G. B. Vico* (Pisa: Pacini, 1975), 34 n. 37, takes notice of this. Martello's text is much shorter than Vico's but it follows the general plan of Porcìa in describing his studies, etc. See *Raccolta d'opuscoli scientifici e filologici*, 2 (1729), 273–92. Incidentally, in a much later issue of the *Raccolta* appears the autobiography of Francesco Spinelli, who had been a private pupil of Vico and who Vico mentions in the *Autobiography* as calling attention to three errors in the *Second New Science* (195–7/82–4). See *Raccolta d'opuscoli scientifici e filologici*, 49 (1753), 465–526.

[69] Costa, 'Enduring Venetian Accomplishment', 49–50, 53 n. 37. Costa claims: 'In any case, we know that only two scholars wrote their autobiographies at the request of Porcia: Vico and Muratori' (49–50). But there was at least one other, Martello. See above, n. 68.

[70] Costa, 'Enduring Venetian Accomplishment', 50.

Arcadia erected a memorial inscription to Vico (209/96).[71] I believe that Costa is correct that in stylistic terms Vico's text is influenced by the life of Chiabrera and the Arcadian tradition. Chiabrera's autobiography casts its first sentence in the third person as does that of the above-mentioned autobiography of Pier Jacopo Martello in the second volume of the *Raccolta*. I suggest that the autobiography of Chiabrera may be the source of Vico's third-person style. This should be considered when reading Fisch's view that 'The very choice of the third person is a reaction from the ubiquitous "I" of the *Discourse*'.[72] Vico's third person may be a stylistic counter to Descartes, but it also is in accord with Chiabrera's 'Gabriello Chiabrera nacque in Savona l'anno della nostra salute 1552 a' 8 di giugno . . . .'.[73]

In stylistic terms it probably exerts an influence on Vico, but in terms of intellectual structure Chiabrera's text does not provide the basis of Vico's unique work. Chiabrera's 'Vita di Gabriello Chiabrera scritta da lui medesimo', written a little more than a decade before his death (just after 1625), is a sketch of less than ten pages in length. He does not give a genetic account of his studies except to say he was enrolled in the 'Collegio de' Padri Gesuiti', where he heard stringent lectures in philosophy. He also gives no systematic account of the development of his thought in his adult career but focuses on his connections with persons in high places in the clergy and the aristocracy, describing their interest and responses to his

---

[71] The Arcadia met for the first time in 1690. The prime mission of the Academy of Arcadia was to restore a classic taste in poetry. Giovan Mario Crescimbeni (1663–1728) was among the founders of the Academy of Arcadia and was the first *custode*. He collected the members' lives in the five-volume work to which Costa refers above. Vico was elected to membership in 1710, the same year as the publication of the *Ancient Wisdom*. The Arcadians were interested in Vico as a poet, not simply because of his developing status as a philosophical thinker. Crescimbeni had asked him to send a poem to be included in a collection, which Vico did. See also B. Donati, 'L'iscrizione del Vico all'Arcadia e il primo annunzio del *De Italorum sapientia*', in *Nuovi studi sulla filosofia civile di G. B. Vico* (Florence: Le Monnier, 1936). Concerning the Arcadia in general something can be learned from the critical-historical selections in L. Caretti and G. Luti, *La letteratura italiana per saggi storicamente disposti: Il settecento* (Milan: Mursia, 1976), 99–119, and A. Piromalli, *L'arcadia* (Palermo: Palumbo, 1963). Piromalli's work includes recent figures of the Arcadia such as Croce, Fubini, and Bruno Maier.

[72] Fisch, Introduction to *Autobiography*, 7.

[73] G. Chiabrera, 'Vita di Gabriello Chiabrera scritta da lui medesimo', in *Canzonette, rime varie, dialoghi di Gabriello Chiabrera*, ed. L. Negri (Turin: UTET, 1952), 507–16.

works, including a reprint of a letter from Pope Urban VIII. In this regard Chiabrera's account is reminiscent of the first portion of Vico's continuation of his autobiography of 1731, where he engages in similar descriptions.

Although Chiabrera's ten-page document has some possibilities of connection with parts of Vico's text, it cannot be taken as a true model or precedent. Pons, like Fisch, holds that there are no geunine models that Vico is following except for his explicit opposition to Descartes. Among lives of the seventeenth century, Pons[74] says one can cite only that of Hobbes and that of the English deist, the *Life of Herbert of Cherbury Written by Himself*.[75] There is little about the life of Herbert of Cherbury that would have interested Vico, if indeed he knew it, except that it is written in the vernacular. But the life of Hobbes would have held some interest. As Nicolini suggests, Vico may have seen the frontispiece of the original edition of the *Leviathan* of 1651 and conceived the figure of metaphysic in the frontispiece of the *New Science* as an allegory of spiritual values in contraposition to the materialistic significance of Hobbes's work. This of course was commissioned by Vico for the 1730 edition of the *New Science*, after the publication of the *Autobiography*, but Hobbes is one of the natural-law theorists against whom Vico is writing in the 1725 *New Science* and whom he admires and borrows from more than he ever says.

Toward the end of his life, at the age of 84, Hobbes wrote his autobiography in Latin verse, and he also left a short prose autobiography, published by Richard Blackbourne in London in 1681. The verse version contains his famous statement that his mother, frightened by the impending arrival of the Spanish Armada, 'did bring forth Twins at once, both Me, and Fear'. It seems unlikely that Hobbes's autobiography served Vico in any substantial way as a model, if he knew it. Its first sentence has a certain parallel to Vico's first sentence: 'Thomas Hobbes, natus Aprilis 5, 1588, Malmesburiae, agri Wiltoniensis.'[76] Vico begins:

[74] A. Pons, Introduction to *Vie de Giambattista Vico écrite par lui-même* (Paris: Grasset, 1981), 25.

[75] *The Life of Edward, First Lord Herbert of Cherbury Written by Himself*, ed. J. M. Shuttleworth (London: Oxford University Press, 1976).

[76] T. Hobbes, *Opera philosophica*, ed. G. Molesworth (5 vols. London: Bohn, 1839–45), vol. i, p. xiii. A more direct model is Petrarch's *Epistola ad posteros* (c. 1370). See Pons, Introduction to *Vie de Giambattista Vico*, 44–5 n. 13, and my discussion in Chapter 5.

'Il signor Giambattista Vico egli è nato in Napoli l'anno 1670 . . .'. But as noted above this is also true of Chiabrera's and Martello's texts, which begin by referring to the fact of their birth with the statement of their full names, as if in a biography. And this has precedent in the third-person style of Roman and humanist autobiography.

It is worth keeping in mind that Vico was himself a biographer, the author of the *Life of Antonio Carafa* (1716). In beginning this work Vico advances a conception of the development of biography. He claims that biographies were first written about men of virtue in accordance with the mores of archaic society. Biographies are later written of men whose qualification is that they hold real political power. And, finally, biographies are written in more decadent times about men simply because they are prominent. In approaching the writing of his own life nearly ten years later, Vico must have reflected to some extent on these distinctions and the style with which he formulated this biography.

Besides Descartes (and, as I wish to show, Augustine), the possible relation of Vico's work to *De vita propria liber* (*The Book of My Life*) of Girolamo Cardano (1501–76) should not be overlooked.[77] Cardano, born at Pavia near Milan, was one of the strangest figures of his century, but an intellect and original thinker of the first order. His autobiography is not the life of an adventurer, like Cellini, but of a scholar, like Vico. It reveals Cardano as a lonely figure, who underwent many humiliations and endured the professional bigotry of his rivals. Not the details of his career, which are quite different from Vico's, but aspects of his spirit and the forces affecting it could be allied to Vico's melancholic temperament. Vico could to an extent identify his own situation with Cardano's. But Cardano's work itself is not analogous to Vico's. His life is not presented as a narrative but as a series of fifty-four achronological essays, in which he probes each part of himself, going deeper and deeper, like the physician he in fact was, probing each symptom or set of symptoms, seemingly seeking the underlying cause. Anna Robeson Burr in her comparative study of the lives of Caesar, Augustine, and Cardano says that Cardano approaches

---

[77] H. Cardanus, *De vita propria liber*, *Opera omnia*, vol. i, 'Fascimile edition of the Lyon edition of 1663', ed. A. Buck (Stuttgart and Bad Cannstatt: Frommann, 1966), and J. Cardan, *The Book of My Life*, trans. J. Stoner (London: Dent and Sons, 1931).

himself 'as if he were a new species of animal which he never expected to see again'.[78]

Cardano is a scientist, applying his own manner of thought to himself, interpreting himself by means of that manner of thinking by which he has made his own discoveries. In this sense he is a very modern writer, and is exactly parallel to Vico who, as the discoverer of the philosophical order of history, applies this historical manner of thought to himself. Where Cardano approached himself as a scientist, Vico approached himself as a historian and philosopher of history. I do not think that Vico takes any one autobiographical text as a model, but if he takes any as models or partial models, Cardano has also to be considered.

None of the previous analysis says why an author would choose to write his own life. It is traditionally said that the pedagogical nature of Porcìa's proposal appealed to Vico, whose own original philosophical viewpoint arose from a conception of pedagogy and who took himself seriously as a teacher throughout his career. Arthur Melville Clark, in an early study, *Autobiography: Its Genesis and Phases* (1935), states quite clearly what a number of writers on autobiography mention but do not discuss fully. Clark says: 'Every autobiographer, I fancy, has passed through a kind of crisis, short and intense or protracted and cumulative in its effects, affecting mind, body, or estate, private or shared with others though on them it made no comparable impression. This experience is, in biological terms, the releasing stimulus. It has somehow isolated him from his fellows and produced a degree of loneliness, a kind of need, more insistent than his normal mistrust of his fellows, for either sympathy, or self-justification, or appreciation, or communication.'[79]

Vico wrote the first draft of his autobiography in 1725, while still in the wake of his loss of the university chair and while writing the *New Science*. He ends his continuation of 1731, as described above, with remarks on his loneliness, ascending to his desk as a 'citadel', recounting his abuse from associates, and comparing himself to the singleness of Socrates. This must be reckoned with as more than a psychological point in the text; it is an objective

---

[78] A. R. Burr, *The Autobiography: A Critical and Comparative Study* (Boston: Houghton Mifflin, 1909). Quoted by Stoner in *The Book of My Life*, p. ix.

[79] A. M. Clark, *Autobiography: Its Genesis and Phases* (Edinburgh: Oliver and Boyd, 1935), 22.

part of what it is and involves the philosopher's classic relationship to the world that goes back to Vico's adduction of himself as melancholy and ingenious, at the first of the text. It is probably true that Vico's aim is pedagogy, but philosophical pedagogy is never ordinary teaching. Vico's autobiography may offer a unique standpoint on the lonely relation to the world that is at the heart of every act of autobiography.

Near the end of his 114 axioms of the *New Science*, Vico states: 'Doctrines must take their beginning from that of the matters of which they treat' (*Le dottrine debbono cominciare da quando cominciano le materie che trattano*) (314; axiom 106). This axiom has the appearance of an afterthought. Vico, in fact, says it might have been placed among his first, general axioms rather than among the final, specific ones, because this conception of doctrines applies to all the subject-matter of the *New Science*. This principle suggests that 'autobiography' is a category that might be applied to Vico's philosophy itself. In a sense Vico's aim is to write the autobiography of humanity.

In Vico's view to understand something is to discover its origin and to recreate its genesis, bringing forth the causes of its development. Only when we can remake the thing in thought in accordance with how it was itself made can we have a true doctrine of it. When this is accomplished, the mind understands the object not simply from the mind's own perspective, but from this perspective modified by the reality of the object as remade in thought.

To understand the object by beginning where the object itself begins holds that all things have their own particular origins, that their causes are internal to their natures, and that these causes emerge in the development of their natures. This way of thinking depends upon the 'rhetorical' sense of language, that is, the power of the word to express rather than simply to define and designate the nature of something, and the power of the word to draw the mind into the perspective of the thing in question, as the orator draws his audience and himself into the perspective of his subject. To understand in this sense is to regard the object as a kind of 'topic' from which a speech can be drawn forth that truly reflects its nature, that adduces the causes of its own particular sequence of development.

To begin doctrines from where their subject-matters themselves begin is to approach knowledge, truth, and the world in autobiographical terms. Galileo's famous view in *Il saggiatore* (The assayer), that physical nature is a book to be read in mathematical characters, is transferred by Vico to the civil world, which is to be read in 'poetic characters' (*caratteri poetici*), his discovery of which, Vico says, is the master key to the *New Science* (34). The human or civil world is a book originally written by the first humans in mute gestures, customs, and deeds accomplished through their power to form particulars into universal meanings through their imagination (*fantasia*). These were later given articulate, linguistic form through the *fantasia* of the first poets in their production of fables, their mythic speech. The philosophers or the Vichian philosophers, the practitioners of the new science, can make the human world understandable by recovering, in so far as it is possible, the *fantasia* of the origin and developing their doctrines of the principles of humanity from this original imaginative order of the first humans and the poets.

The autobiography of humanity is the book of this civil world that is written through all things that depend upon human choice, 'all histories of the languages, customs, and deeds of peoples in war and peace' (7). It is an autobiography in that humanity writes this actual book about itself, an expression of its own nature, but guided by the eye of providence because the order to be found in it ultimately displays a divine structure. To read this actual book is the practice of the new science. The philological contents are to be read in philosophical terms, that is, with the aim of establishing their causes. The events of the civil world are to be read (to juxtapose the *Autobiography*) while 'meditating the causes, natural and moral, and the occasions of fortune' (182/71).

The fact that 'the world of civil society has certainly been made by men' (331) means that its text is written by them in their actual deeds and can be read by those among them who meditate on the content and causes of these deeds. The text itself is the actual autobiography of humanity; he who tells its story is not so much humanity's biographer as its autobiographer because he simply speaks for humanity, since its general story can only be realized in a particular text. The Vichian philosopher is a kind of biographer-autobiographer, since he is both apart from and the subject of the causes he relates. There remains his own particular story, which exists within that of humanity and which includes the discovery of the principles of humanity's life and is itself recountable as a philosophical history by applying these principles to it.

Dilthey's conception of autobiography as connected to lived experience, as an activity of self-reflection wherein the writer gives literary form to what is naturally there in the being of the human self, is quite close to what may be called the Vichian conception of autobiography. And Dilthey's conception that self-reflection 'makes historical insight possible' is highly suggestive for interpreting the significance of Vico's autobiography as connected to his philosophy of history. Apart from Dilthey's attention to autobiography as a philosophical idea, and Misch's attempt to use this as a guide for a history of autobiography, little has been done to understand autobiography in philosophical terms. Even the fairly large range of broad-based works of literary criticism on autobiography offer little systematic thought on the nature of autobiography.

From such works a characterology of autobiography might be constructed, in that they focus on the senses in which the author must be seen as telling the truth, the text must be coherent, the author constructs a myth of himself, orders his life as a discourse, etc. But the relationship of autobiography to conceptions of human knowledge and the human self is not accomplished by an understanding of such characteristics, although they are certainly useful to the reader of autobiographies.[80] I think not only that Vico offers the first philosophical autobiography done in modern terms but also that his work offers, implicitly, the first conception of autobiography as a philosophical idea. In writing his autobiography Vico employs a conception of knowledge, philosophy, and history upon which autobiography as a philosophical enterprise can be based.

In the remainder of this chapter I wish to expound in general terms Vico's conception of autobiography. My aim is to answer two questions which guide the historical and textual analyses which follow. First, what conception of autobiography underlies Vico's work and what does this conception contribute to our understanding of philosophy, in particular the philosophy of

---

[80] For such a characterology, see A. Fleishman, *Figures of Autobiography: The Language of Self-Writing in Victorian and Modern England* (Berkeley, Calif.: University of California Press, 1983), 7–35.

history? Secondly, how does Vico's autobiography add to our understanding of Vico's own philosophy? These are questions I will come back to from time to time in the chapters which follow, but I wish to give a provisional statement of them here at the outset.

The starting-point of Vico's philosophy is a conception of human education and human knowledge both in the sense that these themes dominate his early work and in a systematic sense as the logical ground of his ideas. Vico starts with the human self and with the self's need for a knowledge of itself. Vico's early orations are guided by the ancient project of self-knowledge. In the first oration he quotes the Delphic Oracle, 'Know thyself.'[81] The principle that what is true is what can be made and that what is made is something true has within it the sense of self-knowledge, that is, that the object known is part of the knower and is encompassed and defined in the knower's activity.[82] In accordance with this principle the knower is always confronting his own nature in what he by his powers can make actual.

In the law and in history Vico finds the model of the interlocking between the individual and the universal. Within any particular law, law itself, or right, is present. In the particular historical event the historical itself is present and is what gives the event its universal significance. This interlocking of particular and universal is characteristic of self-knowledge because such knowledge is not simply the 'knowledge' a subject uniquely has of its own existence (of its own psychological state), nor is self-knowledge simply a knowledge of the object, independent of the self's activity of knowing. Self-knowledge occurs within the unique speech of an individual knower, but what is revealed in this speech is what is true of the speaker's universal human condition.

Vico's philosophy generally and his own autobiography particularly is dominated by the Socratic ideal, the quest for self-knowledge. In Vico's view the prime object of philosophical investigation is the knower himself; it is not a knowledge of physical nature or of the gods. The aim of the *New Science* is a knowledge of civil things—that is, the human world, and underlying this is Vico's

---

[81] 'Oratio I', *Opere di G. B. Vico*, vol. i, ed. G. Gentile and F. Nicolini (Bari: Laterza, 1914), 7.

[82] For an exposition of this and the ideas that follow see below, Chapter 4.

knowledge of himself as the philosopher who can know these things. Vico's aim in his theory of *sapienza poetica*, 'poetic wisdom', is a solution to the ancient problem of the relationship between philosophy and poetry, to the ancient quarrel between philosophy and poetry which Plato describes in the tenth book of the *Republic*.

Vico's solution to this quarrel is neither to assign wisdom to the poets nor to divorce it from them and assign it only to the philosophers. Instead he develops an account of poetry or myth as a form of original or primordial wisdom out of which philosophy develops in the course of the life of any nation. Philosophy develops itself as a transformation of this wisdom, which also becomes a renunciation of the form of imaginative universals that dominate the manner of thinking of poetic wisdom. Vichian philosophy is based on a revival of philosophy by directing the natural inclination of philosophy toward the abstract universal back in contact with its origins in the imaginative or poetic universal, a reunion of the concept with the image and the metaphor.

Vico concludes the autobiography with lines from Phaedrus' *Fabulae* concerning Socrates. In his oration *On the Heroic Mind* Vico recalls Socrates as the ideal thinker who did not separate virtue from knowledge, who was a complete university of studies in himself.[83] Vico's thought is dominated by a search for balancing the claims of the ancients and the moderns, something he states as his special aim at the beginning of *On the Study Methods of Our Time*. If the theory of poetic wisdom which is at the basis of Vico's *New Science* is a transformation of an ancient problem, is this also true of his *Autobiography*? I think it is, and the sense in which this is true holds the answer to the Vichian conception of self-knowledge as the basis of autobiography as a philosophical idea.

Among modern philosophical autobiographies which in some sense consciously follow Vico are those of Croce and Collingwood. Croce's work is constructed rather closely on Vico's; Collingwood's is less obviously so built, but is influenced by Vico's. Croce begins his autobiography with reflections on the nature of autobiography, distinguishing what he will say from confessions,

---

[83] 'On the Heroic Mind', in G. Tagliacozzo, M. Mooney, and D. P. Verene, eds., *Vico and Contemporary Thought* (2 vols. in 1, Atlantic Highlands, NJ: Humanities Press, 1979), ii. 233.

recollections, or memoirs, concluding with an assertion that he will write a history of himself, an assertion very like Vico's, although Croce does not assert the strong sense of providential direction that is to be found in Vico. Croce says: 'What, then, am I to write, if not confessions or recollections or memoirs? I will try in plain terms to sketch a criticism, and therefore a history, of myself; that is, of the contribution which, like every other man, I have made to the common stock of work done: the history of my "calling" or "mission".'[84] Croce sees his work as an act of self-knowledge achieved by means of a 'critical' history of himself as a philosopher, a history that will bring out himself not simply as a unique thinker but as a figure illustrating the universal pursuit of human knowledge.

Collingwood in his *Autobiography* says that 'the autobiography of a man whose business is thinking should be the story of his thought'.[85] In his tenth chapter, 'History as the Self-knowledge of Mind', Collingwood connects self-knowledge with history as a type of knowledge and with the historian's own knowledge of himself. Collingwood says: 'If what the historian knows is past thoughts, and if he knows them by re-thinking them himself, it follows that the knowledge he achieves by historical inquiry is not knowledge of his situation as opposed to knowledge of himself, it is a knowledge of his situation which is at the same time knowledge of himself.'[86] He concludes that the historical thinker 'must be, in fact, a microcosm of all the history he can know. Thus his own self-knowledge is at the same time his knowledge of the world of human affairs.'[87] A knowledge of history or the philosophy of history depends upon the historian being able to think the process of history in terms of his own self, to make history his *alter ego*, to make his own need for self-knowledge become interlocked with the knowledge of the world of, in Vico's terms, 'civil things'.

Croce and Collingwood are both historicists in their conceptions of knowledge. Their Hegelian reading of Vico does not allow them to take into account the sense in which the *New Science* does not

---

[84] B. Croce, *An Autobiography*, trans. R. G. Collingwood (Oxford: Clarendon Press, 1927), 23.

[85] R. G. Collingwood, *An Autobiography* (London: Oxford University Press, 1939), Preface.

[86] Ibid. 114.

[87] Ibid. 115.

exemplify a principle of *Aufhebung* in the movement from *corsi* to *ricorsi* in the life of nations. But the extent to which Croce's and Collingwood's conception of Vico's philosophy of history agrees with Hegelian thought as they hold it is not my concern here. What interests me is their insistence on the importance of 'story' as the basis for autobiography, that is, that an autobiography is a 'history' and that, in Collingwood's words, the historian's 'own self-knowledge is at the same time his knowledge of the world of human affairs'. These are hallmarks of autobiography as a philosophical idea, as is Dilthey's claim that self-reflection 'makes historical insight possible' and that autobiography is philosophically important because it is the transformation into literary form of the process of self-reflection that is present as a process natural to any individual. These views, I think, presuppose the transformation of the ancient project of 'Know thyself', of self-knowledge, into the project of autobiography or autobiographical thinking that Vico first accomplishes in his *Autobiography* and which is of a piece with his philosophy of history.

The problems of the pre-Socratic philosophers are centred on the creation of a philosophy of nature and the possibilities present in the development of logical forms of thought to replace the mythological orderings of experience. Socrates shifts philosophical questioning to a new intellectual centre. As Cassirer puts it in *An Essay on Man*: 'Only one question remains: What is man? Socrates always maintains and defends the ideal of an objective, absolute, universal truth. But the only universe he knows, and to which all his inquiries refer, is the universe of man. His philosophy—if he possesses a philosophy—is strictly anthropological.'[88] Socrates never offers a definition of man, but it is clear that the pursuit of this question involves immediate intercourse between human beings.

In the Platonic–Socratic philosophy of the *Republic* the nature of the soul can be found writ large in the structure of the ideal community as it is writ small in the individual. The truth about the human is different from the truth about an empirical object. Man is a creature constantly in search of himself. The maxim 'Know thyself' is connected by Socrates to the activity of philosophizing

---

[88] E. Cassirer, *An Essay on Man: An Introduction to a Philosophy of Human Culture* (New Haven, Conn.: Yale University Press, 1944), 4.

as the essential human activity, in his famous declaration that the activity he is engaged in daily, of talking about all subjects important to man, examining what he himself thinks and what others think, 'is really the very best thing that a man can do, and that life without this sort of examination is not worth living' (*Apology*, 38 A). Cassirer says: 'This first answer has, in a sense, always remained the classical answer. The Socratic problem and the Socratic method can never be forgotten or obliterated.'[89]

Cassirer's own solution to the Socratic problem is not unlike that found in Vico. Cassirer, having defined man in terms of his symbolizing activity, sees the nature of man as writ large in the system of symbolic forms of human culture as Vico sees the human writ large in the historical *corsi* and *ricorsi* of the world of civil things. Cassirer understands the 'crisis in man's knowledge of himself' in contemporary thought as the failure to find a common element that runs through all of man's activities, and he holds that he has found such a common element in his conception of the symbol. The power to form experience in terms of symbols, whether this be through aesthetic images, words of natural languages, or mathematical symbols and numbers, is the key to giving a functional meaning to the classical definitions of man as rational and as social animal. Man as *animal symbolicum*, whose activity of symbols is manifest in the making of the historical world of culture, unites the rational and social into a common human order. Like Vico, Cassirer sees the basis of all culture, the whole of the civil world, as arising from (though not wholly determined by) the mythological ordering of experience.

Although Cassirer is one of the great revivers of the Socratic question in modern philosophy, he, unlike Dilthey, and unlike Croce and Collingwood in their autobiographies, misses the importance of the idea of autobiography for the question of self-knowledge and the historical world of the *Geisteswissenschaften*. Cassirer throughout his career saw Vico as the founder of the philosophy of the human sciences,[90] but he bases this only on his reading of the *New Science* and does not see the sense in which the *New Science* is the autobiography of humanity, although he does

[89] Cassirer, *Essay on Man*, 6.
[90] For a description of the references throughout Cassirer's works to Vico, see my 'Vico's Influence on Cassirer', *New Vico Studies*, 3 (1985), 105–11.

regard culture as the nature of the human writ large, as I have said. In his approach to culture as the individual writ large Cassirer is very like Collingwood in his conception of culture in *Speculum Mentis*[91] and Croce in his conception of culture in his *Aesthetic*.[92] Such approaches take the ancient problem of self-knowledge in the direction of a theory of culture, but they miss the importance of 'autobiography' as the modern response to the ancient question of self-knowledge and the examined life. Vico is certainly the founder of the philosophy of culture, as he is the founder of the philosophy of history. But in his work we also encounter the idea of autobiography as the modern form of the ancient problem of self-knowledge.

In the Platonic *Dialogues* we are presented with a *portrait* of Socrates, which is crucial to our understanding of the idea of self-knowledge, but we are not presented with an *autobiography* of Socrates. This is to say that we are not presented with the history of Socrates. There is no 'story' of Socrates. In the famous 'last days' sequence of the *Dialogues*, the public defence of Socrates in the *Apology*, his conversation with the business man Crito while in prison, on the meaning of public opinion, in the *Crito*, and from his discussion of immortality and soul, and the death scene in the *Phaedo*, we learn a great deal of who Socrates is, that is, we find a certain picture of his character and he reveals some of the details of his life and thoughts, how things have struck him at certain times. For example, he reveals that he has been writing some poetry in an effort to clarify the meaning of certain dreams he has had (*Phaedo*, 60 D ff.), and he tells how he once heard someone reading from a book of Anaxagoras and of the effect it had on him (*Phaedo*, 97 B ff.).

We also learn much about Socrates the person in the *Dialogues*, such as in the *Symposium* and the *Phaedrus*. In addition there are the portraits of Socrates by Xenophon in the *Memorabilia* and in Aristophanes' *Clouds*, both of which Vico mentions in the *New Science* (336, 808, 906, 911). Socrates, at least the Platonic Socrates, appears as the figure who illustrates the philosophical life. Like the philosophers or lovers of wisdom before him, he

[91] R. G. Collingwood, *Speculum Mentis or the Map of Knowledge* (Oxford: Clarendon Press, 1924).

[92] B. Croce, *Aesthetic, as Science of Expression and General Linguistic*, trans. D. Ainslie (rev. edn., New York: Macmillan, 1922).

represents a particular type of person who, while not a god and not a poet nor a politician (not an 'expert' in any field), lays claim to a certain relationship to wisdom.[93] Socrates' unique claim is to a wisdom in human things (*Apology*, 20 D). Socrates' wisdom is what can be derived from the self taking its own nature as its object of knowledge, placing the human at the centre of all questions.

Of course there is no autobiography of Socrates, in the sense that Socrates writes nothing. Anything we know of Socrates is only biographically 'autobiographical'. But in another sense all that Socrates says is autobiographical because it proceeds from his character, from the actual life that is his. Socrates leads a particular life, the subject of which is not nature but man. He is philosophy, the love of wisdom, in human form. The figure of Socrates as the figure of philosophy itself dominates the Western imagination.[94] What Socrates expresses is 'autobiography', since its source is his own being and his being as thoroughly interwoven with the being of the Greek *polis*. The Socratic philosophy of 'Know thyself' is made from the reality that is Socrates, not from anything else. Part of that reality is the Forms, and the mind, which is itself not a Form.

Socrates as he appears in the language of the *Dialogues* is the medium through which we can understand what a life which involves this sense of reality is like—the reality of the Forms and mind. Only if we can think as Socrates does can we possibly grasp the sense of the 'unseen' reality that motivates him. Self-knowledge means nothing apart from the persona of the philosopher, who is defined, at least according to received tradition, by Pythagoras not as wise, for only the gods are wise, but as a lover of wisdom.[95] Ultimately self-knowledge for the Platonic Socrates is the grasp of the 'beyond' of the world, the Forms, as somehow also present in what is 'here' and 'now'. Socrates is himself the master key to the problem of the presence of the unseen in the seen.

---

[93] W. Jaeger, 'On the Origin and Cycle of the Philosophic Ideal of Life', Appendix II of *Aristotle: Fundamentals of the History of His Development*, trans. R. Robinson (2nd edn., London: Oxford University Press, 1948), 426–61.

[94] H. Spiegelberg, ed., *The Socratic Enigma* (Indianapolis: Bobbs-Merrill Library of Liberal Arts, 1964).

[95] As reported by Cicero, *Tusc.* v. iii 7 ff. See also, H. B. Gottschalk, *Heraclides of Pontus* (Oxford: Clarendon Press, 1980), 23–35.

Socrates modifies the ancient definition of the philosopher as only the lover but not the possessor of wisdom, because Socrates claims to possess human wisdom but not divine wisdom. Socrates also modifies the Pythagorean claim that the philosopher is a pure spectator like the spectators at the games at Olympia.[96] Socrates appears, at least in the *Apology*, as both the spectator and actor, performing the service of being the conscience of the *polis*, on which he bases his claim for a pension in the *Apology*. We apprehend Socrates as a locus of self-knowing, as an activity in which the unseen is pursued within the order of what is seen. Socrates is the heroic figure of mind whose dimensions can be elaborated in the narration about what he is and what he thought, but Socrates has no history.

How we are to understand self-knowledge in the Platonic *Dialogues* is a problem in its own right. It involves the relation of the soul to the Good, and such knowledge as itself part of *epistēmē* generally requires a knowledge of the *archē*, the origin. Self-knowledge is also connected with *sōphrosynē* as discussed in the *Charmides* and the problem of separation of theory and practice in Platonic thought.[97] No matter how we are to understand the Platonic–Socratic conception of self-knowledge in relation to intuition (*noēsis*), to the proper order of the soul, or the relation to practical intelligence (*phronēsis*), self-knowledge in the Platonic *Dialogues* is distinguished from self-consciousness.

The project of self-knowledge is understood as distinct from any notion of the subjective development of the self. There is no concept of dialectic as a genetic process in which the individual confronts the various stages of his own development. The power to recollect (*anamimnēskesthai*) plays a role in the Platonic conception of knowledge and reality as in the well-known questioning of Meno's slave boy and in the classroom problems of the knowledge of the Forms (*Meno*, 80 D–86 C). In the *Phaedo* it is said that this process of recollection is possible concerning all subjects studied by dialectic (75 C–D). But recollection is not presented as central to self-knowledge; whatever relevance it may have it is not the master

---

[96] Jaeger, 'On the Origin and Cycle', 432.
[97] This thesis is developed by S. Rosen, '*Sōphrosynē* and *Selbstbewusstsein*', in *The Ancients and the Moderns: Rethinking Modernity* (New Haven, Conn.: Yale University Press, 1989), 83–106.

key to the self's knowledge of its own nature and the consequences that may proceed from such knowledge for practice.[98]

The modern notion of the self and of self-knowledge is understood in terms of self-consciousness, with self-consciousness being understood as a dialectical confrontation the self has with itself, with its own past states. Self-knowledge is understood as grounded in self-consciousness and self-consciousness is grounded in a process of recollection. William Earle in *The Autobiographical Consciousness* divides this modern sense of self-consciousness into two acts which describe the essence of memory: 'Our awareness of the past, then, focuses itself between two acts of consciousness, the present recollecting act and the past recollected act; and while our attention directs itself to the object of that past experience, we have a lateral awareness that it is an object once experienced. The conjunction of past and present occurs within reflexive mind, and is a genuine conjunction of the actual past of consciousness with the actual present of consciousness, and has nothing to do with images, copies, or representations of anything.'[99]

Earle's account of autobiographical consciousness is an attempt to portray the 'life of the transcendental ego' based on insights of Husserl's phenomenology. But the conception of the two acts of recollection described in the above passage is just as much grounded in the phenomenology of Hegel, in the concept of *Selbstbewusstsein* of the *Phänomenologie des Geistes*. Hegel's *Phenomenology* is the great treatise of modern consciousness which places the ancient project of self-knowledge within the idea of self-consciousness, and this conception of self-consciousness is founded in a conception of recollection (*Erinnerung*).[100] Human subjectivity comes about by means of the two recollectible moments that Earle relates, which in Hegel's terms are the act in which consciousness apprehends the object (which is in a sense actually itself) as something 'in-itself' (*ansich*) and then apprehends the fact of its apprehension as its own, as something 'for-itself' (*fürsich*). Because of the basing of self-knowledge in the phenomenological states or

---

[98] See the remarks on Platonic recollection in R. Sorabji, *Aristotle on Meaning* (Providence, RI: Brown University Press, 1972), ch. 3.

[99] W. Earle, *The Autobiographical Consciousness* (Chicago: Quadrangle Books, 1972), 157.

[100] See my *Hegel's Recollection: A Study of Images in the Phenomenology of Spirit* (Albany, NY: State University of New York Press, 1985).

stages of the human's apprehension of itself and the grounding of this process in recollection as a dialectical process, Hegel makes knowledge 'autobiographical'. The question of what is beyond the autobiographical in this sense of the subject's dialectical apprehension of itself rests on how Hegel's notion of 'absolute knowing' (*das absolute Wissen*) is to be interpreted.

However it is to be regarded, the absolute occupies the place of the divine in Vico's *New Science* as the autobiography of humanity. The divine order in Vico's metaphysics is a true beyond in the sense that for Vico God is ultimately transcendent of the human world of civil things, yet the divine is the basis of the providential order of the courses of history and the order of the events of Vico's own life in his autobiography. In the movement from act of recollecting to act of recollection in the self's recollection of itself there is, as Earle claims, no image or representation that intervenes between the two acts of consciousness. The self's consciousness of its past is immediate, just as there is no 'mediation' between the two moments of Hegel's phenomenology of the subject; one moment necessitates the other. Mediation enters when the two interlocking and mutually dependent moments of self-consciousness are given expression in discourse, when in Vico's terms they are meditated and narrated by the self to itself.

This requires the actual process of consciousness as autobiographical in form, as the movement between the two types of recollective acts to be externally expressed. In this act the self *portrays* itself to itself as having a history and as finding the truth of its being as present in the recollective process in which it encounters its own being. In this the self becomes a text for itself. It is not just a text in the metaphorical sense of being a living book to be read by the self recalling its own past life; this past life becomes expressed in the power of language. This is the philosopher's philosophy as written down, his systematic narration of the world. Or it is in addition the actual autobiography of the philosopher himself formulated in accordance with the principles and truth of his philosophy. But what dominates the modern account of the self is the portrayal of the self as generated in time, as a reality that develops such that self-knowledge in the modern sense comes forth as the product, so to speak, of the development of self-consciousness.

The Vichian conception of autobiography, as I am conceiving it here, is based on narrative, but it is the narrative of history, not the narrative of the myth. Myth, as Vico says, is true story, but it is true story because it is the only story. In this sense myth is like a perception—it is true because it is simply a presentation of what is wholly and uncritically the content before the mind. Myth embodies the first claim of the *Theaetetus*: 'perception [*aesthesis*], then, is always of something that *is*, and, as being knowledge, it is infallible' (*Theaet.* 152 C). The perception gains this power of being true simply because of its selectivity, excluding all else and perceiving just what is there. The myth gains this not by selecting from what is there but by its ability to include all that is there or seems to be there—the myth is a perfect composite of all there is.

Vico's concern is to show that self-knowledge can take the form of historical narrative in addition to what I will call 'mythical' narrative. How can the ancient project of self-knowledge be revived in a world that has entered historical time? Vico must embody the ancient sense of mythical narrative which surrounds the figure of Socrates as the archetypal philosophical life in the historical narrative. How can the ancient project of self-knowledge that characterized philosophy in the last period of the *corso* of the ancient world be revived in the barbarism of the *ricorso* of Vico's own modern age? Self-knowledge requires the presence of an actual philosophical self in order for it to live and flourish. Vico must invent himself as a historical being, a being who has a history. But this history will also have the overall structure of a myth or fable. Vico becomes the modern Socrates.

Vico's portrait of himself has a beginning, middle, and end, but this beginning, middle, and end is not a simple story of his genesis; it is at the same time a fabulous history, guided by providence. Thus Vico absorbs the mythic narrative within his historical narrative to make himself the discoverer of the great patterns of the self-knowledge of humanity, captured in his *New Science*. This requires Vico to pass beyond the *res gestae* form of Renaissance and Roman telling of lives. It also requires Vico to have first established myth as the basis of the historical world itself. This he accomplishes in the conception of history in the *New Science*, in which he shows that poetic wisdom which is based on the formation of imaginative universals is the beginning of human history. Society and the forms of human life are born in the primal scene of Jove the thunderer being the first god of the first men, the fearful experience through which the first humans come to realize their separation from nature and their own sense of presence in the world. The separation that the first humans make between god as in the sky and world as the earth, as a response to their fear, establishes the possibility of the human self as a reality. The question of self-knowledge comes only later, with the appearance of the philosophers, which requires the disintegration of the mythical consciousness which names the gods and takes auspices and which later governs human affairs in terms of the figures of heroes.

What Vico calls ideal eternal history is the apprehension of human history as composed of nations which each pass through three stages, the first of which is an age in which men think and live communally in terms of gods. The founders of families are those who can take the auspices of the actions of the divine powers. Thus the heads of families possess the necessary power of knowledge upon which all humanity depends to live. The age of gods dissolves into the age of heroes such as Achilles and Ulysses, who are the embodiment of human virtues prior to humanity's ability to express in conceptual or literal language the meaning of these virtues through which society and thought are guided. What is required for thought and life is present in the stories of the heroes.

Only with the decline of the power and reality of the heroes do thought and language begin to order experience in terms of abstract or intelligible universals. Men begin to think and act according to the class concepts and syllogistic thinking found in Aristotelian logic. The power of the reflective intellect brings with it patterns of life and thought cut off from natural virtues and the gods. As Rousseau puts it, 'finally men chased the gods out in order to live in the temples themselves',[101] a line Vico might himself have formulated. In this world of reflective thinking the self becomes for the first time a problem. It can no longer gain what it needs for its existence from its contact with the divine or from its natural embodiment and motivation to virtue in heroic acts. Reflection empties the self of its vital contact with the world and places the object at a distance. Thought does not live in the world, the world

---

[101] J.-J. Rousseau, *The First and Second Discourses*, ed. R. D. Masters and J. R. Masters (New York: St. Martin's Press, 1964), 54.

lives as an object of thought. The self has achieved the stance necessary for science, but it lacks a science of itself.

The self must recover the power of the poets, not the power to discover a truth in the object but the power to *make* (*poiein*) something as true. This is the essence of self-knowledge. The philosophical project is truly born out of the attempt to have a *speculative* sense of knowledge in the face of the newly found powers of reflective knowing typical of the third age of man. This speculative knowing is the notion of a *speculum*, a mirror that the self can hold up to itself, the rediscovery of its own nature by its powers, or recovery of its powers of *fantasia*, its power now not to form the world itself in terms of images but to form its own reality in terms of images. In this act of speculation, as opposed to its newly found powers of reflection, the self remembers the power of the image. The image is what guides speculative thinking.

The key to speculative thinking is the human problem of self-knowledge. Autobiography is not a project of reflection in this sense; it is always a project of speculation. Reflection allows thought to adjust its form perfectly to the object as independent of thought. The self becomes the knower, knowing the known which is not of its own making. Reflection in this sense is simply the fascination with the object as external to the thinker, a kind of thinking in which the object is neutral to the thinker and not as such a part of the thinker's being. Reflection thus becomes a kind of witnessing of the given in experience. Imagination is necessary for reflection only to the extent that the object must be given a concrete form so that it can be conceptually thought and ordered. But imagination in the sense of *fantasia*, the fundamental sense of imagination endorsed by Vico as the basis of his science of the principles of humanity, is the power of the image to bring a truth into being, to form a starting-point for thought and for life.

Reflection can generate method in thought but speculation cannot. There is never a method for self-knowledge. The so-called Socratic method becomes on inspection no method at all, because it is essentially guided by rhetoric—a certain skill with ordinary words that allows the thinker to reach new senses of what the words mean. Reflection precludes the need for rhetoric or makes rhetoric an appendage for communicating truths found by its formulation of the object. Speculation is essentially rhetorical in form because it depends upon the image as 'topical', that is, the image that the self can form becomes the ground from which thought must draw forth meanings to make its reality in words. The way in which the self can think about itself is dependent upon how the self can form its reality linguistically. Self-knowledge, like poetry, is a linguistic art. Self-knowledge is contained in the complete speech that the self can make about itself and that speech is always made by a particular speaker who makes his own reality in the act of the speech produced. Autobiographical knowledge, which is certainly self-knowledge, is dependent upon a move in thought from reflective understanding to speculative thinking in which the self becomes the maker of the truth of its own being.

In Vico's view the beginning of history is the myth and the overall structure of history as ideal eternal is 'mythic' in the sense of history being a self-contained order in which time is mastered as a closed circle, each nation being an entity that undergoes the same stages but at varying rates. Myth is at both the beginning and end, so to speak, of historical process. The narrative of the life of a nation is bounded by the limits of the three ages of its ideal eternal pattern of rise and fall. The *New Science*, which portrays in words these patterns, is the autobiography of humanity and as such is the self-knowledge of humanity, for it shows how humanity makes itself. The *New Science* is the complete speech of the nature of humanity made on its behalf by Vico, its spokesman, in which humanity finds out what its nature is.

To write a philosophy of history in Vico's view, then, is to write the autobiography of humanity. And, as Collingwood's comments quoted above suggest, this grand sense of self-knowledge that is to be found in our philosophical apprehension of human history must be grounded in the self-knowledge of the philosopher. Moreover, I would add that the basis of the philosopher of history's grasp of history depends on his ability to grasp his own reality, the reality of his own selfhood in terms that are a microcosm of the macrocosm of historical life. His own sense of self-knowledge, the narrative or potential narrative of his self, must be accomplished in terms of the same principles whereby the life of the collective is understood. For the philosopher of history, in Vico's terms, the Greek *polis* becomes all of history or, as Vico puts it in Augustinian terms, 'that great city of the human race'. Thus as providence is present in terms of the cyclic order of history, so Vico systematically interprets the events of his life, what I will call the fable of himself, in terms of a providential ordering.

Although Vico writes his *New Science* of history before he writes his autobiography, it is his ability to conceive of himself as a reality that has narrative form which contains the same principles of the *polis* of humanity that allows him to have the philosophy of history that he does, and to be assured of its truth. If Vico could not actually make a narrative of his own individual humanity, in terms of principles adopted from those of humanity in general, how could he be assured of the truth of the *New Science?* The phenomenological proof of the truth of his science is Vico's hermeneutic of his own life. But Vico's formation of his own reality cannot be the story of a unique individual, and this may be what makes his autobiography different from that of Rousseau, who sees himself as a unique individual or at least rhetorically employs this principle. Vico's autobiography is the portrait of the modern philosopher as the mythic narrative of Socrates is the portrait of the ancient philosopher. Vico's fable of himself is set in terms of his isolation as thinker in the midst of an age of barbarism and barbaric thinkers and barbaric, reflective philosophizing. In this Vico is the seeker of the Socratic ideal of self-knowledge who is placed in the modern position of the thinker cut off from the *polis* and confined to his study, in the manner established for the figure of the philosopher in Descartes's *Discourse* and *Meditations*.

Vico's autobiography of humanity is not a work born of conversation in the *agora* but is a giant meditation born from his isolation. An 'autobiography' of Socrates does not exist not simply because Socrates did not write anything but because Socrates has no autobiographical existence. His pursuit of self-knowledge is an activity conducted in public, not in the study. Vico makes discoveries that not only are not understood but also go largely unrecognized and ignored. His autobiography becomes a necessary text to justify their existence and to make them evident to those who can listen.

The project of self-knowledge requires that the philosopher himself appear on the stage of the world as the medium through which the reader or listener can model his own existence, can grasp the philosophical dimensions of his own life. Vico's autobiography is not simply a portrait of the unique thinker of Naples, suffering his particular injustices and misfortunes, it is the portrait of the modern philosopher. As Rousseau says of Socrates, in the modern world he would not be condemned to drink the hemlock but would simply be forced to suffer all the indignities of the thinker who attempts to think in the barbarism of the modern age.[102] We only know what self-knowledge is in the Socratic sense by careful attention to the living figure of Socrates. Self-knowledge is not some particular type of knowledge that can be conveyed by means of a method or a doctrine. It exists only through our apprehension of the figure of Socrates as a player on the stage of the world who is both actor and spectator. We can only apprehend that sense of acting and spectating that is necessary for insight into the problem of self-knowledge and its pursuit by attention to the mythic narrative of Socrates, the examiner of his life. The image of Socrates himself is the key.

The ideal of self-knowledge is clothed in the figure of Socrates and no one else. This suggests that any philosophy can be seen as a theatre of self-knowledge and that behind it is a particular type of human being, the philosopher, whose construction of reality is in fact a construction of his own reality, even if he keeps his own reality largely hidden from his thought. I am calling the narrative of Socrates mythic because it is static. In Vichian terms Socrates is a heroic figure, who is not a true heroic figure like Achilles or Ulysses, because his contact with virtue is through his power of thought rather than a power of deed, a power to enact things in the world.

Autobiography as a philosophical idea is what emerges when we as moderns take up the task of self-knowledge because our reality is developmental or historical, and thus the self can be apprehended as a story. The self can come to know its own reality as a process in time, which requires a memorial grasp of its origin and a construction of its own reality in genetic terms. If this is done in philosophical terms this genesis has a necessity of development. Like history itself it has an overall meaning, or what Vico understands as providential structure. Autobiography is never simply historical because it is always an attempt to recover the origin and in that sense is mythic.

The project of self-knowledge is in fact always metaphorical at bottom, because the self comes into existence only by the forging

102 Rousseau, *Discourses*, 46.

of some metaphor which allows the self to write itself. And it is metaphorical in the sense of a transference because in the act of autobiographical writing the self transfers its being into words and thus the reality that it makes for itself in words is never what it itself is. The mythic drive to see the world as an *alter ego* becomes the model for self-knowledge. When the power of the myth is lost, the sense of the *alter ego* that was once attached to all of the world itself is transferred to the pursuit of the self as *alter ego*—the pursuit of self-knowledge. The *alter ego* of the self becomes its autobiography.

As a philosophical idea understood in Vichian terms autobiography depends upon the distinction between ancient and modern. In terms of Vico's conception of history the ancient world enters the third and final stage of its *corso* with the arrival of philosophy and the essence of this is the ground of philosophy in the pursuit of self-knowledge first framed by Socrates. The narrative in which we encounter Socrates is a 'mythic' narrative. It does not tell the story of Socrates in genetic terms. It relates the nature of Socrates in terms like those used of the mythic hero. Socrates is Plato's replacement for the Homeric figure who acts by acting. Socrates acts by thinking. There is no autobiography of Socrates wherein we learn of his genesis, his early education, and the development of his thought. We encounter him in terms of the traits of his character and his death.

The modern world requires the same pursuit of self-knowledge, the kind of knowing that only philosophy can supply in the face of the barbarism of the third age of the *ricorso* of the West, in which we and Vico find ourselves. Vico lives in a historical world that encompasses in its memory the Socratic figure of the philosopher. But self-knowledge can no longer be pursued in strictly Socratic terms. There is no *polis*. The philosopher stands in isolation as the Cartesian thinker in his study, an isolation that Descartes does not himself invent but simply reflects. The revival of self-knowledge must take a form that is responsive to the modern condition. This form is autobiographical thought.

Just as metaphysics must take the form of a philosophy of history, self-knowledge and the rediscovery of the nature of the philosopher must take a new form. Autobiography as a philosophical act is the attempt by the philosopher to make a historical narrative of himself which ultimately functions as a means to reach the elements of the mythic narrative of the Socratic—which I will later call Vico's fable of himself. Socrates is a tranformation of the figure of the hero. He is in direct contact with the divine order, with the Forms. He is both a part of the *polis* and dangerous to it.

Vico draws the portrait of the modern philosopher who is in contact with the divine order as the providential order of his own historical time. His power of self-knowledge is not based upon an immediate or direct involvement with the divine. Modern or Vichian self-knowledge is reachable only by going through history to its divine order. Vico's statement in the *New Science*, that its proof rests on the reader meditating and narrating it to himself, taken back in the direction of his concept of autobiography, is to say that this proof also entails the reader meditating and narrating his own reality in terms of its divine principles (349). This then is what in modern terms will give the philosopher access to that human wisdom which Socrates claims to possess in the *Apology*.

As a literary pursuit autobiography is part of the literature of the human self and is subject to all of the techniques of the criticism and analysis of the text. As a part of philosophy, autobiography is grounded in the ancient project of self-knowledge, and in Vichian terms autobiography is the centre of the problem of philosophizing in the modern world.

3

Augustine's *Confessions* and Descartes's *Discourse*

St Augustine was of particular importance to Vico. He cites the *City of God* directly in several places in the *First* and *Second New Science* and paraphrases its title in several other places, applying it to the central concept of his own project. In the *First New Science* (1725) he speaks of 'the nations united together as in a great city of the world' (bk. 2, ch. 5), and of 'the universal law of the gentes observed in this great city of the human race' (bk. 4). In the *Second New Science* (1730, 1744) he says that providence, often against the designs of men, 'has ordered this great city of the human race' as it undergoes its development in history (342), and in the conclusion to his work Vico says that no matter what else we may have learned from his science, the simple observation we can make of the fall of corrupt nations and their regeneration through their reapprehension of the virtues in their returned bestial state, 'would lead us to say certainly that this is the great city of the nations that was founded and is governed by God' (1107). Vico's metaphor for the 'common nature' of nations is that of Augustine's 'earthly city'.

In the late summer of 1731, a few months after finishing the continuation of his autobiography, Vico signed his extensive 'third' set of 'Corrections, Meliorations, and Additions' to the *Second New Science* with the declaration that St Augustine was his 'particular protector': *Terminato la vigilia di santo Agostino (27 agosto), mio particolare protettore, l'anno 1731* ('finished on the eve of the feast day of St Augustine (27 August), my particular protector, the year 1731').[1]

In the *Autobiography*, when describing his inaugural oration of 1719, in which he announced his project of a new theory of universal law (which led to the three books to which he gave the

---

[1] *L'autobiografia, il carteggio e le poesie varie*, ed. B. Croce and F. Nicolini, 2nd rev. edn., *Opere di G. B. Vico*, vol. v (Bari: Laterza, 1929), 377.

general title *Il diritto universale* and with which he hoped to win
the concourse for a university chair of law), Vico says he based his
remarks on the Augustinian tripartite division of *nosse* (knowledge), *velle* (will), and *posse* (power) (156/46), because these are
the principal elements of all divine and human learning. In his
general introduction to his work on *Universal Law* Vico states that
the whole work derives from his reading of a passage of the *City
of God* which caused him to think of a passage in Varro, in which
Varro propounds that the Roman gods were made according to a
formula of nature. From this Vico thought of the idea that natural
law is the formula and idea of truth that demonstrates the true
God, infinite, incorporeal, and one.[2] Varro is also the source of
Vico's three ages of gods, heroes, and humans in the *New Science*
(6). In the second chapter of *De uno universi iuris principio et fine
uno* (On the one principle and the one end of universal law) (1720)
Vico cites the *Confessions* and the above tripartite division as the
basis for his definition of God. He says: 'God, as St Augustine
defines in his *Confessions*, as divine philosophy demonstrates, and
as our religion professes, is infinite Power, Knowledge, and Will'
('*Deus, ut divus Augustinus in* Confessionibus *definit, philosophia
divina demonstrat et nostra religio profitetur, est Posse, Nosse,
Velle infinitum*').[3]

Vico repeats the distinction of *posse, nosse*, and *velle* at the
beginning of *De constantia iurisprudentis* (On the constancy of the
jurisprudent) (1721)[4] and mentions it in his notes on both books.[5]
He emphasizes here, at the beginning of the second book, the sense
in which these three elements are the basis of the definition of God,
and also are the principles necessary in the mind for any science
and for virtue. Vico understands these elements as a circle that
goes from God to man to God, from the infinite mind to the human
mind, and that takes the human mind back to its dependency on
the divine.

In referring to the *Confessions* for this tripartite division Vico

[2] *De universi iuris uno principio et fine uno*, ed. F. Nicolini, *Opere di G. B. Vico*,
vol. ii (Bari: Laterza, 1936), pt. 1, p. 33. The passage where Varro speaks of the
formula naturae is *City of God*, iv. 31. See also *New Science*, 1045 and 364.

[3] *De uno principio*, 42 and 43 (ch. 2).

[4] *De constantia iurisprudentis*, ed. F. Nicolini, *Opere di G. B. Vico*, vol. ii (Bari:
Laterza, 1936), pt. 2, p. 272.

[5] *Notae in duos libros*, ed. F. Nicolini, *Opere di G. B. Vico*, vol. ii (Bari: Laterza,
1936), pt. 3, pp. 600 and 615–16.

apparently has in mind Augustine's discussion in Book 13, where he speaks of some resemblances of the Trinity that exist in man. These are *esse, nosse,* and *velle* ('*Dico autem haec tria: esse, nosse, velle*') (xiii. 11). Instead of *posse* in this list is *esse* (cf. the triad *memoria, intellegentia, voluntas* in *De Trinitate*, x. 11). Augustine says that man can look into himself and see that he is, that he knows, and that he wills. Like the Trinity, these three are distinct yet are in one single mind or soul. Although from these we cannot know whether these correspond one for one with the Trinity or whether all three are in each person, or precisely how their relationship can be expressed, from their existence in man we can have an impression of our connection with the divine.

In the last philosophical work of his career, his address before the Academy of Oziosi on 'the relation between philosophy and eloquence' (1737), Vico closes with a prayer that invokes Augustine and is both pagan and Christian at once. He says: 'having collected all my powers in a thought of highest reverence, the formula being dictated to me by the great Father Augustine, under whose protection this Academy stands resigned, I conceived this prayer with these solemn and consecrated words—Hear, humbly I pray you, hear, not fabulous Minerva, but Eternal Wisdom, generated from the divine head of the true Jove, the omnipotent Your Father.'[6] St Augustine was one of several saints who were *protettori* of this Academy; the others were St Jerome, St Thomas Aquinas, and St Teresa, whom Vico does not mention.[7] Vico selects his own *protettore* for this layman's prayer which, like the philosophy of Augustine itself, unifies the meaning of the pagan wisdom under the eternal truth of the Christian doctrine, the same project which Vico himself undertook in the *New Science*.

Vico says that one of the principal aspects of his science is that it is 'a rational civil theology of divine providence' (342). He certainly has St Augustine in mind, because he ends this paragraph with one of the above-mentioned references to Augustine's city of God.

---

[6] 'The Academies and the Relation between Philosophy and Eloquence', trans. D. P. Verene, in *On the Study Methods of Our Time*, trans. E. Gianturco, reissued with a preface by D. P. Verene (Ithaca, NY: Cornell University Press, 1990; orig. pub. 1965), 90. See *Opere di G. B. Vico*, vol. vii (Bari: Laterza, 1940), 36–7. See also Vico's poem, 'In onore di Sant'Agostino', which he recited on 31 Aug. 1735 at the Academy of Oziosi, in *Versi d'occasione e scritti di scuola*, ed. F. Nicolini, *Opere di G. B. Vico*, vol. viii (Bari: Laterza, 1941), 117.

[7] Nicolini, ed., *Opere* (Milan: Ricciardi, 1953), 941 n. 3.

Vittorio Mathieu in his essay 'Truth as the Mother of History' points out that in St Augustine providence is a biblical providence, that is, the expression of God's *deliberate* will exercised in carrying out a predetermined pattern. Mathieu says: 'Whereas Vico's providence, though never explicitly opposed to the Biblical conception, is much closer to the Plotinian *prónoia*, that is, to an *automatic* manifestation of divine unity which endows the sensible world with its admirable order but which also, in a manner likewise automatic, leaves behind it *hiati*, imperfections, contrasts, for the very reason that this unity takes place on a level which is not its own: the level of sensible dispersion.'[8] In Mathieu's understanding of the Vichian project, history becomes a sequence of things done for the wrong reasons but which have good outcomes; adversities, violence, and negativity are the birth conditions for the good, true, and beautiful in human history. The divine is born upside-down in history.

St Augustine (AD 354–430) wrote the *Confessions* at about the age of 45 (*c*.400) and may have conceived the *City of God* as early as ten years later. There is certainly a parallel between the two works, in that the *Confessions* reveals God's action in man and the *City of God* reveals God's action in the course of the world's history. Is there a similar parallel between Vico's *Autobiography* and his *New Science*, the two versions of which were written in an interlocking fashion with the two divisions of the *Autobiography*, that of 1728 and the continuation of 1731? In the early books of the *Confessions* Augustine narrates the events of his life as moving toward the event of his conversion under the providence of God's will, as he narrates the historical development of Roman civilization toward Christianity in the *City of God*. Vico regards every adversity and misfortune of his career as in actuality part of a providential course, moving him toward the discovery and production of his new science. As with the life of nations, the positive is never born directly but arises through its opposite, and can be recognized initially only by those who are attuned to reading the events of historical cycles.

Vico, through his own use of Augustine's concept of the city of

---

[8] V. Mathieu, 'Truth as the Mother of History', in G. Tagliacozzo and D. P. Verene, eds., *Giambattista Vico's Science of Humanity* (Baltimore: Johns Hopkins University Press, 1976), 118.

God and the city of men in the *New Science*, makes it evident that
the *City of God* is an important source for his *New Science* and
the work on *Universal Law* that leads up to it. Is Augustine's
Confessions a source for Vico's *Autobiography*? Are there textual
and conceptual parallels between these two works? Vico mentions
Augustine only once by name in the *Autobiography*, an incidental
mention in relation to a work of 'Richardus' (Étienne Deschamps)
which he read while at Vatolla (119/11). He does not mention
Augustine in connection with his conception of his autobiography.
As said earlier, the only 'autobiography' Vico mentions directly is
Descartes's *Discourse*. But Augustine's *Confessions* is the *Urtext*
for any philosopher's reflection on his own life. The parallels I have
mentioned could not have escaped Vico—St Augustine as his
'particular protector', the reference to the *Confessions* at the
beginning of the *Universal Law* as the source for the tripartization
of *nosse, velle,* and *posse,* and his indirect reference to Augustine
through his remarks on these in the *Autobiography*, their shared
Neoplatonism, religion, and interest in the joining of pagan
thought with Christian doctrine and history, their profession of
rhetoric—all these point to a connection between the two autobiographies. William Spengemann in *The Forms of Autobiography* says,
'St. Augustine set the problem for all subsequent autobiography:
How can the self know itself? By surveying in the memory
its completed past actions from an unmoving point above or beyond
them? By moving inquisitively through its own memories and ideas
to some conclusion about them? Or by performing a sequence of
symbolic actions through which the ineffable self can be realized?'[9]

My aim in what follows is not to develop an independent
interpretation of the meaning of Augustine's *Confessions*. This is
an important problem in itself, and beyond the aims of this essay.
To the extent that I have an independent view of the *Confessions* I
agree with that of Ann Hartle, as she has set it off against
Rousseau's *Confessions* in *The Modern Self in Rousseau's Confessions: A Reply to St. Augustine* (1983)[10] and as she has made it
part of her study of the autobiographical nature of philosophy

---

[9] W. C. Spengemann, *The Forms of Autobiography: Episodes in the History of
a Literary Genre* (New Haven, Conn.: Yale University Press, 1980), 32.
[10] A. Hartle, *The Modern Self in Rousseau's Confessions: A Reply to St.
Augustine* (South Bend, Ind.: University of Notre Dame Press, 1983).

interwoven with the Socrates of the *Phaedo* and Descartes's *Discourse* in *Death and the Disinterested Spectator: An Inquiry into the Nature of Philosophy* (1986).[11] My aim is to approach Augustine's *Confessions* from the perspective of Vico's *Autobiography*, to look at it in Vichian terms, and to ask what light it may throw on how to understand Vico's project. One question should be answered directly: Why does Vico not mention the *Confessions* in writing his own life? In one sense it is unnecessary, as anyone would know it, and know it as the archetypal model of the writing of a philosophical life. It would be indiscreet or even irreligious of Vico to suggest direct comparison, for the reader, between his own life and the life of a saint, and this fact alone would preclude any mention of Augustine in his text.

Vico's problem is to invent the true art of autobiography against the feigned autobiography of Descartes. To what grand model is he to turn? Augustine is the inventor of the art of autobiography itself, or at least the inventor of philosophical autobiography as an enterprise involving the full narration of his life. Although philosophers have spoken about themselves and have even been profoundly 'autobiographical', as Hartle has shown of Socrates in the *Phaedo* (and as Misch has shown of a number of ancient figures), Augustine is nearly totally original in his project. In this connection one might also think of the autobiography of the Jewish historian Josephus (AD 37–c.100) to whose histories Vico makes reference in the *New Science* and whose autobiography in many ways reads almost as a modern work. But there are no specific similarities with Vico's work, and it is unlikely to have been a model for him, except in its being a prominent ancient work.

Augustine's project is set against the tradition of Roman biography and Roman lives, few examples of which survive. According to Tacitus (*Agricola*, 1), the writing of such lives was common in the time of the Republic. Varro wrote *De vita sua* in three books. Marcus Aurelius wrote the well-known *Meditations* (*c.* AD 170). Julius Caesar's *Commentaries*, which is not a true autobiography but a series of notes recording the year-by-year conquest of Gaul, is prominent amongst ancient lives. But the Romans wrote such

[11] A. Hartle, *Death and the Disinterested Spectator: An Inquiry into the Nature of Philosophy* (Albany, NY: State University of New York Press, 1986).

works as *mémoires pour servir*, as a document that would serve to ensure their place in posterity.[12]

In opposition to this tradition Augustine might be seen as offering a new type of biography. He confronts the pagan rhetorical and philosophical arts of biographical expression by placing biography in the hands of the subject and having the subject speak about itself as subject, not simply as agent, as creator of actions, laws, political improvements, military achievements, and doer of deeds. If this is in some sense true, Augustine is devising his new art of writing against a feigned version of what he wishes to produce. In a fashion analogous to Vico's opposition to Descartes, Augustine presents the truth of the Christian religion in a form that confronts the 'feigned' pagan sense of telling of truths about lives which are guided by no eternal pattern, which have only accidental, not providential, structure, and which present the subject as a kind of shell rather than as an instantiation of the forms of eternal light and truth. Augustine is using his own life as a means to transform a pagan tradition into a higher form, in accord with Christian doctrine, not as a work of *res gestae*. This is a rhetorical step that must be taken to give Augustine an original place from which to present his philosophical views.

St Augustine is original in that he creates not a new kind of writing of one's own life but the idea of doing so as a philosophical instrument. The *Confessions* can be divided into three parts. Books 1–9, which comprise somewhat more than half of the total text, present Augustine's narrative of his life from his birth to his conversion, ending with his mother's death. Books 10–12 present Augustine's philosophical views on memory, time, and creation. Book 13 is a final profession of faith and affirmation of man's place in relation to God. After ending book 9 with his prayer for his mother, Augustine ceases the narrative of his own life and also

---

[12] A. F. West, *Roman Autobiography* (New York: De Vinne Press, 1901), claims that autobiography is completely an invention of the Romans, 'a native form of Latin literature' that is 'unknown in classical Greek literature' (1 n. 1). This view, which has become a standard one, has been challenged by A. Momigliano, *The Development of Greek Biography* (Cambridge, Mass.: Harvard University Press, 1971), who shows that the development of the writing of autobiography and biography has a much more complex history, and that Latin *vitae* have a basis in Greek *bioi*. See also P. Cox, *Biography in Late Antiquity: A Quest for the Holy Man* (Berkeley, Calif.: University of California Press, 1983), esp. her discussion of the relation between the writing of histories and the writing of ancient biography.

ceases to connnect what he says with events in it. The second half of his work has much of the appearance of a free-standing set of philosophical ideas and presentation of the Christian doctrine. Eugene Vance, following the leads of French thinkers such as Jacques Derrida, has given a reading that deconstructs the references to Augustine's life of the first nine books, turning them into a meditation on language and interpreting the 'conversion' as a movement from corporeal or referential language into a language of the self, the 'self as language' of the later books.[13] This would make the *Confessions* not a 'life' at all.

In the first part of his *Autobiography*, the original 1728 text, in contrasting his approach to Descartes's, Vico says he wrote his life as a historian; in the second part, his continuation of 1731, he adds that he wrote it as a philosopher. In these passages he emphasizes his intent to narrate and meditate the causes of his particular development as a man of letters (113/5; 182/71). As he turns away from the narrative of his own life of the first half of the *Confessions*, Augustine, at the beginning of Book 10, enquires into the purpose of his work: why should other men hear these confessions? Why should he not simply confess privately before God? What is to be the fruit of his confessions? (x. 3). He says that people 'wish, therefore, to hear me confess who I am within' (*volunt ergo audire confitente me, quid ipse intus sim*) (ibid.) because, he says, this is what they cannot derive from their eyes and ears in their external apprehension of him. He then says that

---

[13] E. Vance, 'Augustine's *Confessions* and the Grammar of Selfhood', *Genre*, 6 (1973), 1–28. Vance states that, for Augustine, 'language is not really "about" life or the world, but rather, life is "about" language. Indeed if one reads the narrative portion of the *Confessions* with such priorities in mind, one quickly discovers that the events of Augustine's life are chosen, in the main, to illustrate his life in language: narrative, accordingly, assumes a function that may be called metalinguistic. Thus, the progress depicted in the *Confessions* is not merely one of a rhetorician moving toward conversion to the word, but it is also one of a developing meditation on language that penetrates more and more deeply beneath the worldly surfaces of language to reach fundamental questions about the origins and existence of speech—and of speech as existence. As we shall see, the switch from narrative to exegesis in the *Confessions* is less radical than it may seem, for in each sphere Augustine's concerns with origins and with language remain constant' (17). Cf. P. Ricoeur's discussion of Augustine's conception of time in *Time and Narrative*, vol. i, trans. K. McLaughlin and D. Pellauer (Chicago: University of Chicago Press, 1984), and also R. A. Markus, 'St. Augustine on Signs', in *Augustine: A Collection of Critical Essays*, ed. R. A. Markus (Garden City, NY: Anchor Books, 1972), 61–85.

the true fruit of his confession is not simply to relate what he has been, but what he is: 'This is the fruit of my Confession, not what I have been, but what I am' (*Hic est fructus confessionum mearum, non qualis fuerim, sed qualis sim*) (x. 4). Hartle claims that, 'In its being addressed to God and in its being written for other men, *The Confessions* is primarily intended as a way of discovering truth. . . . Confessing is a "doing" (*facere*) of the truth. . . .'[14]

Augustine's purpose in the *Confessions* is pedagogical, to share his inner truth with his fellow pilgrims and citizens. But in doing this he says it is also an act of self-discovery. He implies that this act of self-discovery, although its purpose is not to judge himself (God is the only true judge), will increase his understanding of his true nature and his relationship to God, that is, the understanding of the Christian doctrine as it resides in him as a particular person.

Vico's purpose in narrating and meditating the causes of his development is pedagogical. The prime reason for Porcìa's proposal, besides its patriotism, is the pedagogical value of learning how thinkers writing their own lives accomplished their discoveries, a point that was at the heart of Leibniz's original suggestion. Vico's own first and last interest is pedagogy, in the sense of promoting *paideia* or *Bildung*, 'human education'. He says at the end of the *Autobiography* that he attempted to teach in accordance with the principles of his oration, *On the Study Methods of Our Time* (198–9/86). Vico says in the sixth oration that pedagogy and the cycle of studies is to have a Christian end. But Vico's *Autobiography* and Augustine's *Confessions*, although related, are different projects. Both believe in the Socratic ideal of self-knowledge. This is Vico's theme of his first oration: 'self-knowledge is the greatest incentive for anyone to complete in the briefest time the whole cycle of the fields of knowledge.'[15] Vico throughout his career identifies self-knowledge with mastery of the whole of human wisdom or *sapientia*. This is something acquired, not by learning everything there is to learn, in terms of the content of all fields, but by the mastery of the arts of erudition—the powers of metaphor, topics, and argument employed by the faculties of memory, imagination, and ingenuity that allow us to combine philological

---

[14] Hartle, *Death and the Disinterested Spectator*, 87.

[15] *Le orazioni inaugurali, il De Italorum sapientia e le polemiche, Opere di G. B. Vico*, vol. i, ed. G. Gentile and F. Nicolini (Bari: Laterza, 1914), 5.

and philosophical ways of understanding into a grasp of the whole that is expressible in language. In this sense, Vico sees human self-knowledge writ large in culture, the world of 'civil things' (*cose civili*).

Augustine's conception of self-knowledge or self-discovery is based on the confessional study of oneself. To confess is truthfully to say what happened, to acknowledge motives, to admit one's sins. In making the confession the self is unburdened of what has weighed upon it, but it is not the judge of the causes or significance of its acts and motives. The judge of its revelations is the confessor, God or God's intermediary. As Augustine says, he does not decide what he is or judge: 'But I do not judge myself' (*sed neque me ipsum diiudico*) (x. 4). I do not determine what I am; that can only occur through my relationship to God and He is all-knowing. My self-knowledge depends upon this relationship. When Augustine narrates the course of his life, in the first nine books of his work, he says what happened, but he does not meditate it as a development that generates its own internal causes, as Vico does with the narration of his career. Augustine's life as he relates it has a coherence, but the element of coherence is derived by God operating as final cause. The movement of his life is toward the moment of his conversion. Each small step of his narration is punctuated by his noticing and reporting God's presence and plan in each incident he relates.

Through Augustine's adversities God is always the presence directing them toward the final end of the realization in Augustine's life of the Christian truth. But providence here is God acting deliberately to bring events in Augustine's life to the proper point. God is the transcendent and final cause whose providential pattern can be discerned in retrospect. In his autobiography Vico portrays himself as making himself. The adversities and negativities are turned to advantage and rights because Vico himself has the power to realize the providential structure that is present as the permanent possibility of their meaning within the events of his life. As in Mathieu's description, quoted above, of Vico's concept of providence in history, Vico's life-events involve *hiati* that are not directly bridged by deliberate divine guidance but are bridged by Vico at his own level of existence, making the specific truths of his own actions which in retrospect fit within the providential pattern of his discovery of the new science.

Augustine, I think, confesses in three different modes that follow the three divisions of time. In the first nine books he confesses his past ignorances and sins; in books 10–12 he confesses his present philosophical ideas on the memorial nature of the mind, the temporal character of human existence, and his understanding of the order of creation; in the final, thirteenth book he confesses his stance against the future; that is, he confesses his ultimate faith in the divinity of God's works and in the divine plan, and in God who is at the end of time. In the tenth book Augustine says that he will speak of himself as he is. The three parts of his *Confessions* thus reflect his state of existence at the age of 45 when writing them, his life not yet over, but his past overcome, and his future the continued truth of the Christian faith. Thus he stands before the reader in all three senses of time (see xi. 27).

In what sense does Vico's account of himself parallel Augustine's? There are certain points of contact. The general facts of Augustine's life are as follows: he was born at Tagaste in North Africa, the son of a pagan father who was very supportive of his education and a Christian mother who was an abiding influence on his life and who moved with him about the ancient world. He studied rhetoric and became a teacher of grammar at Tagaste. He was supported by his family to continue his education at Carthage, where he became a teacher of rhetoric. Beginning at the age of 19, and continuing for a period of nine years, he was a member of the Manichees. About 383 he moved to Rome, and shortly thereafter to Milan to hold a professorship of rhetoric, being attracted by the philosophy of the Neoplatonists and the Sceptics. Through the study of Paul's letters and the preaching of St Ambrose he was converted to Christianity; he resigned his chair of rhetoric in Milan in 386 and was baptized by Ambrose in the spring of 387.

Augustine gives a description of his childhood, saying that he learned the names of things by mute gestures, which he calls that 'natural language, as it were, of all nations' (*tamquam verbis naturalibus omnium gentium*) (i. 7). This reminds one of Vico's mute language, that he says was the first language of the first men, the 'children of the human race' that he speaks of in the *New Science* (209, 376, 401), although Vico gives no such description of his childhood. Augustine gives an account of his father and of course an extended portrait of his mother. Vico only classifies the respective characters of his parents. Augustine reports that as a boy he suddenly fell ill with a pain in his stomach such that it was presumed he might die. His mother prepared him for accepting the sacraments. But he recovered without his baptism being completed. He says that upon his recovery his baptism was deferred 'as if it were necessary' (*quasi necesse esset*) that he be further defiled and experience more sinful life before coming to Christ (i. 11).

The one event which Vico relates from the early period of his childhood is his head-first fall from the ladder, his lying near death, and his recovery, in which his character as a melancholy and profound thinker was determined. Vico is reborn from his cheerful and active disposition as a boy before the fall to the thinker he is to become through the ladder accident. It is as if the fall were necessary to accomplish this. Augustine is not baptized at the point of his illness and thus is not reborn at that moment, but he is fixed on his course toward his ultimate conversion and baptism. He must live longer, but the die is cast. Augustine describes the course of his studies in some detail, as does Vico in even greater detail. His father plays a supportive but basically unimportant role, as does Vico's, but Augustine's mother, as presented in his famous portrait of her, is a crucial guide for him. Vico in his fall acquires his mother's melancholy temperament and not his father's cheerful nature. It is his mother's nature that guides Vico throughout his career, even to his reflections on the problematic character of his melancholy at the end of the autobiography.

Vico presents himself, although in a sense following some courses of formal instruction, as essentially an autodidact, withdrawing from formal instruction to master texts on his own, such as his withdrawal to study the grammar of Alvarez and, later, to read the works of Suárez. Augustine reports that at the age of 20 he read Aristotle's *Categories* on his own, and when he compared his notes with those of his teachers at Carthage, he was astonished by how little they understood of it, in comparison with what he had taught himself. Generally Vico's and Augustine's courses of studies have elements in common: they study many of the same classical authors, prepare themselves in rhetoric and in legal studies. Both become professors of rhetoric. However, Augustine lives a licentious life of pleasures, taking a mistress, etc., and Vico marries soberly as soon as he acquires an income.

There is a certain parallel and an important difference between Augustine's famous sin of robbing the pear-tree, at the age of 16, and Vico's rejection for promotion to a higher grade in the Jesuit school, at the age of 13. Augustine's theft of the pears was a wanton and wasteful act, as he neither needed nor even fully ate the pears and had no purpose in the theft other than theft itself. In this act Augustine learns what sin is because, as he says, he discovered he loved nothing but the illicitness of the act itself (ii. 8). He saw in this the power of sin, that sin was not simply straying from a proper path, but involved a transformation of the soul itself, an alteration of the personality. He experienced a dimension of the real order of things of which he did not have personal knowledge, and which altered his relationship to the world. It was an experience that increased his inner strength. This prepared him for the insights that led to his conversion much later.

In the Jesuit school Vico, attempting to push himself ahead of others on the basis of his merits (and with some support from at least one of his teachers), experienced not sin but injustice. With the best intentions Vico attempts to gain something from the institutional order on the basis of his true merits, only to find it given to another, for unjust reasons. This crisis causes him to withdraw from the school but also sets a lifelong pattern of shaping himself and his inner strength by reliance on his sense of virtue; virtue is something he must make, it is not simply given in the institutional order. Each of these youthful events is completely typical of each author—for Augustine the first experience of personal sin in a career bound for salvation; for Vico the first experience of personal injustice in a career in which he hoped for intellectual acceptance and respectability. What both seem to imply, but which emerges only later in the account of each, is the sense in which piety and wisdom are the sources of strength against the adverse dimension of the objective order. Vico ends the *New Science* with the phrase that this science is inseparably connected to the study of piety, and 'that he who is not pious cannot be truly wise' (*se non siesi pio, non si può daddovero esser saggio*) (1112). And Augustine, criticizing the Manichees, quotes Job 28: 28 that 'piety is wisdom' (*ecce pietas est sapientia*) (v. 5; cf. x. 38).

There is in a sense a parallel between Vico's sojourn at Vatolla and Augustine's involvement with the Manichees. Manicheism is the false spiritual doctrine out of which Augustine must work his way in order to undergo conversion to the truth of Christianity. It is a laborious process, not accomplished without seeing through the intellectual falsehoods and inadequacies of Manicheism at least as Augustine describes it. The parallel here for Vico is obviously his attachment to the corrupt style of poetry that, he says, he was fond of when he went to Vatolla and which he cured by his programme of reading the Tuscan and Latin classics, and, more importantly, his attachment to Cartesianism. As Fisch points out, Vico's poem 'Affetti di un disperato' 'could not have been written by a devout Christian'.[16] As mentioned earlier, Fisch also maintains that Vico was a Cartesian until about the age of 40, that is, until his formulation of the position of the *Study Methods*.[17] Vico himself claims to have both avoided and to some extent worked his way through Cartesianism as an unacceptable physics and metaphysics during his nine years at Vatolla. He claims to have arrived back in Naples as a stranger in a climate of Cartesianism.

Both the pear-tree incident and the working through of the false doctine of Manicheism are turning-points that might, in one sense or another, map on to many lives, but their existence as part of Augustine's *Confessions* is one reason why it is archetypal for subsequent texts of self-knowledge, and Vico's autobiography is no exception. A final point of comparison, in terms of Augustine's life-narrative of his first nine books, is the parallel between Vico's loss of the concourse for the morning chair of law and Augustine's course of action connected with his conversion and baptism by St Ambrose. When Augustine is converted he describes (ix. 2) how he gives up his professorship of rhetoric at Milan. He is now free to withdraw from the world of professional teaching and scholarship and to study and write the truth as he sees it. Augustine in one sense does this deliberately, but in another sense it is done to him. He is converted by a voice (viii. 12); his conversion is not a voluntary act, like a career change. This change is determined for him by divine or providential force, outside his control. He no longer can nor needs to carry on in the usual manner.

Vico sees his loss of the university chair as a providential turn. It is not a conversion to a new doctrine, but his loss of the con-course—the greatest disappointment of his university career—was his salvation as a scholar and discoverer of an original science. The

---

[16] Fisch, Introduction to *The Autobiography of Giambattista Vico*, trans. M. H. Fisch and T. G. Bergin (Ithaca, NY: Cornell University Press, 1983), 36.
[17] Ibid.

terms in which he puts this to his friend Father Bernardo Maria Giacco, in a letter of 25 October 1725, are quite significant. He sent this letter just after the publication of the *First New Science*. He says that his loss of the chair has set him free to write his major work. Previously he had written in order to become professionally successful and obtain such a chair. Had he obtained it he would have spent the rest of his life expounding paragraphs of the *Pandects*. But now he sees that the course he had taken was in fact to lead him to his great discovery of the new science. Vico writes: 'Forever praised be Providence, which, when the weak sight of mortals sees in it nothing but stern justice, then most of all is at work on a crowning mercy! For by this work I feel myself clothed upon with a new man.'[18]

Augustine leaves the professorial life for the religious life, for a life of writing, preaching, and teaching outside the university. Vico does not literally leave his position, but he leaves the university in the sense that he abandons any ambitions he had in it for himself. It now becomes a place for him to write the truth as he sees it and to teach according to the manner and methods he sees fit for whomever wishes to listen. In both cases providence arranges events such that each is put on a course to pursue truth in his own terms. Augustine is quite clear in the *Confessions* that although God's truth and wisdom is objective and known properly only to God, he presents only what he himself understands it to be.

The two most remarkable parallels between Vico's and Augustine's texts are their respective life-threatening childhood experiences that set each on course to develop his ultimate character—Vico as the philosopher and Augustine as the Christian; and the act of providence that relieves each from the course of his professional career and releases each to pursue his own truths, which turn out to have a strong connection, that between the *City of God* and the *New Science*. Each produced his masterwork by recasting the meaning of his previous philosophical studies. In Augustine's case it is to reconceive the pagan philosophy in connection with Christian revelation, and in Vico's case it is to develop his conception of universal law as a total philosophy of history and the civil world.

Vico, as Augustine and as perhaps any autobiographer must,

---

stands between past, present, and future. The narrative of Vico's life, up to the loss of the concourse (his text written in 1725, what in the Fisch and Bergin translation is called Part A), corresponds to Augustine's narrative of his own life in Books 1 to 9. Vico's final pages of his original autobiography, which he added after the publication of the *First New Science* and sent with the revised first portion to Venice in 1728 (Fisch and Bergin Part B), corresponds to Augustine's Books 10 to 12. Like this portion of Augustine's work it does not relate Vico's life-events, but summarizes his philosophical ideas of that present moment; it presents the principal ideas of the *First New Science*. Vico's continuation of his autobiography of 1731 corresponds in principle to Augustine's Book 13, if this is seen as Augustine projecting the framework of his future. Vico's continuation is largely a retrospective of earlier events, with details of the publication of the *Second New Science* and his invitation to write the earlier part of his autobiography. In these respects this continuation overlaps with both portions of Augustine's work. But Vico is aware of his own mortality, speaking of his illnesses, saying that he intends nothing beyond the discovery he has attained in the *New Science*, and bringing into view the prospect of his own death with his quotation from Phaedrus on Socrates. As Augustine's final book is a profession of faith in the truth of creation, Vico's leaves the reader with a final profession of his faith in the philosophical truth of his new science. And it is at this point that he makes his only confession, when he says he was 'choleric to a fault' (*peccò nella collera*). He says that he often reacted too strongly and inappropriately to errors or misconduct of other scholars against him, and that he should have reacted with more Christian charity and, as a true philosopher, overlooked or pitied such rivals (199/86) (cf. *Confessions* on praise and dispraise, x. 37). But it is a small confession, and Vico immediately proceeds again to attack his attackers, by speaking of the 'caitiff semi-learned or pseudo-learned' who called him a fool, thus showing that he is not very repentant, and indeed 'choleric to a fault'.

I wish now to turn to Vico's relation to Descartes. Descartes's relation to Augustine is well known, especially Augustine's formulation of *si fallor, sum* (*De libero arbitrio*, II. iii. 7) as a forerunner of Descartes's *cogito, ergo sum*. It is through a criticism of Descartes's *cogito* as a first principle of metaphysics that Vico approaches Descartes, and this criticism lies behind his attack on Descartes's *Discourse* in the *Autobiography*. In a letter written in Leiden in November 1640 (to whom is not known) Descartes writes: 'I am obliged to you for calling to my attention the passage of St Augustine to which my *I think, therefore I am* has some relation. I have been to read it today in the town library, and I find he does truly use it to prove the certainty of our existence.' Descartes's reference is to the *City of God* (xl. 26; cf. *De trinitate*, x. 10 and *De libero arbitrio*, II. iii. 7). Descartes goes on to distinguish Augustine's use of this in connection with the Trinity from his own purpose, which is to prove that the conscious *I* is an immaterial substance. He concludes, 'And such a thing is of itself so simple and natural to infer—that one is from the fact that one is doubting—that it could have fallen from the pen of anyone; but I am quite pleased to have been in agreement with St Augustine, if only to close the mouths of those small minds who have tried to quibble about this principle.'[19] In the *Confessions* Augustine, in considering the truth of God's existence in his creation, quotes Exodus 3: 14, 'I AM THAT I AM', and concludes that he would 'sooner doubt that I did not live, than that Truth is not' (*faciliusque dubitarem vivere me, quam non esse veritatem*) (vii. 10). Although Augustine speaks of doubting his own reality, God, not the I, is the first principle of his metaphysics, which places Augustine closer to Vico than to Descartes.

Vico's *On the Most Ancient Wisdom of the Italians* begins with a refutation of Descartes's *cogito*. Vico places this within a scene from Plautus' *Amphitryo* (441–7). In so doing Vico finds a different and less dignified precedent for Descartes's first truth. In Plautus' play, while Amphitryon, the commander-in-chief of the Theban army, is away at war, he is cuckolded by Jupiter, who assumes Amphitryon's guise. As the guise is so perfect, the wife of Amphitryon (Alcmena), who is wholly innocent, presumes Jupiter to be her husband. In this comedy of errors Mercury assumes the guise of Amphitryon's slave Sosia. Following the prologue, Sosia, now returned with his master from war, discovers his double, and begins to doubt his own existence when Mercury, in his guise as Sosia, tells Sosia that he is mistaken about his own identity, and

---

[19] Descartes, *Œuvres de Descartes*, ed. C. Adam and P. Tannery (12 vols., Paris: Cerf, 1897–1910), iii, 247–8.

that in fact he, Mercury, is Sosia. The passage that Vico quotes in
the *Ancient Wisdom* is introduced by Mercury saying to Sosia:
'Oh, you can have the name when I don't want it; *I'm* Sosia and
you're nameless. Now get out!' Sosia then looks in the mirror and
begins to develop his 'Cartesian' proof, which concludes, 'But,
when I think, indeed I am certain of this, that I am and have always
been' (*Sed quom cogito, equidem certo sum ac semper fui*).[20]

Vico finds Descartes's famous first truth in the burlesque of
Mercury with a simple-minded slave. Descartes intends his principle of the *cogito* to be more than what Vico finds uttered by
Sosia, because, as he says in the above-quoted letter, he intends it
to establish the *I* as an incorporeal substance. The key word in
Sosia's reaction to his mirror image, for Vico, is *certo*, that he is
certain of his being. Vico's claim is that Descartes's first truth is a
certainty (*certum*) but not a 'true' (*verum*). It is not sufficient for a
first principle to be certain; such a principle must be true.

Vico also finds a precedent in ancient thought for Descartes's
doubt, his 'malignant demon' by which he comes to this principle.
Vico always associates Descartes with the Stoics; for example, in
his letter to Abbé Esperti (1726), Vico associates his description of
the Stoic idea of 'deaf necessity' with Descartes, contrasting it to
the 'blind chance' of Epicurus.[21] Descartes, in his third maxim of
Part 3 of the *Discourse*, associates himself with Stoic philosophy.
In introducing the passage from Plautus Vico cites Cicero's *Academica*, saying that the Stoic uses the same device as Descartes.
Vico seems to be referring to the argument that it is just as plausible
that an omnipotent god could cause impressions that are purely
phantasmal as it is that they proceed from realities (*Academica
priora*, II. xv. 47), the parallel being that for the ancients, dreams
were generally held to be the result of divine interventions, and
that since the god causes the false impression of the dream, the god
could be presumed to be capable of interfering with the reality of
any one of our impressions. Behind this is Zeno's distinction, and
that of the Stoics generally, between true and false impressions,
defining a true impression as one that allows the mind to seize the
object and feel certain that it has been rightly apprehended, which

---

[20] *De antiquissima Italorum sapientia*, ed. G. Gentile and F. Nicolini, *Opere di
G. B. Vico*, vol. i (Bari: Laterza, 1914), 139. Reading with Plautus' text *Sed cum
cogito* instead of Vico's *Sed quom cogito*.
[21] 'All'abate Esperti in Roma', *Opere di G. B. Vico*, v. 201–3.

leads to the Stoic definition of the individual 'irresistible impression'. In the ancient tradition of Scepticism deriving from Pyrrho, Arcesilaus advances the view that arguments for and against the trustworthiness of sense impressions exactly balance each other.

Vico does not relate such details in his connection of Descartes's principle with the Stoics, but they bear on his criticism, because in essence Vico's point is that Descartes's *cogito, ergo sum*, as a first principle of metaphysics, does not answer scepticism. Vico's reference to this passage in Cicero implies that he regards Descartes's principle of the *cogito* as an attempt to fulfil the original Stoic conception of a true impression by adducing an archetypal example of a clear and distinct idea—the idea or impression that the mind has of itself. Against this model of certainty Vico places his principle that 'the true is the made', *verum esse ipsum factum*.

Descartes's procedure in metaphysics is suppositional; he supposes the possibility of ultimate doubt, through his device of the demon, in order to arrive at the certainty of the *I*. But once Descartes has arrived at this certainty, the suppositional method can be applied to the nature of the *I*, and the problem of in what its being consists can become the subject of sceptical doubt. Descartes's special form of the Stoic 'true impression' is entangled in a complex of objections which is just what historically occurred with Descartes's announcement of the *cogito*, resulting in the Cartesian 'objections and replies'.

A principle of certainty is not a truth, because it does not tell us the nature of the thing of which we are certain. It does not provide us with its form or cause. That is, it does not make it intelligible for us. *Verum* here is best understood to mean 'intelligible'. Fisch explaines *verum* as follows: 'Vico's *verum* means the true, not the truth, and its plural *vera* means not truths but the trues or intelligibles; that is, the things, other than sentences or propositions, that are true in the transcendental sense of intelligible.'[22] What can be known to be true or what is intelligible to the knower is what the knower makes (*factum*), what the knower can convert. Vico takes his first principle of metaphysics from God, who is both

[22] Fisch, 'Vico and Pragmatism', in G. Tagliacozzo and H. V. White, eds., *Giambattista Vico: An International Symposium* (Baltimore: Johns Hopkins University Press, 1969), 408.

knower and maker, and who makes by knowing. Human knowledge, Vico says, 'imitates divine knowledge'.[23] The model for this which Vico gives in the *Ancient Wisdom* is mathematics. Mathematical truths, Vico claims, are true because we make them. The mind can fully know their nature because it is reflecting on what it itself has made. Vico restricts the term science (*scientia*) to thought in which *verum* is convertible with *factum*. This occurs perfectly only in the divine mind, but is imitated in certain acts of the human mind.

Science is distinguished from consciousness, or what Fisch helpfully calls the 'witnessing consciousness' (*conscientia*). This *conscientia*, 'conscience' or 'consciousness', is not the self's or knower's relation to itself. *Conscientia* describes the knower's relation to what is external to the knower, the object as already begotten by God, and of which the knower can become aware. Thus the sciences of nature as we normally conceive them are elaborate and useful means for 'witnessing' the world. But our thought in these sciences is in principle closed off from making their objects fully intelligible, because we do not make the object; it is not a *factum*.

With his distinction between *scientia* and *conscientia*, based upon his principle of *verum ipsum factum*, Vico has absorbed Descartes's certainty into the true, and has stood the traditional conception of knowedge and consciousness on its head. He has, in fact, shown the sciences of nature for what they are—forms of consciousness—and has made way for what, in his later work, becomes a science of metaphysics, based upon a science of the civil world that has 'certainly been made by men'. Vico regards this attack on Descartes and Cartesianism in 1710 as decisive, the conclusion of what he had published, the previous year, in his criticism of the conception of studies that derives from the empiricist and rationalistic mentalities. In the *Autobiography* it is presented as the fruit of his living as a stranger in his own land, upon his return to the Cartesianism in Naples from his period at Vatolla, in 1695, when he found Aristotle's metaphysics to have become a 'laughing-stock' (*era già divenuta una favola*) (132/23).

In the fourth paragraph of the *Autobiography*, just after having described how his too early attempt to study scholastic metaphysics had caused him to despair of his studies for a year and a half, Vico

---

[23] *De Italorum sapientia*, 137.

suddenly says: 'We shall not here feign what René Descartes craftily feigned as to the method of his studies simply in order to exult his own philosophy and mathematics and degrade all the other studies included in divine and human erudition.' He concludes that 'with the candour [*ingenuità*] proper to a historian, we shall narrate plainly and step by step the entire series of Vico's studies, in order that the proper and natural causes of his particular development as a man of letters may be known' (113/5).

From the *Study Methods* Vico has erected his philosophy against his criticism of Descartes, his other foes being, as they emerge in the *New Science*, the seventeenth-century natural-law theorists. The three whom Vico most frequently mentions are Grotius, Selden, and Pufendorf (Grotius also being extensively cited in the *Universal Law*). But in 1725, in the *Autobiography*, Vico carries forward his opposition to Descartes, now putting himself against Descartes's use of himself in the presentation of his conception of knowledge in the *Discourse*. Since Vico's own thought involved a struggle to free himself from the dominance of Cartesianism, Vico is in one sense also putting one part of himself against another. In doing so he takes seriously the fact that the *Discourse* is autobiographical philosophy. Having attacked the *I* as an inadequate metaphysical principle in Descartes's philosophy, Vico now attacks the rhetorical and autobiographical *I* as a support for Descartes's conception of the philosopher.

In a letter from Guez de Balzac to Descartes, written in Paris on 30 March 1628, Balzac says: 'Moreover, Monsieur, remember, please, *De l'Histoire de vostre esprit*. It is awaited by all our friends, and you have promised it to me in the presence of Père Clitophon, who is commonly called Monsieur de Gersan. It will be a pleasure to read your various adventures in the middle and in the highest region of the air; to consider your feats against the Giants of the School, the path that you have taken, the progress that you have made in the truth of things, etc.'[24]

The editors, Adam and Tannery, point out in their footnote to this letter that Descartes kept his promise, at least in the sense that there is a letter from Descartes to Balzac from Leiden on 14 June

---

[24] 'Balzac à Descartes (Paris, 30 mars 1628)', *Œuvres*, i. 570–1. On the meaning of the nickname 'Père Clitophon', see Descartes, *Correspondance*, ed. C. Adam and G. Milhand, vol. i (Paris: Alcan, 1936), 447–8.

1637, written only a few days after the *Discourse* appeared, and accompanied by a copy of the book.[25] However, the *Discourse* hardly seems to give the *l'histoire* of Descartes's *esprit*, to give the 'path that [he] has taken' (*le chemin que vous avez tenu*), etc., although Descartes claims exactly this. To have done this would have been to come very near the conception of Vico—to narrate the 'series of all his studies' (*la serie di tutti gli studi*).

Descartes's *Discourse*, published in Leiden on 8 June 1637, was presented as the introduction to his essays on three sciences. It bore the full title of *Discourse on the Method for Rightly Conducting One's Reason, and Seeking Truth in the Sciences. Plus the Dioptrics, the Meteorics, and the Geometry, Which are Essays on This Method*.[26] The *Discourse* was written in French, but a Latin edition was published in Amsterdam in 1644, the same year as the publication of Descartes's *Principia philosophiae*. Given Vico's comment in the *Autobiography* about his decision not to learn French (134/25), the Latin text may be the version he employed, although, given the closeness of Italian and French as Romance languages, it is very likely that Vico could have compared it to the original. In fact, one cannot help but wonder if Vico's claim about not learning French is not an aspect of his *fictio* about his relationship to Cartesianism, given the discourse on the nature of the French language and its grammar which he enters into in the *Study Methods*.[27] Vico hardly seems ignorant of French, or certainly not as ignorant as he claims in the *Autobiography*.

The *Discourse* describes a four-step method of problem-solving, a logic for the rational establishment of a truth. Descartes intended the work to be a comprehensive plan for a complete body of knowledge, based on a method that could solve any problem the human mind could pose. The title he planned for it, in 1636, was *Plan for a Universal Science Capable of Raising Our Nature to Its Highest Degree of Perfection. Plus the Dioptrics, Meteorics and*

[25] 'Descartes à Balzac (Leyde, 14 juin 1637)', *Œuvres*, i. 381.
[26] *Discours de la méthode pour bien conduire sa raison, & chercher la verité dans les sciences. Plus La dioptrique, Les météores, et La géométrie, Qui sont des essais de cette Méthode* (Leiden, 1637). For an analysis of Descartes's claim to a method as a rhetorical device see J. A. Schuster, 'Cartesian Method as Mythic Speech: A Diachronic and Structural Analysis', in J. A. Schuster and R. R. Yeo, eds., *The Politics and Rhetoric of Scientific Method: Historical Studies* (Dordrecht: Reidel, 1986), 33–95.
[27] *On the Study Methods of Our Time*, sect. 7.

*the Geometry, Where the Most Curious Matters the Author Could
Have Chosen to Give Proof of the Proposed Science, Are Explained
So That Even the Uninstructed Can Understand Them.* The essays
were intended by Descartes to be specimens of how his method
could solve problems in the sciences. In the *Dioptrics* he treats
questions of vision, light, and the best arrangements of lenses; in
the *Meteorics* the same method is used to construct hypotheses
concerning atmospheric phenomena, such as clouds, storms, and
rainbows; in the *Geometry* he showed how the method could yield
results in previously unsolvable mathematical problems.

My aim here, regarding Descartes's *Discourse*, as with Augustine's *Confessions*, is not an independent or full interpretation of
Descartes's text, but to regard it from a Vichian perspective, and
to treat it as autobiography. The account with which I most agree
is David Lachterman's suggestive essay, 'Descartes and the Philosophy of History'. Lachterman states 'Descartes substitutes the tale
of his own life for the exemplary histories and fables of the past.'[28]
Lachterman has in mind the fact that Descartes, while eliminating
the histories and fables of the ancients from the conception of truth
that he outlines in the *Discourse*, says, in the same breath: 'But this
work is put forth merely as a history, or, if you like it better, as a
fable . . .' (*Mais, ne proposant cet écrit que comme une histoire,
ou, si vous l'aimez mieux, que comme une fable . . .*).[29] And,
following the classical understanding of the use of fables and

---

[28] D. R. Lachterman, 'Descartes and the Philosophy of History', *Independent
Journal of Philosophy*, 4 (1983), 39. There are not many discussions that consider
Descartes's *Discourse* as autobiography. I find very convincing Ann Hartle's chapter
on Descartes in *Death and the Disinterested Spectator*. R. Kennington, 'René
Descartes', in L. Strauss and J. Cropsey, eds., *History of Political Philosophy*
(Chicago: Rand, 1963), regards the form of the *Discourse* as autobiography (385).
From a different direction, J. M. Bernstein, *The Philosophy of the Novel: Lukács,
Marxism and the Dialectics of Form* (Brighton, Sussex: Harvester, 1984), calls the
Discourse 'Descartes's ur-novel' (165) (see also ch. 5, sect. 2, 'The Cartesian
Novel'). D. Simpson, 'Putting One's House in Order: The Career of the Self in
Descartes' Method', *New Literary History*, 9 (1977), 83–101 holds that the self is
an ironic device in the *Discourse*. See also D. Judovitz, *Subjectivity and Represen-
tation in Descartes: The Origins of Modernity* (Cambridge: Cambridge University
Press, 1988); and R. Elbaz, *The Changing Nature of the Self: A Critical Study of
the Autobiographic Discourse* (Iowa City, Ia.: University of Iowa Press, 1987), ch.
4. For a view of Descartes as a transformer of the Augustinian conception of the
self, see C. Taylor, *Sources of the Self: The Making of Modernity* (Cambridge,
Mass.: Harvard University Press, 1989), ch. 8.

[29] Descartes, *Discours de la méthode*, chronology and preface by G. Rodis-Lewis
(Paris: Garnier-Flammarion, 1966), 35.

histories to teach prudence, Descartes adds that the reader may find in it examples to imitate, but also adds that there will be many others that it will be well not to follow. In the 'Author's Letter' that appears with the French translation of the *Principles*, Descartes says it should be read through first as a *roman*.[30]

The criticism of the *Discourse* as unreliable in some of its autobiographical details overlooks what Descartes says regarding his conception of the text.[31] Vico's charge that Descartes 'feigns' (*finse*) his autobiography is not the charge that Descartes has overlooked certain details of his life. It is that Descartes has pretended to show us the path to his discovery of his method, but has not done so. In the fourth paragraph of the *Discourse* Descartes claims 'But I shall be delighted to show, in this discourse, what paths I have followed, and to represent my life as in a picture . . .' (*Mais je serai bien aise de faire voir, en ce discours, quels sont les chemins que j'ai suivis, et d'y représenter ma vie comme en un tableau . . .*).[32] Descartes then says, in a manner analogous to his comment following his remark on reading his text as a history or fable, that he has done this in order that everyone may be able to judge his methods for themselves. Descartes's term 'tableau' is well chosen because, unlike Vico's narration of causes, he simply places himself as the *I*, the subject, the thinker in the tableau of the stove-heated room.

The picture that Descartes gives of himself, that remains in the reader's memory, is that of the first page of Part 2, in which he says he stayed in Germany during the winter, while returning to the military campaign from the Emperor's coronation and, since he was not troubled in any way, he spent the whole day alone in a *poêle*, or stove-heated room, 'where I had complete leisure to discourse with myself about my own thoughts' (*où j'avais tout loisir de m'entretenir de mes pensées*).[33] Descartes (1596–1650) joined the Dutch army in 1618 as a gentleman volunteer under Prince Maurice of Nassau, after completing his education at La Flèche, and two years after taking a law degree at Poitiers. In Breda he met a Dutch doctor, Isaac Beeckman, under whose influence he

---

[30] Descartes, *Œuvres*, ix. 11.
[31] See Lachterman, 'Descartes and the Philosophy of History', 39 n. 47.
[32] *Discours*, 34–5.
[33] Ibid. 41.

experienced an intellectual awakening to the nature and importance of science. He left Breda for Copenhagen, planning a very
indirect route via Amsterdam and Danzig (Gdańsk), then through
Poland and eventually Austria and Bohemia. He arrived in Frank-
furt in September 1619, in time to be present at the coronation of
Ferdinand. He broke his journey in Germany at Ulm, in the winter
of 1619, and in a house near Ulm he gave himself over to intense
reflections on methodological questions. These led him, on
10 November 1619, to experience a daytime vision and three
dreams, which revealed to him his life task: to develop a science
that would unify the sciences.

Descartes's tableau, of spending a day in his room with his
thoughts and arriving at the four-step method he presents in Part 2
of the *Discourse*, as well as the other views which follow, is hardly
an account of the paths that led to his discovery, which involved
his encounter with Beeckman and his intense meditations in the
house at Ulm, and the developing realization of the possibility of
unifying a long list of sciences under a mathematical order.
Descartes does offer reflections on his education and its faults that
led up to his discovery and reports some details of the aftermath,
but it is his tableau of this day of self-discourse that dominates his
account.

In Part 3 he says that he decided to pursue his thought by going
back out in the world, saying that he spent the following nine years
(the same number of years Vico spends at Vatolla) roaming about
the world, 'attempting to be a spectator rather than an actor in all
the comedies that play there' (*tâchant d'y être spectateur plutôt
qu'acteur en toutes les comédies qui s'y jouent*).[34] In a notebook
begun on 1 January 1619 and completed during the course of the
next few years, Descartes says: 'Just as comedians are warned not
to allow shame to appear on their brows, and thus put on a mask:
so I, about to step upon the theatre of the world, where I have so
far been a spectator, come forward in a mask.'[35]

Descartes's mask, his persona, his fable of himself, of the *I*,
Descartes, is carried out in the *Discourse*. But, like every true
autobiographer, he insists that he will tell the reader only the truth,
and continually invites the reader to judge for himself, not to
imitate all of what is told, for although it is the path he has taken

---

[34] *Discours*, 55.   [35] Descartes, *Cogitationes privatae*, in *Œuvres*, x. 213.

it may not be the path for everyone (a claim reminiscent of Augustine's insistence that his confession is to be understood as only his alone). The reader is urged to practice an art of criticism concerning what should be valued in Descartes's tale, while at the same time being taken in to believe that what is being told is the true picture of Descartes. The reader is warned that 'those who govern their conduct by examples from history are liable to fall into the extravagances of the paladins of romance and undertake projects beyond their power to complete'.[36] Descartes adds that in the pursuit of truth eloquence is unnecessary. If what is said is clear and intelligible it matters not if the person speaks only *bas breton* and has never learned rhetoric.[37] The truth is eloquent in itself.

But the *Discourse* is based on rhetorical principles, on Aristotle's first principle in the *Rhetoric* (1377^b15–1378^a30), that what convinces most is the character of the speaker. The audience must perceive the speaker to be telling the truth. This is achieved by Descartes through the principles of repetition and authority. His repetition of the *I* makes himself an authority for the reader. The traditional appeal of the speaker to authority, to the embellishment of what is said by quoting authority, is replaced by Descartes's sincerity of the *I*. Descartes offers a modern version of the ancient principles of discourse. The *I* becomes the master *topos*, metaphor, and maxim (I am, I exist) from which Descartes draws forth his credibility as a speaker.

Is there a model for Descartes's autobiography of his *I*? I think that it lies in Montaigne's *Essais*. With his principle of the certainty of the *cogito* Descartes hopes to answer the scepticism of Montaigne. Montaigne may be the source for Descartes calling his three works that follow the *Discourse* by the title *Essais*. The conception of certainty of the *Discourse* is an answer to the scepticism of Montaigne's *Essais*. In a sense, Montaigne assumes the Cartesian stance prior to Descartes; realizing that none of the rational and scholastic opinions concerning the external order of things offers certainty of knowledge, Montaigne turns to himself. He says in his address 'To the Reader' in the *Essais*, 'I am myself the matter of my book',[38] and similarly in the last essay, 'Of Experience': 'I study

---

[36] *Discours*, 37.   [37] Ibid.
[38] M. de Montaigne, *The Complete Essays of Montaigne*, trans. D. M. Frame (Stanford, Calif.: Stanford University Press, 1958), 2.

myself more than any other subject. That is my metaphysics, that is my physics.'[39] Montaigne's response to his scepticism, a scepticism that pervades the sixteenth century, is to investigate himself, to explore his self-portrait. Descartes does not in fact disagree with Montaigne's scepticism, but his answer, in the *Discourse*, is to carry the sceptical project to its limits in an effort to arrive at a point of certainty which will serve as a model for all thinking and be the basis of a method of truth. Thus in Part 4 of the *Discourse* Descartes says that he found this truth in the assertion '*je pense, donc je suis*', and that it was so firm and assured a truth 'that all the most extravagant suppositions of the sceptics would not be able to shake it' (*était si ferme et si assurée, que toutes les plus extravagantes suppositions des sceptiques n'étaient pas capables de l'ébranler*).[40]

The *Discourse* is not only an answer to the *Essais*, through the adduction of a certainty in the midst of their scepticism, the *Discourse* is an *Aufhebung* of Montaigne's *I*. Montaigne's view that the only business he has is with himself, that his study of himself is the whole of his metaphysics and physics, is taken up into the Cartesian *I* and transformed into an objective first principle. The source of Descartes's autobiographical style in the *Discourse* must be Montaigne. It is Montaigne's rhetoric of the self connected to the production of a mathematically based conception of objective truth. Here, at the hands of Descartes rather than Montaigne, the self is not offered through a portrait of how he sleeps, eats, walks, etc., as in Montaigne's essay 'Of Experience'. These are seen as accidents of the self as thinking substance. The models for the *Discourse*, the first work Descartes published, are the 'essay' and the 'self-portrait', the two powerful rhetorical instruments of scepticism.

Alexandre Koyré says that the *Discourse* 'could be called the Cartesian *Confessions* or his *Itinerarium Mentis in Veritatem*, his *Journey of mind towards Truth*', and he holds that it is a response to the scepticism of Montaigne.[41] But Descartes, unlike Augustine,

---

[39] Montaigne, *Complete Essays*, 821.   [40] *Discours*, 60.
[41] A. Koyré, Introduction to *Descartes's Philosophical Writings*, trans. and ed. E. Anscombe and P. T. Geach (Indianapolis: Library of Liberal Arts, Bobbs Merrill, 1971), p. xiv.

does not confesss a path of errors; his 'confession' is distinctively that of the modern researcher into truth—the revelation of his successful results, accompanied by a superficially modest picture of himself as the researcher. In his *Aufhebung* of Montaigne's *I*, Descartes has cancelled its flesh and blood and pride in its own experience. The *I*, in its new, non-Renaissance form, becomes the bare and modest worker of the method, but a figure not ashamed to claim its objective, verifiable successes.

Cicero in *De inventione* (i. 27), as Lachterman points out, claims that there are three species of narration in which rhetoric is involved.[42] These are *fabula*, which is not true nor similar to the true; *historia*, which recounts a remote deed held in memory; and *argumentum*, which Cicero says is 'something feigned but which still could have occurred' (*ficta res, quae tamen fieri potuit*). Lachterman asks: 'Why does Descartes blur or transgress the line dividing history from fable?'[43] His answer is that Descartes wishes in this way to challenge the authority of other authors and what others think, and does not wish straightforwardly to install his own authority. As Lachterman rightly says, Descartes's 'relation to the reader necessarily blends allurement and detachment'.[44] Vico charges Descartes with 'feigning' an account of himself and his discovery. Nicolini, as mentioned above, charges Vico with feigning at least his account of his involvement with and awareness of Cartesianism during his Vatolla period, calling it Vico's *fictio*.[45] This *fictio* is much wider in Vico's text than just this Vatolla period.

Vico, while charging Descartes with pretence, also blurs the line dividing history from fable. He does this by consistently referring to himself in the third person. Thus he writes of himself as 'Vico', in the way that a biographer might. If Descartes draws the reader in, by continually inviting the reader critically to judge for himself, while all the while enticing the reader to place himself in the direct position of the *I*, Vico creates the force of truth in his narration by the apparent 'objectivity' of the third person, and by simply using his own name. Descartes, in his use of the first person, the style of a personal narration, places a narrative element within the objectivity of a discourse. Vico, while actually using the form of a historical

[42] Lachterman, 'Descartes and the Philosophy of History', 39.   [43] Ibid.
[44] Ibid.   [45] Nicolini, ed., *Opere*, 25 n. 1.

narration, suggests the sense of a discourse, with his systematic use of the third person. Vico stands Descartes's project on its head in order to create a different sense of the transgression of the classical distinction between history and fable.

The one place where Vico varies from his consistent use of the third person is in the above-quoted passage in the fourth paragraph of the autobiography, where he accuses Descartes of 'feigning' the method of his studies (113/15). Here Vico uses the future impersonal to describe his own historical approach to his studies, saying *non fingerassi (si fingerà)* and *si narrerà*, which Fisch and Bergin render well in this context as 'we shall not feign' and 'we shall narrate'. Because of his strong opposition to Descartes, Vico steps out of the narrative he is giving of his studies and makes a normative statement about the nature of his own narrative. In this one place Vico becomes actively present in his own narrative. In the continuation of his autobiography of 1731, Vico speaks *about* himself as author, saying that 'he wrote it as a philosopher, meditating the causes, natural and moral, and the occasions of fortune' (182/71). But in accusing Descartes of feigning, Vico speaks directly *as* author, at this moment declaring his intent to employ a conception of knowledge and self-knowledge that will show the falsity of Descartes's presentation of himself, which leads, Vico says, to the degradation of all 'human and divine erudition'.

Quintilian, in *Institutio oratoria* (II. iv. 2–3), distinguishes between three forms of narrative, in a way similar to Cicero. Quintilian says there are the fictitious narrative we find in tragedies and poems, which is not true and has little resemblance to the true (*fabula*); realistic narrative, as found in comedies, which is also not true but which has a certain verisimilitude (*argumentum*); and historical narrative, which exposits actual fact (*historia*). He says the first two of these rightly belong to the teacher of literature (*grammaticus*) and the third belongs to the rhetorician; and he adds (a line Lachterman quotes)[46] that 'the rhetorican who makes his start with history will be stronger the more truthful he is' (*apud rhetorem initium sit historica, tanto robustior quanto verior*).

Quintilian says he will delay his presentation of the best method

---

[46] Lachterman, 'Descartes and the Philosophy of History', 39.

of narration until he treats narration in the courts. He presents this in his fourth book (IV. ii) as the *narratio*, or statement of facts as employed in legal cases. In his detailed explanation of the nature of such narration he considers the question of whether the statement of the facts of a case needs to be plausible if it is in fact a true history of what has happened, concluding that the question of plausibility is extremely important, because there are many things that are true but hardly credible (IV. ii. 3). Narration of facts is a rhetorical act and depends upon eloquence. The narration need not present the facts in the actual order of their occurrence (IV. ii. 83), but a plausible picture must be given so as not to create doubt or anxiety (IV. ii. 123–6). Quintilian says that he holds that the statement of facts, more than any other portion of the speech (the *exordium*, proofs, *peroration*), must be done with utmost grace (IV. ii. 116).

Both Descartes and Vico, in their narratives of themselves, are transgressing the lines of these classical classifications. Both blur the line between Cicero's *fabula* and *historia*, in favour of a narrative that would better fit his conception of *argumentum*, offering the reader a fiction of themselves, but not a pure fiction. If each offers the reader a *ficta res* ('something feigned'), how does each accomplish the second part of this definition? How do they offer what is feigned as *quae tamen fieri potuit* ('but which still could have occurred')? Descartes, I think, places his narrative in the form of the comic as classified in Quintilian's second point, his conception of *argumentum*, which he identifies with comedy. This form fits Descartes's conception of truth as comic, for reasons I will suggest shortly. Quintilian's order of narratives indicates that Descartes's narration is part of poetic rather than rhetoric. Seen in this way, Descartes is giving a direct answer to the fables of poets, which, he says, 'make imaginable various events when they are not'.[47] His fable of himself becomes a comic text for his philosophical position, that can in this way be viewed as an answer to Plato's 'ancient quarrel with the poets' (*Republic*, x), in modern terms, forming the text itself by poetic principles, but to express a truth that separates poetry from truth.

Vico's transformation of Cicero's narrative of *argumentum* is different. It is related to Quintilian's third form of narration, not

---

[47] *Discours*, 37.

in the sense of relating actual historical fact, but in the sense of the narration of facts in a legal case. Vico's fable of himself enters at the point concerning whether the narration of the facts is also to be plausible. Quintilian's third point (*historia*) is the property of the rhetorician, not the teacher of literature. Aristotle says, in the first sentence of the *Rhetoric,* 'rhetoric is a counterpoint of dialectic'; that is, they make a pair, like strophe and antistrophe. Rhetoric creates the speech of the probable. Vico insists that, in contrast to Descartes, he speaks in his autobiography as 'a historian'. But the narration of facts can never be simple. Truth never speaks for itself, as Quintilian knows; but Descartes wishes to claim just the opposite in his statement about the possibility of truth speaking in *bas breton.* Historical *narratio* always requires the element of plausibility, an element that must be derived from fables, from the myth, which Vico always equates in the *New Science* with *vera narratio.* Vico's answer to the poets is, as I wish to suggest, to rediscover the original connection between poetry and history, to rediscover the common root of these two classical forms of narrative.

Descartes blurs the distinction between history and fable to accomplish his end, but Vico redefines it, and his narration of his life cannot be understood apart from this redefinition. If Descartes's *I* is a transformation of Montaigne's *Essais* (1580–8), Vico's history is a transformation of Castelvetro's *Poetica d'Aristotele vulgarizzata et sposta* (1576).[48] In the *New Science* Vico says: 'The truth understood by Castelvetro, [is] that history must have come first and then poetry, for history is a simple statement of the true but poetry is an imitation besides. Yet this scholar, though otherwise most acute, failed to make use of this clue to discover the true principles of poetry . . .' (812). Vico then concludes that 'Inasmuch as the poets came certainly before the vulgar historians, the first history must have been poetic' (813).

Vico's view is achieved by taking Aristotle's view in the *Poetics* (ch. 9, 1451^{b}5 ff.), that poetry is more philosophic than history, and by making the first history poetic in form, he makes poetry, or fable, the source of both philosophy and history. This requires the additional reconception of the nature of fable, from that stated by

---

[48] L. Castelvetro, *Poetica d'Aristotele vulgarizzata et sposta,* ed. W. Romani (2 vols., Bari: Laterza, 1978–9).

Cicero as his first species of rhetorical narration, *fabula*. Vico says: 'The fables in their origin were true and severe narrations, whence *mythos*, fable, was defined as *vera narratio*. But because they were originally for the most part gross [*sconce*], they gradually lost their original meanings, were then altered, subsequently became improbable, after that obscure, then scandalous, and finally incredible' (814). Thus Vico, by redefining fable as the original meaning of true narration and history as based in poetry, collapses the first of Cicero's three species into the second, so that history requires a 'fabulous' sense of truth, and the merger of these becomes the basis of *argumentum*, which is the form in which a truth of memory can be recaptured. Vico stands to the story of his own life as a modern teller of *vera narratio*, that is, as a *mythos* or fable that is told in terms of conscious philosophical principles. In this he is both close to and far from Descartes. Vico is close in that he, too, is engaged in a kind of feigning, but he is far because it is a kind of feigning that derives from very different principles, principles that Descartes to some extent uses, when he writes his discourse and invites the reader to regard it as a history or fable, but which he strongly excludes from his method of rightly directing the mind in the sciences.

Augustine is certainly a figure who philosophically stands behind both Vico and Descartes—behind the 'great city of the human race' and behind the doubting *I* of the *cogito*. Augustine is also a figure whose autobiography sets the form for subsequent self-discourse. Vico is writing against Descartes, and under the protection of Augustine. The cycle of Augustine's narrative has significant parallels with the narrative of Vico's career. Yet Vico's narrative of his life-events is not the confession of errors, but, like Descartes's *Discourse*, it is the story of a successful breakthrough and discovery of a new conception of knowledge. Descartes, like Augustine, is outside the text for the reader, confessing something of himself in the text, stated in personal terms, and, also like Augustine, Descartes insists that what he says is only as he understands the truth he has found. Vico, for the reader, is in the text, developing himself with the reader through his turns and adversities. His use of the third person, his reference to himself as Vico, is 'fabulous' in that it is the tale of a hero who is born and is presented by the gods (providence) with trials, but who fulfils his quest—of finding what no one has ever found before but which is the one thing needed for the completion of human wisdom—a true science of the human itself. And, as with Augustine's discussions of creation, Vico's science demonstrates the presence of God in the world. Unlike Descartes's first principle of the *cogito*, that in the *Meditations* becomes the springboard for the proof of God's existence, both Augustine and Vico begin with the divine, and unfold its order in the world through their respective conceptions of time and memory.

Descartes speaks of his mask or persona, that he wears, with the comedians, on the stage of the world. As a modern, in fact the first true modern, Descartes has a comic conception of knowledge; that is, a conception of knowlege that has no relation to the negative.[49] Because his method is an instrument that begins with something evidently true and reliable and proceeds to something more that is true and reliable, Descartes's conception of knowledge is forever a happy one, that never enters into what Hegel, for example, calls 'the labour of the negative' (*Arbeit des Negativen*). Descartes's conception of knowledge never 'stares the negative in the face'. Behind Descartes's mask there can be a frowning uncertainty, waiting to be made certain, but his comedy is not connected, nor can it, in principle, be connected to tragedy.

'Comic' and 'tragic' are not commonly used as epistemological categories. A comic conception of knowledge regards knowledge as essentially 'progressive', regarding thought as working from better and worse suppositional principles that allow experience more and more to be brought under these principles, yielding an ever happier result. Science is seen as a series of 'happy endings', a drama in which more and more desired results are attained, each set against the ultimate happy ending when cognition has come full circle on itself and the order of things is finally fully investigated and mastered. The project of human knowledge, equipped with the right method, is always considered as only temporarily short of this happy future state—the logicians' paradise, where all arguments are *sound*. A tragic conception of knowledge regards knowledge as in need of recovering the origin, the *principium*, the point where thought and its object are born. We arrive at our ways of

---

[49] I agree with Hartle that 'Descartes's detachment allows confusion, error, and uncertainty to appear in a comic light. There is no comparable mention of tragedy in the *Discourse*, and nothing is even described as pitiable' (*Death and the Disinterested Spectator*, 146).

thinking at a point that is always past this original state of the vital connection of thought and object and we are in need of recovering some sense of its nature in order to guide our thought about the present. A tragic conception of knowledge is always connected to the project of self-knowledge, and memory, not method, is what is fundamental to it. The form natural to memory is the narration that can bring together the forces of past, present, and future.

Vico's viewpoint is in its nature tragic because it is an attempt to recover the origin, which is never recoverable, and it is never recoverable because all origins are tragic, having within their moment of birth the seeds of their own destruction. In the *Discourse* Descartes can simply abandon the wisdom of humanism and the arts of human erudition for the comedy, the happy certainty of mathematics. Vico can hope, as he does in the *Study Methods*, to discover a balance between the ancients and the moderns. He must live with the moderns, and is himself a modern or a modern-ancient, a combination that he attempts to sustain even in the title of his major work, beginning it with the modern terms 'new' and 'science' and ending it with a special notion of the *polis*, 'the common nature of the nations'. Vico ends the account of his own life, to the point he has written it, as being within the unresolvable dialectic of the greatness of his discovery of the *New Science*, his satisfaction in his success, and the total lack of recognition of it by his associates, and his lack of friends—Vico, the solitary, 'stoic' figure, at the citadel of his desk, whose science is based on the idea of 'the great city of the human race', truth as found in the common bonds of humanity.

4

Vico's Conception of His Own Philosophy

A NEW METHOD OF STUDIES

In interpreting a philosophy two courses are commonly followed: the philosopher's work is divided into its major ideas and these are discussed in terms of their logical meaning, coherence, and truth, or its ideas are placed within certain traditions of thought, with emphasis placed on discovering their sources and on discussing the philosopher's views as reflections, modifications, and fulfilments of earlier views. Many interpretations employ aspects of both of these approaches, and either may be emphasized, whether the philosopher's work is discussed developmentally or considered as a single set of views.

Both seem to be 'objective' ways to interpret a philosophy, the first because it applies ordinary standards of logic and criticism and the second because of its appeal to history. Both, however, risk violating Vico's second axiom in the *New Science*, of judging what is unfamiliar by 'what is familiar and at hand' (122). All interpretation incurs this risk, because to interpret is to make what is 'distant and unfamiliar' comprehensible and thus familiar. Even if the aim of the interpretation is to overturn established and familiar views of a thinker's work, the newly established interpretation brings its own sense of familiarity.

I wish to take a different approach. It involves the same second-axiom risk. My aim is to enter into Vico's thought to discover the lever and fulcrum Vico uses to lift the world. My authority for this is Vico's invitation to the reader in his section on 'Method' in the *New Science* to meditate and narrate for himself the principles of this science and in so doing to make for himself its proof (*pruova*) (349). This proof for the *New Science* requires meditating the truth of its principles through a narration of the full materials of history. I would like to accept a version of this invitation—to meditate for myself the points in thought from which Vico's principles them selves are generated. I wish to enter into Vico's mode of thought not in a psychological sense, but in an epistemological and metaphysical sense, in an effort to present a sketch of the origin and generation of his position.

In Chapter 1 Vico's life was presented as a series of stages in his career, following the order of his presentation of them in his autobiography. In this chapter I wish to go through this course a second time, now as a series of philosophical thoughts. In the following chapter I wish to go through this a third time as a series of textual structures. The central issue in these three modes of consideration is Vico's claim to have given the proper causes, both 'natural' and 'moral', of his development. The first account of his life, that of Chapter 1, relates the external causes of the turns of his career and thought—his fall, his sojourn at Vatolla, his failure in the concourse, and difficulties with the publication of the *New Science*—the basic story-line of his development. What I wish to do now is to invite the reader to think through the course of Vico's thought as a philosopher, as a sequence of ideas with one point naturally leading to another.

I think three things dominate Vico's thought and career: pedagogy, law, and the search for a science of wisdom. Vico claims to have discovered something new in each of these areas, and these fundamental discoveries have led him to interlocking discoveries about language, mythology, society, and history. Vico is led from pedagogy and law to his conception of wisdom. The medium of pedagogy and law is rhetoric. His mastery of rhetoric in these areas leads him to a rhetorically based conception of philosophy—to the 'new critical art' upon which the *New Science* in both its first and second versions rests. Vico does not reduce philosophy to rhetoric. The *New Science* is not simply a modern version of Cicero's *De republica*. Vico rejoins philosophy with its roots in ancient poetic and rhetoric and with its Renaissance ties to these humanist activities, but he does so in order to accomplish a philosophic vision of truth. It is an original vision, a new philosophy that is genuinely 'new'; its 'newness' is not derived simply from a new arrangement or comprehension of earlier humanist ideas.

The *New Science* is a book of wisdom—a book in which are to be found all the keys to Western thought and consciousness held in one place, available to the reader who can meditate their meanings with its author. It is a work built on repetition, repetition of its ideas from page to page and on repetition of other books. The *New Science* is a book about other books. The 'new science', like pedagogy, teaches what has already been taught; like the law, it makes its decisions on the basis of what has already been decided, i.e. it thinks from the precedents of its case. How, then, is the new science 'new'? The answer to this, I think, lies in Vico's conception of *method* in the *New Science*. The understanding of this lies in getting to the heart of Vico's concern with pedagogy and with what is philosophical about the law: how does the law offer a model of philosophical truth? Because I wish to answer such questions in a short space, I will attempt to pursue them in as direct a manner as possible, keeping the main points in view, and trying to visualize how Vico moves from one to the next.

At the beginning of *De nostri temporis studiorum ratione* (1708–9), the so-called *Study Methods*, Vico says that if he is not mistaken the theme he wishes to treat is new (*'Res nova est, ni fallor'*); 'but the knowledge of it is so important, that I am amazed it has not been treated yet'.[1] Vico returns to his point of newness at the end of his oration, saying that just because it is new is not in itself a recommendation, and that the reader will have to decide for himself whether it is praiseworthy and not simply a novelty or monstrosity (sect. 15). Vico's theme is: 'Which method of studies is most correct and better, ours or that of the Ancients?' (sect. 1).

In raising this question as his theme Vico appears to be entering the *querelle des anciens et modernes* which took shape in France in the works of Fontenelle and Perrault in the late 1600s, while Vico was educating himself at Vatolla. The 'quarrel between the ancients and moderns' had taken its own natural shape within the rise of modern science, a great dividing point being Galileo's shift from Aristotle's description of motion and rest in terms of substance and qualities, that is based upon Aristotle's subject–predicate analysis of language, to the conceptualization of motion and rest in terms

---

[1] *De nostri temporis studiorum ratione*, *Opere di G. B. Vico*, ed. G. Gentile and F. Nicolini, vol. i (Bari: Laterza, 1914), sect. 1. *On the Study Methods of Our Time*, trans. E. Gianturco, reissued with a preface by D. P. Verene (Ithaca, NY: Cornell University Press, 1990; orig. pub. 1965). Hereafter cited in the text by section number common to the Italian and English editions. I have in some instances modified Gianturco's translation.

of relations and quantities symbolizable in mathematical nota-
tions.[2] A version of this quarrel was formulated by these French
thinkers within the tradition of letters, raising the question of
whether the writers of the modern age were equal or superior to
the ancient poets.

Vico's 'quarrel' is neither that of modern science nor the French
querelle of letters, which spread beyond France. Vico's theme is
rooted in the more fundamental question of the difference between
the ancient and modern worlds, in the mentality of the 'new' of the
modern versus the view that the modern world is a palimpsest of
the ancient. The freedom of the Renaissance was to reinscribe upon
the tablets of the ancients. But the mentality of the moderns is
what Vico met upon his return from Vatolla—the view that
thought through its powers of logical supposition and evidence
could provide its own origin, that the new involved the destruction
of the old. Or, as Rousseau puts it in the *First Discourse*, Socrates
in the modern world would not be put to death; instead he would
simply be met with insult, mockery, and contempt and cast aside.
The tension in Vico's quarrel between the ancients and moderns is
between the ancient notion of 'self-knowledge' and what took
shape later as the modern notion of 'self-consciousness', that finally
became the German idealist theme of *Selbstbewusstsein* and later
became the occupation of 'psychoanalysis'.

Because Vico's quarrel is philosophical and not literary or
scientific, it is grounded in pedagogy in the sense of a theory of
human education, not in the sense of methods of classroom
instruction and school administration, which is where pedagogy
finds itself today, as a 'social science'. Vico declares that his answer
to his question is not an argument for the ancients over the
moderns. It is an attempt to discover the merits of each. But his
aim is not to draw up a kind of balance sheet, listing the advantages
and disadvantages of each. His aim is more to find the ground of
each in the human faculties and in the natural course of human
development in order to fix on them in terms of a kind of mean. If
we add to this Vico's conception of the title of his oration of
slightly more than two decades later, *De mente heroica* (1732) (*On
the Heroic Mind*), the mind is at its zenith, like the heroic, when it

---

[2] E. Cassirer, 'The Influence of Language upon the Development of Scientific
Thought', *Journal of Philosophy*, 39 (1942), 309–27.

can balance its opposites, each of which has its rightful claim. The
heroic is never a choice of good against bad, of light over darkness,
but rather a surmounting of the two in some way, never actually
joining or synthesizing them.

The true theme behind Vico's question concerning the ancients
and the moderns is the question of self-knowledge. In his seventh
oration, the *Study Methods* of 1708–9, he takes up the same
question that was the theme of his first oration of 1699, but in a
much deeper way, that is, in terms of a full conception of mind.
His theme is the same because in the first oration he asked what
could meet his listeners' expectations, what would not fall below
their hopes and dignity. His answer is that the only proper
motivation for education and study is the possibility of self-
knowledge. He quotes the Delphic Oracle: *Nosce te dicit. Hoc
dicit: Nosce animum tuum* (Know thyself. This means: Know your
own soul).[3] Self-knowledge, or the grasp of one's own mind and
spirit, is to be gained not by introspection but by mastery of the
whole cycle of human studies, which for Vico are grounded in
language, the medium distinctive to human nature. Thus self-
knowledge is the result of being taught and learning. The key to
the human is pedagogy. And the key to pedagogy is the order of
studies.

The translated title of Vico's oration, *On the Study Methods of
Our Time*, is problematic or even misleading. 'Study Methods',
corresponding to the part of Vico's Latin title that is *studiorum
ratione*, reverses the singular and plural; the translation is literally
'method of studies'. The title might better be rendered 'On the
method of studies of our time'. What does Vico intend by *ratio* in
his title and in his text? Although 'method' is one of the less usual
meanings of *ratio*, Vico intends it to be taken in this sense, himself
using *metodo di studiare* in referring to it in the *Autobiography*
(140/31). His use of *ratio* can be taken in two senses: as a counter
term to Descartes's and the Port-Royalist sense of *méthode*, stand-
ing for Vico's endorsement of the method of *ars topica* against the
'analytic' or 'critical' method of the moderns. It is also to be taken
in its more central sense of an ordering or arranging of something,
as a 'system of studies'. Vico's purpose in his oration is not just to
counter the modern sense of the method of thought with the

ancient method of topical thought; his further aim is a new ordering of studies that will promote the attainment of wisdom in the face of the modern quest for simple certainty and intelligence. Without this second sense of a natural ordering of studies, his opposition to the Cartesian ideal of truth is unsuccessful.

Part 4 of the *Port-Royal Logic* of Arnauld and Nicole, *L'Art de penser*, published in 1662, concerns the conception of method, and it distinguishes two kinds of methods of thinking: analysis and synthesis. Method is generally described as 'the art of arranging well a succession of various thoughts, or for discerning the truth when we are ignorant of it, or for proving it to others when we already know it'.[4] Two types of method are then distinguished: 'one for discovering the truth, which is called *analysis*, or *method of resolution* and that also can be called *method of invention*; and the other for making it understandable to others when it has been found, that is called *synthesis*, or *method of composition* and can also be called *method of doctrine*'.[5]

Vico accuses Arnauld of considering the *ars topica* to be useless (sect. 3), yet as Gianturco points out, Arnauld in the *Port-Royal Logic* never explicitly attacks the *ars topica*.[6] The attack is more general and more serious. The *ars topica* is in Vico's view identified with *inventio*.[7] 'Topics', Vico says, 'is the art of finding the middle term (what the Scholastics call *medium* and the Latins call *argumentum*)' (sect. 3). To understand this we should recall that in Aristotle there are two ways to consider the syllogism.[8] One way is to regard the syllogism as an instrument of demonstration; the other is to regard the syllogism as a means for the generation of ideas. In the first of these the middle term plays the role of stating the class through which the classes of the major and minor terms are connected. The middle term is present only in the premises

---

[4] A. Arnauld and P. Nicole, *La Logique ou l'art de penser: contenant, outre les règles communes, plusieurs observations nouvelles, propres à former le jugement*, critical edn. by P. Clair and F. Girbal (Paris: Presses Universitaires de France, 1965), 299.

[5] Ibid. 299–300.

[6] *Study Methods*, 17 n. 10.

[7] E. Grassi, 'Critical Philosophy or Topical Philosophy? Meditations on the *De nostri temporis studiorum ratione*', in G. Tagliacozzo and H. V. White, eds., *Giambattista Vico: An International Symposium* (Baltimore: Johns Hopkins University Press, 1969), 45–7.

[8] Aristotle, *Rhetoric*, i. 1–2 and ii. 20–3; *Prior Analytics*, ii. 27; *Topics*, i. 1.

and it disappears in the statement of the conclusion. In the second sense of the syllogism the middle term is all-important because it is the commonplace or *topos* out of which the other two terms of the syllogism are drawn forth.

This second sense looks at the syllogism from the perspective of how arguments are created, how they come into being, not how they are tested for their validity when they are already in hand. The *ars topica*, understood in this way, requires that the speaker who wishes to assert a connection between two terms must find a third term to act as a middle, a meaning that is held in common between the speaker's intention and his listeners, i.e. a commonplace. This can often take the form of a maxim or be formulated within an enthymeme. From such common ground the speaker can then 'draw forth' the connection of the terms of his conclusion, bringing the understanding and agreement of his listeners along with him. Lane Cooper states: 'But the sound rhetorician does draw one thing *from* another. Thus we come to the preposition *ek* (or *ex*), which is characteristic of Aristotle's thought, but often is hard or impossible to translate directly. The speaker is supposed to have resources, *from which* he draws his arguments and illustrations.'[9]

From Vico's perspective, logical methods of thought or what he calls 'criticism' or 'philosophical criticism' (sect. 3) require *ars topica* as the means to establish the beginning points of their judgements. Although Arnauld does not attack topics, what, in his view, stands in the place of topics in human reasoning? As quoted above, the *Port-Royal Logic* designates *analysis* as the *method of invention*. As Gianturco notes, Vico uses the word 'analysis' in two senses.[10] One is the general sense associated with the second step in Descartes's four-step method of reasoning and truth in the *Discourse*: 'to divide each of the difficulties that I examined into as many small parts as possible and as was required for the best solution' (pt. 2). From this position, according to the third step, the reasoner is to ascend little by little from the simplest to the complex. The other sense of 'analysis' as used by Vico designates analytic geometry, pioneered by Descartes. Sometimes Vico uses

[9] *The Rhetoric of Aristotle*, ed. and trans. L. Cooper (New York: Appleton-Century-Crofts, 1960), p. xxiii.

[10] *Study Methods*, 8 n. 3.

'analysis' to mean both of these senses at once, and rightly so, because the second is in effect derived from the first, and because analytical geometry is essentially the application of the above process to the study of geometrical curves.[11] It should be remembered that the *Geometry* was one of the *Essais* which the *Discourse* introduced.

Why is Vico so much against the idea of analysis? It is the unifying theme of his dissatisfaction with the modern conception of thought and education. The answer, I think, lies in the fact that it stands in the place of the *ars topica*, the function of which in thought is *inventio*. In the *Port-Royal Logic* this power of thought is converted (or the attempt is made to convert it) into analysis as a *method*. Invention now appears to be open to everyone who possesses the Cartesian *bon sens*. In the *Port-Royal Logic* Descartes's method of the *Discourse* is turned into a theory of education. Analysis parallels *inventio* and synthesis parallels *demonstratio*. Rhetoric is robbed from the mind by logic and with it go prudence and eloquence, the two keys to human wisdom.

Descartes's *bon sens* is characterized by its anonymity because anyone who can employ the method can engage in discourse that is independent of the speaker's subjectivity or sense of place in a particular human community.[12] Each subject should be replaceable in the reasoning process. As members of the human community and historical subjects we are left just with Descartes's stoical rules of the third part of the *Discourse*; morals are placed in a permanently provisional state. Against Descartes's anonymous *bon sens* is Vico's *sensus communis*, which Vico understands as 'communal sense' (sect. 3) such as might be associated with Aristotle's principle of the human being as a social animal. Humans exist within a political community under specific recurrent historical conditions. Thus the individual must possess the ability to recognize and assess the situations in which he finds himself. Vico says 'it is an error to apply to the prudent conduct of life the abstract criterion of reasoning that obtains in the domain of science' (sect. 7).

This faculty for the individual to assess where he stands in a

---

[11] Ibid. 26 n. 20.

[12] Grassi, 'Critical Philosophy or Topical Philosophy?', 40. In the *De antiquissima Italorum sapientia* (ch. 7, sect. 5) Vico, quoting Terence (*Eunuchus*, 62–3), says that to attempt to order practical life by the geometrical method would be to go mad rationally and that such a method provides no basis for public discourse.

particular situation was called *phronēsis* by the Greeks and *pruden-tia* by the Romans. *Res* and *verba* must be joined in a mode of thought and expression in which the individual does not abstract from the situation, but in which the situation can be portrayed as a whole without losing its particular details. Eloquence is the prime feature of this expression of a situation as a whole. Such speech must be copious, that is, it must be encompassing of all that is there. That is why Vico admired Demosthenes. In his oration to the Academy of Oziosi on the relation of philosophy and eloquence (1737) he said that Demosthenes came forth from the Platonic Academy 'armed with his invincible enthymeme, which he formed by means of a very well-regulated excess, going outside his case into quite distant things with which he tempered the lightning flashes of his arguments, which, when striking, amazed the listeners so much the more by how much he had diverted them'.[13] And he credits a similar power to Cicero.

There is no wisdom for Vico without prudence and eloquence. He asks: 'What is eloquence, in truth, but wisdom speaking ornately and copiously in words appropriate to the common sense of the human race?' (sect. 15). In the *Autobiography*, as mentioned previously, Vico claims to have conducted his own teaching by this view (199/86). In the end Vico's complaint against the modern, Cartesian conception of pedagogy is twofold: that it fragments knowledge, the true object of which is the whole, and that it is unnatural to the development of the human faculties. The mind that could be truly educated by the Cartesian ideal will greet the particular historical situation with a blank stare.

In regard to the first point, fragmentation, the modern simply denies the humanistic arts of language and cuts the mind in half, as Descartes does with his speaker of *bas breton*, or the modern, while denying the truth to the *ars topica* of the ancients, employs them as the basis of his own texts in an act of *mauvaise foi*. The attempt to deny the truth of the ancients leads to the problem of the second point, that of the unnaturalness of the modern. Here Vico is adamant: 'Just as old age is powerful in reason, so is adolescence in imagination' (sect. 3). The moderns give us no order

---

[13] 'The Academies and the Relation between Philosophy and Eloquence', trans. D. P. Verene, in *On the Study Methods of Our Time*, 87. See *Opere di G. B. Vico*, vol. vii (Bari: Laterza, 1940), 35.

of studies at all, but offer a single method that is to be mastered and applied in all areas of study. Education must follow the natural course of the development of the faculties. The young naturally excel in the faculties connected to the knowledge of the ancients— memory, imagination, and ingenuity. Training in these gives the basis for the later powers of intellect required for the analytic and critical thinking of the moderns.

Vico says that 'the whole is really the flower of wisdom' (sect. 14) and his whole is a *ratio* of studies connected to the natural development of the human. Self-knowledge is possible only by the individual following such a course, and as he becomes educated in both the *ars topica* and the *ars analytica,* wisdom (*sapientia*) becomes the power heroically to hold both senses of thinking in mind. Pedagogy in Vico's view is not the unification of all the fields of study in some centralized *ratio.* This would, in fact, point in the direction of Descartes. Pedagogy is rightly a kind of 'comprehens-ive' speech offered the student, not by a single person, such as Socrates, who Vico says was a whole university in himself, as ancients often were, but delivered through a system of studies tuned to the natural course of the human faculties in their development. Vico says, 'The most eulogizing epithet that can be given to a speech is that it is "comprehensive": praise is due to the speaker who has left nothing untouched, and has omitted nothing from the argument, nothing which may be missed by his listeners' (sect. 3). And, since pedagogy, in the sense of teaching, is an art of total speaking about a subject done at a particular time and place, no method of analysis or synthesis could itself be its guide, although such method could be a part of what is taught.

Vico's new 'method of studies' is not new in the sense of intending to be something novel. It is the attempt to revive something old—the interest of the ancients in self-knowledge and the basis self-knowledge has in the teaching and practice of humane letters. Vico's objection to the Cartesian view of human education is that it is one-sided and this will ultimately result in a one-dimensional understanding of the human self. In the Cartesian view the self is an agent which can understand the object in all of its dimensions by means of a single unified method of thinking. The whole for the Cartesian is reached not as the flower of wisdom but as the 'unity' that method will bring to the multiplicity of the sciences. Although the self in the Cartesian view can form the object of thought in many different ways, all thought which will result in truth is subject to the four-step method of Descartes's *Discourse*. In this view the sciences offer the thinking *I* a panorama of its *bon sens* at work in the world, but such a panorama does not offer the self that thinks a 'science' of its own historical and social nature.

It is through the ancient arts of language found in rhetorical and poetic speech that the self traditionally has access to its own nature as a social being—to the ways the human self confronts its own nature in the world of its own making. In Vico's view these arts must remain as the basis of the child's education. Only if these arts are absorbed when young can the mature scientific thinker function as a social being and confront his own nature as a distinctively human question. Without acknowledging it the Cartesian method presupposes that there is an actual, historically conditioned self present as thinker, for just the same reason that science is not itself culture, but presupposes society and culture as the medium through which it can be conducted. To begin with something that is clear and distinct, as the Cartesian method affirms as the proper starting-point of its method, presumes that the self has determined a place for itself in the world and that a society exists within which to think.

As there can be no society of philosophers, so there can be no realm of science that is dependent solely on method. Method presupposes a social and personal order which is not itself achieved or maintained by method. Vico's sense of a new 'method of studies' is one in which the ancient arts of poetical and rhetorical speech and historical forms of understanding are placed in a balanced relationship with those purely methodological forms of thinking that have caused the growing successes in the sciences of nature. Science is not self-knowledge, and yet science is a part of the self. That 'method' or 'order' of human studies which mirrors the natural order of development of society itself is the order that should be followed by any system of human education.

The child should first be taught those arts that themselves make human community possible and then proceed to those forms of analytic thought and methodology that make the modern sciences possible, which presuppose and at every turn depend upon the power the self has to make a world for itself. To do otherwise is to forget Aristotle's dictum that man is a social animal and to believe that science is the beginning and the end of culture.

A JURISPRUDENCE OF THE HUMAN RACE

In his discussion of law as one of the studies in the *Study Methods*, Vico says: 'The very designations "art of the law", "art of jurisprudence" seem to ring false. There is only one "art" of prudence, and this art is philosophy.' (*Quamquam quid hoc verbi est 'ars prudentiae', cuius una ars est philosophia.*) (sect. 11). Vico, quoting Horace (*Ars poetica*, 396–9), claims that the Roman jurists preserved the original heroic *sapientia*—the separation of public and private rights, the separation of sacred and profane, the rules of marriage, and the means of establishing communities, etc. In saying this Vico was reflecting the Roman view expressed in the *Digest* and elsewhere that jurisprudence is philosophy and all of philosophy, but Vico develops his own version of this ideal. From this he concludes that both the Roman conception of jurisprudence and the Greek notion of wisdom meant 'the knowledge of things human and divine' (*divinarum humanarumque rerum notitiam*) (sect. 11).

Vico says that the difference between science (*scientia*) and prudence (*prudentia*) rests on their approaches to causality. Outstanding thought in science is based on the ability to reduce a multiplicity to a single cause; excellence in prudential thinking is the ability to portray the widest number of possible causes of an event and to conjecture which from all of them is the true cause (sect. 7). Given this description *scientia* and *prudentia* might appear to be two routes to the same end, or at least to have in common the same end—the one correct cause of something. But their difference is fundamental and depends upon *how* the cause is established, because the way in which the cause is established determines its character, the shape of its content, once it is found.

The aim of science (in the non-Vichian sense) is the dismissal of the particular and the discovery of what is common to a class of particulars, the one universal element they share that makes them what they are.[14] Once the cause is found, science has no interest in the other possibilities present in the particular situation from which

---

[14] Vico's notion of *scientia* is based on the Aristotelian theory of concept-formation, what Cassirer calls the *Substanzbegriff*, rather than what lies behind modern, mathematically based logic (*Funktionsbegriff*). E. Cassirer, *Substance and Function*, authorized trans. W. C. Swabey and M. C. Swabey (Chicago: Open Court, 1923), ch. 1.

the question of cause arose. Science is single-minded in its pursuit of the universal and elimination of all accidental elements of an event or set of events. The cause when established is probable. Prudence is also a means to the probable cause of an event, but its consideration of the widest possible number of causes of an event becomes part of its final understanding of the cause which it conjectures to be the true cause of the event. Prudence is a way of thinking and speaking about the particular that preserves as much as possible of what is in the reality of the particular, including those elements that are not truly its cause but which in contrast to the cause illuminate its meaning. In Vico's view we can have a science of the physical world that is based on the kind of partial consciousness of it we can attain by reducing its particular events to their universal causes. But we cannot have a 'science' of the human or civil world that is not based on prudence, that is, on a form of thinking and speaking that brings to bear on the understanding of a single event the totality of its possible causes.

The prudence of the human world is 'jurisprudence' because law is the cause of the human world. Law is the basis of the human world. A knowledge of human and divine law is the basis of human wisdom. In the *Study Methods* Vico says that the weakness of modern jurisprudence lies in its separation from philosophy (sect. 11). In the sixth oration Vico says that the student will find that jurisprudence is derived from a fusion of moral, civil, and theological doctrines of conduct and thought.[15] In the *New Science*, Vico, citing Dio Chrysostom (*Discourse*, 76) holds that law begins in natural customs which are direct expressions of the fact that human nature is sociable. He says: 'The natural law of the gentes is coeval with the customs of the nations, conforming one with another in virtue of a common human sense [*un senso comune umano*], without any reflection and without one nation following the example of another' (311). Law is rooted directly in the *senso comune* out of which all human society arises. Vico subscribes to Dio's view that law as custom commands naturally, but written law, although derived from custom, commands by force like a tyrant (308), a state of law corresponding to the final stages of a nation's life, in Vico's view. The natural customs which result are expressions of *phronēsis* or *prudentia*, the kind of wisdom through

---

[15] 'Oratio VI', in *Opere di G. B. Vico*, i. 62.

which such basic human actions are taken. The 'art of prudence' or jurisprudence is in truth philosophy, in Vico's view, because to understand the natural wisdom of these customs is for the human to encounter itself. The law, rooted in natural custom, is a theatre of self-knowledge.

How does Vico reach this view? Chapter 12 of the first book of the *Scienza nuova prima* is entitled 'On the Idea of a Jurisprudence of the Human Race'. If there is a 'jurisprudence of the human race', there can be a philosophy of the human race, and such a philosophy will provide us with a knowledge of 'things human and divine' because it will show not only the causes of the things of the human world as they are rooted in human acts of custom and later written law, it will show how in this natural human *prudentia* there is inscribed a divine *prudentia* or *providentia*. Philosophy can then rediscover its ancient mission as the science of human and divine wisdom; it can speak of human wisdom directly and of divine wisdom indirectly as perceived in the providential order of the institutions of human wisdom. The route Vico takes to this view, as he makes clear in the *Autobiography*, is his work on *Universal Law*.

The several works that Vico groups under the title of *Il diritto universale* comprise a study longer than the *Scienza nuova seconda*, and because Vico's treatment of the subject shifts within the two major books of the work, it poses problems of interpretation that are in a sense more difficult than those of his *magnum opus*. It is not my purpose here to attempt to interpret the difficulties of this work in which Vico sketches for the first time his conception of his new science, but to affirm the role it plays in establishing the basis of his philosophy, namely, the idea of *certum*. My view follows that of Guido Fassò, who holds that Vico's concern with the connection between *certum* and *verum*, rather than the principle, *verum ipsum factum*, leads him to the *New Science*.[16] I also hold with Fassò, and on this I hope not to be misunderstood, that the convertibility of *verum* and *factum* is crucial to the *New Science* and certainly employed in it. But without Vico's concern with the relationship of *certum* to *verum* in the law, he would never have

---

[16] G. Fassò, 'The Problem of Law and the Historical Origin of the *New Science*', in G. Tagliacozzo and D. P. Verene, eds., *Giambattista Vico's Science of Humanity* (Baltimore: Johns Hopkins University Press, 1976), 3–14.

achieved his understanding of the relationship of philology and philosophy that is fundamental to his conception of the new science and upon which the order of the axioms is based in the *Second New Science*.

In the Proloquium to *De universi iuris uno principio et fine uno* Vico speaks of the foundation of law on both *ratio* and *auctoritas* and holds that *auctoritas* is *rationis pars quaedam*.[17] In Chapter 82 regarding the relation of *verum* and *certum* in law, Vico says that *certum est pars veri*.[18] Vico's concern is with the relationship between law as rational and universally valid and laws that are made by human will, by *auctoritas*. The certain, what is the result of human will, is part of the true, what is justified as a direct expression of human reason. In introducing his first sketch of his idea of a new science in *De constantia iurisprudentis* (*De constantia philologiae*), Vico says: 'Philosophy secures the consistency [*constantia*] of reason; let us consider whether philology secures the consistency of authority, for as we have said authority is part of reason [*auctoritatem partem esse rationis*].'[19] Thus Vico recalls for the reader the assertion of the earlier book. *Ratio* and *auctoritas* parallel *verum* and *certum* and both are parallel to philosophy and philology.

In his introduction to the idea of the work in the *New Science* Vico says that it is based on a 'new critical art' and that the distinctive feature of this art is that in it 'philosophy undertakes to examine philology' (*qui la filosofia si pone ad esaminare la filologia*) (7). This distinction of philosophy as connected with the true (*il vero*) and philology as connected with the certain (*il certo*) forms the basis for Vico's division in his general axioms (163). At the point of his first conception of his new science, in his chapter on 'Nova scientia tentatur' in *De constantia iurisprudentis*, Vico has worked out only the conception that the certain is part of the true, and he conceives of this as a principle that can be extended from jurisprudence to history, but he has not worked out an understanding of the method or 'new critical art' whereby the certain can always be demonstrated to be within the true, whereby the need

---

[17] Fassò, 'The Problem of Law', 10. *De universi iuris uno principio et fine uno*, *Opere di G. B. Vico*, ed. F. Nicolini, vol. ii (Bari: Laterza, 1936), pt. 1, p. 26.

[18] *De uno principio*, 82–3. See also, Fassò, 'The Problem of Law', 10–11.

[19] *De constantia iurisprudentis*, *Opere di G. B. Vico*, ed. F. Nicolini, vol. ii (Bari: Laterza, 1936), pt. 2, p. 307.

for universality that is native to the true can be achieved in such a way as to incorporate the certain. Vico has demonstrated that there is a *constantia* of reason secured by philosophy and a *constantia* of 'authority' secured by philology. But not until the *New Science* does he reach the point where he can secure a *constantia* that is common to both; for this a new way of thinking is required.

I think Vico arrives at this new unified method of thinking by meditation on jurisprudence, specifically through considering the philosophical meaning of the idea of *ius gentium*. The *ius gentium* in Roman law was originally those principles regarded as common to all peoples as distinct from those applying only to Roman citizens. Such principles were at first matters of morality and not legally binding. As trade and commercial relations developed between Rome and other peoples and with the introduction into the Roman courts of *praetores peregrini*, ideas were adopted from other legal systems and a whole system of law was developed distinct from *ius civile*.

Ius gentium was thus a body of law in concept and in practice that stood between *ius naturale* and *ius civile*. *Ius naturale* is a conception originating in Greek philosophy but taken up by Roman jurists as a conception of justice which is to proceed directly from human reason and be everywhere common to all men and all nations. A standard example of the difference between *ius naturale* and *ius gentium* is that slavery was reckoned as in accordance with *ius gentium* but was usually thought contrary to *ius naturale*. *Ius naturale* is always to be *aequum et bonum*.

Ius civile has different senses. In its earliest senses it was called *ius Quiritium*, the right of a Roman citizen as distinguished from *ius honorarium*, the law introduced by the magistrates to amplify or correct *ius civile* based on their ability to grant *actiones honorariae* not arising from *ius civile*. In contrast to *ius naturale*, *ius civile* is positive law enacted by legislation, that is, created by human will and decision in response to specific situations, not stemming from the human condition generally, as does *ius naturale*. In contrast to *ius gentium*, *ius civile* applies exclusively to Roman citizens, whereas *ius gentium* is that part of Roman law that applies both to Roman citizens and the citizens of all other nations, that part of Roman law shared with all other systems of law or thought to be so shared. In the development of Roman law with the *Constitutio Antoniniana de Civitate*, the same law was applied to both Roman citizens and *peregrini* and the distinction between *ius civile* and *ius gentium* effectively collapsed in practice.

Ius gentium remains an extremely important and suggestive concept in subsequent legal theory and jurisprudence, including the work of Suárez[20] and Grotius,[21] both of whom exert important influence on Vico. In the title of the *Scienza nuova prima* (1725) Vico uses the term *diritto naturale delle genti*. In his shortening of the title for the *Scienza nuova seconda* (1730) this term does not appear, but it appears in the text in his explanation of the idea of the work (31) and elsewhere (e.g. 146), including its designation as the sixth of Vico's list of seven 'corollaries concerning the principal aspects of this science' (394). Vico first formulates this term as the subject of Chapter 136, 'De iure naturali gentium et iure naturali philosophorum', in *De universi iuris uno principio et fine uno* (1720). What does Vico mean by the notion of a *ius naturale gentium*?

Vico combines *ius naturale* with *ius gentium* to forge the fundamental concept upon which his conception of the civil world is based. Unlike Suárez Vico does not regard *ius naturale* as an abstract and perfect ideal of just law, but like Suárez he regards one of the prime contents of the *ius gentium* to be the universality of religion, although forms of religion differ from nation to nation. Suárez's *De legibus* is very likely to have been an influence on Vico.[22] Grotius had shown how *ius naturale* and *ius gentium* must be understood according to different methods for the establishment of their character, but he also showed how they can be seen as mutually supportive. His concentration on *ius gentium* as a bridge between *ius naturale* and *ius civile* points in the direction of Vico but in the end Grotius does not give us a single system in which the philosophy of law can be brought together with the historical study of particular systems of law. B. A. Haddock says in *Vico's Political Thought*, 'What looked like a synthesis of philosophy and history

---

[20] E. Gianturco, 'Character, Essence, Origin and Content of the *Jus Gentium* According to Vico and Suárez', *Revue de littérature comparée*, 10 (1936), 167–72.

[21] B. A. Haddock, *Vico's Political Thought* (Swansea: Mortlake Press, 1986), ch. 4. See also G. Fassò, *Vico e Grozio* (Naples: Guida, 1971). There is a great deal of literature on Vico's relation to Grotius. I have found that of Haddock and Fassò to be among the most helpful. Also very helpful on Vico and law is the work of D. R. Kelley.

[22] Gianturco, '*Jus Gentium*', 171–2.

[in Grotius] actually depended upon the fact that the spheres of the *ius naturale* and the *ius gentium* overlapped in material respects.'[23]

What captures Vico's imagination, I think, is the philosophical meaning of the *ius gentium*. As he asks in the *Study Methods*, 'Why did *ius gentium* arise?' (sect. 11). How can there be a law that both is enacted by human will (*auctoritas*) and yet has the universality of natural reason (*ratio*)? The concept of *ius gentium* is the idea of something in human affairs that is at once certain and true. It is certain because it is not ideal, but actually grounded in the law of a society. Yet it is universal in that it is an embodiment of a truth of human custom that holds for all human societies. Philosophically understood, *ius gentium* is the idea of law writ large, the idea of a particularized universal that is inherent to any law. Any law has to be a *true-certain*; that is, any law can only be such because it embodies in some way right or justice which is universal. *Lex* must always embody *ius*. We encounter *ius* only in its form as a specific law. Yet *ius* has no true meaning in and of itself in human affairs, unless we can see how it is or can be truly embodied in them. All particular laws are attempts to realize *ius* in relation to a specific set of conditions. They are thus acts of prudence, hence the term 'jurisprudence' as the term ultimately to express what the law is.

Ius gentium, like the idea of law itself, is necessary to any society or nation because without it there can be neither *ius civile* nor *ius naturale*. *Ius civile*, which is distinctive only to a particular society, exists as such within a society in contrast to what in it is universal and not simply its own positive law. Thus it can be contrasted to *ius naturale*; but *ius naturale* makes no sense simply as an abstract ideal. This ideal must in some way have actual social and legal content; it must be really present in the life of the *gentes*. Vico's insight is that *ius gentium* is what nations begin with. They devise positive law in the sense of *ius civile* as they develop beyond the state of their natural customs, so to speak, and their philosophers develop the idea of *ius naturale* as an abstraction from the sense of *ius gentium* that is at the basis of human society.

Vico's solution to Grotius's problem of leaving natural law with the philosophers is to merge natural law with *ius gentium*. Vico's three principles of religion, marriage, and burial are at bottom a concept of *ius gentium*. These are the three eternal and universal

---

[23] Haddock, *Vico's Political Thought*, 84.

customs (333) out of which human society arises and in these, understood as the content of *ius gentium*, Vico is quite close to Suárez. All nations develop customs of sacred and profane, and rules of marriage, and establish dominion through the burial grounds of their dead. These three principles are the original jurisprudence of any nation, even in its independent development from all other nations. Such initial customs are both particular to a given nation and universal to all nations.

Vico, in accordance with the etymology of his day and very much in accordance with his procedure of making etymology fit his philosophy, regards *ius* as a contraction of *Ious* or Jove (398). The gentile nations begin with the experience of the fear of Jove as the thundering sky. Social order is first founded upon the taking of the auspices of Jove's actions in the sky. This science of the divine becomes the basis of the ordering of human things. Vico says: 'Thus our treatment of natural law begins with the idea of divine providence, in the same birth with which was born the idea of law. For law began naturally to be observed, in the manner examined above, by the founders of the gentes properly so called, those of the most ancient order, which were called the greater gentes, whose first god was Jove' (398). The basis of the original prudential or jurisprudential order of human society is providential. Human prudence is possible because it is rooted in divine prudence—the divine wisdom speaking in the order of particular historical events. *Providentia* and *prudentia* are not only the same word, they are the same thing.[24]

The tie between two of Vico's most fundamental concepts, that between *ius naturale gentium* and *storia ideale eterna*, can now be seen. The natural law of the gentes is developed in history in accordance with a divine prudence. 'Ideal eternal history' is a jurisprudence of history, a judgement or order of history placed upon any nation in the pattern of development it holds in common with every other nation. Each nation manifests a principle of *ius gentium* in its origin, its natural customs of religion, marriage, and burial, and it manifests a similar principle of commonality of law in the pattern of development its institutions undergo as they move from the age of gods, to that of heroes, to that of humans and

[24] A. Pons, 'Prudence and Providence: The *Pratica della scienza nuova* and the Problem of Theory and Practice in Vico', in *Vico's Science of Humanity*, 442.

decline, all of which is governed by divine providence. Vico's *New Science* as a work which describes this course and recourse of the nations is a work of jurisprudence in the sense of the original meaning which Vico ascribes to the term in the *Study Methods*—a knowledge of human and divine law which is the basis of wisdom. Vico's *New Science* is a book of wisdom in this sense.

Vico transforms the traditional conception of natural law by connecting the idea of natural law with the idea of repetition in history and by connecting this with the idea of providence. He overcomes the remoteness natural law seems always to have from concrete human affairs by claiming a version of natural law that makes it a principle of the development of any nation's historical life. This he calls the 'ideal eternal history' of any nation, the notion that any nation's life is governed by a cycle of rise, maturity, and fall. This pattern, repeated in the life of all nations, Vico regards as the meaning of providence. Providence is God's existence in history. History is 'ideal' in that the stages of any nation's life, while the same in general as those of any other nation, occur at different rates and have varying contents and particular shapes. History is 'eternal' in that all of the civil world is governed by the same divinely ordered repetitions.

The sense in which any nation's history of rise, maturity, and fall makes up a whole, a single course, is the sense in which it has a 'jurisprudence'. The full course of the life of any nation viewed, so to speak, from above will display a 'justice', a sense of internal order of its stages, a proper proportion or harmony of the beginning, middle, and end of its life. This is also a kind of 'prudence' or total economy or eloquence of action that makes the nation what it is, gives it its self-identity. This eloquence is derived from the eternal order in which it participates.

As discussed above in Chapter 2 and elsewhere, in its ideal eternal history each nation passes through an age of gods, an age of heroes, and an age of humans. The existence of these three ages is the jurisprudence of human history itself. In addition to this sense of *ius* in history, there is a sense of *ius* or natural law which prevails within each of these three eternally repeatable ages (31, 311 ff., 922–4). In the age of gods the natural law depends upon the founders of the families interpreting the actions of the gods through augury and sacrifice. The gods are the ultimate order which is at once natural and social. In the age of heroes natural law is what is enacted in the deeds of heroes. In their deeds is the ultimate standard of human conduct. The heroes are the basis of custom and social order.

In the age of humans natural law becomes a concept. Natural law becomes remote as something informing the positive laws of a society. Particular laws are the result of authority and natural law that of reason. As the divine itself retreats from being actually present in the temporal order of life, so natural law becomes remote and reduced to an abstract sense of 'right' that is elusively and problematically attached to the validity of any specific law or body of laws. What constitutes natural law alters relative to the particular state of human society. This relativity of natural law is possible because of a sense of history as ideal eternal.

In Vico's construal of providence in history as a jurisprudence of history, the difference between his conception of providence and the traditional notion of biblical providence can be seen. In the description by Mathieu mentioned above, biblical providence is the expression of God's deliberate will and in its strict form excludes the accidental.[25] In Vico's notion of a divine jurisprudence of history, providential order stands in relation to historical events as *verum* which is inscribed in *certum* or as the philosophical which has undertaken the philological. Jurisprudential thinking is the wisdom to see, in the event that has occurred within the limits of the order of ordinary positive law, the larger order of justice of which it is a part. The truth of what is otherwise just a certain is brought out. In this way Vico's *New Science* joins philosophy with history. It is this prudential way of understanding that allows Vico to see the events of his own life as having providential order.

Providential order understood on the model of jurisprudential thinking is different from necessity. What is done out of necessity involves no act of human will. But *certum* in Vico's view is always *auctoritas*, which is always a part of *ratio*. Thus the things of the civil world are made by men as the things of Vico's career are made by him; that is, they arise through acts of human will that confront other past and present acts of human will. The human world as made always confronts the human world as it has been

---

[25] V. Mathieu, 'Truth as the Mother of History', in *Vico's Science of Humanity*, 118. See my discussion of Mathieu's characterization of Vico's conception of providence in Chapter 3.

made and is being made. But such acts of will are never pure acts; they are always part of *ratio* in the sense of an order that has been there from the beginning in human events and is always in one way or another being worked out as a kind of general narrative. Prudence is the wisdom to act in accord with this larger order.

Vico places the idea of providential order between the 'blind chance' of the Epicureans and the 'deaf necessity' of the Stoics. If we ask Vico how we know there is a providential order and not just chance or necessity, Vico's evidence is the educational process in which the faculties can undergo a cycle of studies that promotes their natural development; that is, the actual use of jurisprudential thinking in ordering human affairs, and, what has not yet been discussed, the human experience of narrative and the power to order events in narrative fashion. That Vico's meditations on the law led him to the *New Science* there can be no doubt, as Vico declares in the title of the fourth chapter of Book 1 of the *First New Science*, 'This Science is Meditated upon the Idea of the Natural Law of the Gentes that was held by the Roman Jurisconsults'. It is through the law that Vico makes his own connection between philosophical and philological knowledge in order to arrive at his new conception of a science of the civil world.

A NEW CRITICAL ART

Vico's purpose in the *Study Methods* was to consider the advantages and disadvantages of the ancient and the modern conceptions of knowledge. This consideration takes the form of the ancient commitment to the art of topics and the modern commitment to criticism and how each of these can be fitted into a conception of education governed by the aim of self-knowledge. Both ancient and modern conceptions of knowledge are rooted in the relation of thought to the thinker, the ancient in 'Know thyself' and the modern in the Cartesian 'I think'. Vico's view is that criticism requires topics and the faculties that the art of topics involves— memory, imagination, and ingenuity—because criticism, being an art of judgement, must make its judgements through arguments, and topics is the means through which the starting-points of arguments can be found. Topics is the art of drawing forth through commonplaces what is needed for the formation of premises from which conclusions can be drawn and judgements made.

Critical philosophy in Vico's view is particularly connected to mathematics, especially analytical geometry, and metaphysics. Vico pursues his views of these two fields briefly and importantly in his unfinished work on the *Ancient Wisdom*, and, as mentioned above, he produced the book on metaphysics but left unfinished the book on physics (except for his now lost treatise on the motion of living bodies), and never wrote the book on ethics, an order of knowledge very closely akin to that of Descartes's tree of knowledge in the 'Author's Letter' to the *Principles*. Instead of pursuing his answer to critical philosophy through the completion of the books of the *Ancient Wisdom*, Vico moved to the side of the ancients and pursued topical philosophy through an analysis of its great repository in Roman law. As the title from the fourth chapter of Book 1 of the *First New Science* quoted above so clearly states, it is his meditations on Roman jurisprudence that lead him to the central concept of his new science, the idea of a natural law that is not a philosophical idea, but is actually there in the life of all nations.

Vico transforms the notion of *phronēsis*, practical wisdom, *prudentia*, into a conception of philosophical wisdom, *sapientia*. Vico's *Universal Law* is not a philosophy of law in the modern critical sense of a philosophical examination of the principles of law as a type of human thought or culture. It is a conception of jurisprudential thinking as itself the fundamental form of philosophical thinking. Vico has to show that the ability to think from the individual situation to the features of the truth that lie within it, rather than thinking from the particular situation to an abstract principle of which it then becomes an instance, is a basic form of human understanding that is taught in rhetoric and which underlies the practice of law and is the basic form of human wisdom required by philosophy. The power to hold together the true and the certain in the jurisprudential thinking of the law suggests to Vico the possibility of a science of things human and divine. This science is new not in the sense of a new revival of ancient notions of jurisprudence and the art of topics. It is new because of how it converts jurisprudence and philosophy. What catches Vico's imagination is that law contains the principles of the human world generally and that the one principle and end of law is the sense in which a specific law made by an act of human will in a particular time and place is also *law*.

Jurisprudence is the ability always to understand things in terms of their particular circumstances, the features of the particular case, while holding in memory the analogies it has with other past cases and showing in speech how certain principles can be extended to it to make evident its truth. What if philosophy, with its natural drive toward mathematical abstraction and metaphysical argument, were to become convertible with this 'art of prudence', which, as mentioned above, Vico in the *Study Methods* says is nothing other than the 'art of philosophy'? This would require the union of philosophy and philology, which Vico defines in the *New Science* as 'all the things [*cose*] that depend on human choice' (7). Such a reform of philosophy, which studies the true, and philology, which studies the certain in human affairs, would require a new art of criticism. Vico says that 'Topics has the function of making minds inventive, as criticism has that of making them exact' (498).

Starting from the division between the ancients and the moderns that he states in the *Study Methods*, Vico aligns himself on the side of the ancients in order to recover their sense of wisdom as tied to prudence and eloquence, eloquence being the power to portray in speech the whole of a situation. Eloquence is not simply the power to adorn a topic, to make it pleasing, but to convey the whole of a situation, to make the situation evident in all its dimensions. Thus eloquence is the natural companion of prudence and is, as Vico mentions at the end of his autobiography, and in his address to the Academy of Oziosi, 'wisdom speaking'. But it is not enough to recover the wisdom of the ancients, even to recover it in a new way. Vico must meet the moderns on their own ground; he must offer an art of criticism to stand in the place of their art of criticism. Seen in terms of Vico's development, this is the intellectual problem that completes his task. In the summary of the *First New Science* with which he concludes the original 1728 Venice text of his auto-biography, Vico is quite clear about this, saying, 'For he discovers this new science by means of a new critical method' (167/56). In the second book of the *First New Science* Vico titles chapter 9 'Idea d'una nuova arte critica', and says it will provide us with a new way to read fables in order to discover the true origins of humanity, concluding that 'This will be the guiding principle for this whole work' (*Che sarà la condotta principale di tutta quest'opera*).[26]

---

[26] *La scienza nuova prima, Opere di G. B. Vico*, ed. F. Nicolini, vol. iii (Bari: Laterza, 1931), para. 93.

In the *Ancient Wisdom* Vico was not yet in possession of his conception of the new critical art, and thus he attacks Descartes's conception of mathematical knowledge and metaphysics directly with his criticism of the *cogito*, as described in Chapter 3. The *Ancient Wisdom* supplies only part of Vico's positive doctrine, centring around his principle of *verum ipsum factum*. To replace the Cartesian philosophy with another philosophy of his own, he requires the further conception of his new critical art based on his researches into jurisprudence. As Vico says in the *First New Science*, 'the duty of anyone who criticizes whole systems of others is to replace them with one of his own'.[27]

This 'new critical art' is the key to what I have called above Vico's third motivating idea, the quest for a science of wisdom. It is in his eyes the *sine qua non* of his science; none of it would be possible without this new art of thinking. It is thus as tied to Vico's project of a master science as Descartes's four-step method is tied to his conception of a unified theory of all knowledge. Vico explains what he means by this art in the section on method in the first book of the *Second New Science*. He identifies this new art with a metaphysics of history, stating: 'To determine the times and places for such a history—that is, when and where these human thoughts were born—and thus to give it certainty by means of its own (so to speak) *metaphysical chronology and geography*, our Science applies a likewise *metaphysical art of criticism* [*un'arte critica, pur metafisica*] with regard to the founders of these same nations, in which it took well over a thousand years to produce those writers with whom philological criticism has hitherto been occupied' (348, my emphasis).

Certainly one of the prime features of this new critical art is the joining of philosophical criticism with philological criticism. Conventional philosophical criticism has presumed that humans have always thought in the ways currently familiar and have not traced thought back to its origins. Philosophy has considered forms of thought simply in terms of how they stand to standards of rationality, with no attention to the philological details or historical conditions out of which thought arises. Conventional philological criticism, that is, the art of judging the meaning and order of customs, languages, and deeds, etc., has begun its considerations

[27] *La scienza nuova prima*, para. 79.

only with later writers, in which a conception of historical detail is already present. Philology has not taken its researches back into the fables and the origin of customs and deeds, and languages themselves. Vico says: 'It follows that the *first science to be learned should be mythology* or the interpretation of fables. . . . By such a method the beginnings of the sciences as well as of the nations are to be discovered, for they sprang from the nations and from no other source' (51, my emphasis).

The basis of this new critical art is mythology. It is a method for creating a science of origins. In the *New Science* Vico adds to his researches into rhetoric and jurisprudence the subject of poetic. He says that the first gentile peoples 'were poets who spoke in poetic characters [*caratteri poetici*]' (34). This insight is the 'master key of this Science' which he says cost him twenty years of his career to discover (34). This is Vico's most original and most complicated idea, which according to my reading is the very heart of the *New Science*.

In *Vico's Science of Imagination* I have attempted to work out the notion of 'poetic characters' or 'imaginative universals' (*universali fantastici*) as the basis of Vico's philosophy and in particular his conception of language and myth.[28] I refer the reader to this as a fuller account than I can give here. Vico's *New Science* intends to show that there is a faculty or power of *fantasia* that is primordial and which is presupposed by the intellect. The first humans form their world through myths. The world is not first thought with the intellect, but felt through the passions and the senses. Through the *fantasia* of the first men the world as felt is formed into images of the world that are narrated in the myths of any nation. The first humans are not merely able to feel the world with their bodily powers, they are able to *form* the world in accordance with how they feel. Feeling cannot be formed conceptually. Feeling is closed to the intellect whose power is to abstract from the world as felt and from particulars and to form universals as separate from sensation.

Natural to feeling is the thought of images. In the image what is sensed or felt can be thought in an immediate form, a form close to sensation and feeling themselves. *Fantasia* is not 'creative

---

[28] D. P. Verene, *Vico's Science of Imagination* (Ithaca, NY: Cornell University Press, 1981).

imagination' so much as it is 'making imagination'. Imagination does not create something novel in this sense, rather imagination as *fantasia* forms or makes into a 'truth' what it feels in the world. The truth that is made is an imaginative universal. The notion of an imaginative universal is the key to Vico's notion of the fable and poetic wisdom as the basis of human language. The fable always tells a universal truth. Like the metaphor (which is a fable in brief) the fable or myth is a universal story or image. But this universal meaning is embedded in a particular content. In the myth the particular is made into something objective and universal by the imagination, not by the intellect. The intellect makes its truths by another sense of universality than the 'story' or image. The intellect derives its power by leaving the particular and our felt sense of the world behind and abstracting what is common to a group, thus forming experience into classes and orders of things. The intellect requires the sacrifice of the particular.

In Vico's view language is in its first form mythical and dependent upon the power of the metaphor. The world of the first men is formed via a series of transferences of the world as felt in particular ways into objectifications of these feelings, which are not originally subjective, but communal—in other words, into gods—particular types of beings or names. The art of forming these names from what is communally felt is the art mastered by the founders of the first families. They are the masters of poetic metaphysics.

Vico's proof of the truth of his conception of poetic wisdom is the subject of the third book of the *New Science*, his 'discovery of the true Homer'. Vico's discovery is that Homer is the mind of the Greek people themselves. Homer represents a total way of forming the world based in *fantasia*. The works of Homer are not particular works of literature in the modern sense of being products of a single author's subjectivity. They are reflections of a total way of thinking about the world that is rooted in the primordial power of the imaginative universal. But neither are Homer's works statements of an esoteric wisdom. Homer is not a philosopher. His works do not contain rational truths that are couched in poetic statement. Vico's discovery of the true Homer is his solution to Plato's ancient quarrel with the poets, as to whether the poets or the philosophers have truth. Homer's wisdom is presupposed by Plato's wisdom. Metaphysics, including Vico's critical art of metaphysics, presupposes poetic metaphysics.

The original art of poetic metaphysics which forms the world in terms of imaginative universals, the thought of the metaphor, is the basis of the human arts and sciences. From poetic metaphysics as from the trunk of a tree come logic, morals, economics, and politics, as well as physics, cosmography, astronomy, chronology, and geography, all poetic in form. Language comes into being in Vico's view by first exercising its metaphorical powers, which are at the same time its metaphysical powers—its powers to give form to the real. From such power all that there is in human thought and human affairs flows.

In Vico's view there is not for the first humans an empirical order of experience that is practical in form and that is then transferred into poetic and religious forms of thought. Instead there is first myth, and myth is, for Vico as for later anthropology, a genuine way of thinking. Myth is not a form of language that is developed from or attached on to man's empirical and practical perceptions of the world. Myth is first and foremost a way of thinking that makes possible the general order of being within which empirical and practical thinking and acting can develop. Vico's own metaphysics must be a recovery of this sense of the original power of language both as a subject-matter to be philosophically understood and as an influence on the very form of modern metaphysics itself, what Vico calls his new critical art. Vico identifies his new science with metaphysics—*questa* Nuova Scienza, *o sia la metafisica* (31)—and it is metaphysic as grounded in myth. The basis of the common nature of nations is a 'poetic wisdom' (*sapienza poetica*) and the basis of this poetic wisdom is a 'poetic metaphysics' (*metafisica poetica*).

In a short chapter intended as an addition to his section on 'Poetic Metaphysics' in the second book of the *New Science*, titled 'Reprehension of the Metaphysics of René Descartes, Benedict Spinoza, and John Locke', Vico sets this conception of metaphysics directly in opposition to modern philosophy.[29] In these paragraphs Vico argues that since metaphysics is the science of being, it must take its beginning where the idea of being itself is first recognized, namely, in the fables of the ancient poets—the body

---

[29] Trans. D. P. Verene, *New Vico Studies*, 8 (1990), 2–18. See *La scienza nuova seconda, Opere di G. B. Vico*, ed. F. Nicolini, vol. iv (Bari: Laterza, 1942), pt. 2, paras. 1212–17.

of myth that is at the beginning of any nation. In human experience being is first apprehended in poetic form by the human power of imagination or *fantasia*. Metaphysics requires an art whereby this original apprehension of being or Jove can be recovered and seen as a principle of the human world in its development from its beginnings.

In modern metaphysics, Descartes, Spinoza, and Locke, each in his own way, believes that being can be reached by a method of supposition (*supposizione*). Having divorced metaphysics from poetry, modern metaphysics supposes that through the idea of my own being I have the idea of Being or God, and this supposition is tested in terms of doubt or evidence of common sense. Although such suppositional method, in Vico's view, can allow us to arrive at *substance* (as with Descartes's, Spinoza's, and Locke's various senses of this), it cannot produce the idea of Being. Myth can directly produce this.

The origin cannot be recovered by the critical art of supposition, doubt, and analysis such as presented in Descartes's *Discourse* and pursued in various ways by both rationalists and empiricists in modern philosophy. A science of being that does not take its beginning from where Being itself begins is no science of being at all. In his section on 'Method' in the *New Science* Vico says that the criterion of his 'metaphysical criticism' (*critica metafisica*) is the 'common sense of the human race' (*il senso comune d'esso gener umano*) (350). Axiom 12 states: 'Common sense is judgment without reflection, shared by an entire class, an entire people, an entire nation, or the entire human race. This axiom, with the following definition, *will provide a new art of criticism* concerning the founders of nations' (142–3, my emphasis). The new art of criticism is rooted in the common sense of the human race and is in fact an extension of this manner of judgement to the level of a method of philosophical understanding. How can this be done?

In Chapter 57 of the second book of the *First New Science*, entitled 'Discovery of the True Elements of History', Vico speaks of 'a certain critical art, like that of jurisconsults' (*una certa arte critica, come quella de' giureconsulti*) who reduce to the certainty of laws the uncertain facts or doubt of reason.[30] Vico then goes on to mention the idea of a 'jurisprudence of the human race' and

---

[30] *La scienza nuova prima*, para. 208.

how this new science of humanity must narrate the rise, progress, stasis, decadence, and ends of the nations by determining their condition in terms of certain times and places according to the 'two eyes of history': chronology and geography. This new art, like the art of jurisprudential thinking, can bring what is uncertain and doubtful to reason into a law-like arrangement of certainties. The power of ordering experience as the result of human will or authority governed by common sense is what generates human institutions. This occurs through judgement without reflection. The new critical art is the power to think in terms of this form of wisdom and to elicit and express the meaning of its activity through a type of thought compatible with it. A metaphysics based on logical supposition or analysis of such activity into its smallest parts could never discover its true elements because they are not reflective truths. They are not the result of reflective judgements and cannot be criticized as such. Rational metaphysics can never penetrate the truths of history and history always appears to it as something accidental. Because of this such metaphysics can never offer a guide to life, a *pratica*.

In the *Second New Science* Vico delineates a set of axioms or elements which he says are to 'circulate as the blood does in animate bodies' and 'course through our Science and animate it in all its reasonings about the common nature of nations' (119; cf. 1133). Vico uses this biological metaphor of the circulation of the blood to explain the action of the elements that are described in the geometrical terminology of Euclid's *Elements*, of axioms, definitions, and corollaries, although in a very loose fashion. As mentioned in Chapter 1, in reporting in his *Autobiography* on Le Clerc's review of his *Universal Law*, Vico calls attention to the fact that Le Clerc says it is 'constructed by "mathematical method", which "from few principles draws infinite consequences"' (164/54). Vico holds plane geometry along with topics as part of the curriculum of the ancients. Euclid's method determined what came to be understood in Western philosophy as the best means of intellectual demonstration, reasoning deductively from *archai*, the truth of which was intuitively known, to what was contained in them. But this sense of thinking seems far from Vico's metaphor of axioms circulating like the blood in the historical body of the nations, revealing the means of their animation.

What is the role of the axioms in this new critical art? I think they are connected to 'deduction' not in the sense of the logician but more in the sense of the jurist, that is, not to the process of affirming one truth on the basis of another but to the question of *quid iuris*, the need to state the right or legal claim relevant to a specific action (the question Kant employs in the first *Critique* but to a different end, the 'deduction' of his categories). The axioms of the *New Science* are a kind of legal geometry, which, given any fact of a nation's life, provide the basis through the convergence of philological and philosophical criticism by which it may be judged to be a rightful part of a nation's ideal eternal history. All facts of a nation's life are part of its history but the rightful place of each must be determined. The axioms circulate like the blood in that they may be consulted in any order to be brought to bear on the interpretation of the law of nations, to provide a judgement of the specific meaning, that is, joining the certain and the true, to make a particular of a nation's history understandable within its ideal eternal history.

In the above sense the axioms are the conditions for the proof of the meaning of any particular point within the compass of the new science. But what of the proof of the new science itself, of its general philosophical validity? Vico gives a direct answer to this question, but it is not a comfortable one for the philosophical mind which still holds to the Cartesian sense of method even in a small degree, or which holds to the view that there can be a reflective science of history or even that history is a dialectical theatre of reason, although this is closest to Vico's view. Vico says, 'The decisive sort of proof in our Science is therefore this: that, since these institutions have been established by divine providence, the course of the institutions of the nations *had to be, must now be, and will have to be such as our Science demonstrates*' (348, my emphasis). Vico then says, 'Indeed, we make bold to affirm that he who *meditates* this Science *narrates* to himself this ideal eternal history so far as he himself makes it for himself by that proof "*it had, has, and will have to be*"' (349, my emphasis). And, he concludes, addressing the reader directly: 'O reader, that these proofs are of a kind divine and should give thee a divine pleasure' (349), his point being that since we are both the maker and the narrator of history, our action is mimetic of the divine, in which making and knowing are one.

Vico puts his proof of 'it had, has, and will have to be' ('*dovette, deve, dovrà*') in quotation marks, which, so stated, becomes a citation of the ancient wisdom and ability attributed to the Muses in Hesiod's *Theogony* (36–9) and, by tradition, generally throughout the ancient world. The Muses, through their mother, who is Memory (*Mnemosyne*), are associated with the faculty of *memoria* (which Vico says includes *fantasia* and *ingegno*, 819) and with Jove, who is their father. This proof is far from that which might be based in Descartes's *bon sens*, but it is not so extravagant as it may seem when its connection to Vico's *senso comune* is understood. The Muses are in fact a model of prudential wisdom. One way to see this is perhaps to consider a maxim of the Renaissance historian, Francesco Guicciardini, from his *Ricordi*: 'All that which has been in the past and is at present will be again in the future. But both the names and the surfaces of things change, so that he who does not have a good eye will not recognize them. Nor will he know how to grasp a norm of conduct or make a judgement by means of this observation.'[31]

The form of this kind of wisdom is narration. The new critical art forms its meditation as a narrative because narrative allows for repetition common to both *fabula* and *historia*. The meditation of events as having a providential pattern gives Vico a conception of prudence that is based not on particular examples in history but on the very order of history itself. This order is a kind of divine wisdom which originates in the songs of the Muses and is thus connected to the fables of the poets and also, as Vico claims, originates in divination practised by the founders of poetic wisdom. This sense of divine recurrence has behind it not only the Muses but the great tradition of the Renaissance conception of history and human affairs, understood in a practical sense.

Vico's proof is objective in the sense that it is a narrative; it is not introspective meditation, but meditation that brings the philological certains of history together with the philosophical history of ideas. In the *First New Science*[32] and in the *Autobiography* (172/61) Vico distinguishes between two forms of wisdom—*sapienza volgare* and *sapienza riposta*. In Book 4 of the *First New Science*,

---

[31] 'Tutto quello che è stato per il passato e è al presente, sarà ancora in futuro; ma si mutano e nomi e le superficie delle cose in modo, che chi non ha buono occhio non le riconosce, né sa pigliare regola o fare giudicio per mezzo di quella osservazione.' F. Guicciardini, *Ricordi* (Milan: Rizzoli, 1977), 131.

[32] *La scienza nuova prima*, para. 247 and bk. 4, esp. para. 398.

which concerns the proofs which establish the science, he stresses that the *sapienza riposta* or esoteric wisdom must always be at the service of the *sapienza volgare*, the vulgar or common wisdom. The truths of the former are derived from and dependent upon the latter. But moreover, he says, the *sapienza riposta* must act to correct and aid the *sapienza volgare* when it goes astray. This is accomplished, Vico says, by judging the state of nations in terms of how much they are brought together or drawn apart by the three maxims of humanity—religion, marriage, and burial—and the extent to which the philosophers as possessors of esoteric wisdom assist the nations in being brought together around these three principles. Thus part of the proof of the new science is a praxis.

In the fourth book of the *First New Science* Vico says that of the proofs for his science, two of them are practical: 'Of these, one is a new critical art which serves as a torch to distinguish the true in obscure and fabulous history. In addition to this, the other practic is like a diagnostic art [*un'arte come diagnostica*].'[33] This diagnostic art, he says, is regulated by the wisdom of the human race (*la sapienza del genere umano*) and assesses the order of human things (*cose*) in terms of necessity and utility. In other words, Vico means that by this diagnostic art the Vichian scientist can examine the state of the institutions of a given nation and assess its present position in relation to the pattern of ideal eternal history that governs any nation. In the *Second New Science* Vico states this pattern as follows: 'Men first feel necessity, then look for utility, next attend to comfort, still later amuse themselves with pleasure, thence grow dissolute in luxury, and finally go mad and waste their substance' (241), and he makes a very similar statement in the *First New Science*.[34] Vico says that this diagnostic art provides 'the principal end of this Science of recognizing the indubitable signs of the state of nations'.[35]

Vico does not speak of the diagnostic art as such in the *Second New Science*, but the concept of it is present in the short chapter on the 'Pratica della scienza nuova' that he wrote as an addition to the conclusion of the *Second New Science*.[36] Fisch interprets Vico's conception of this diagnostic art connected to the *Pratica* as

---

[33] *La scienza nuova prima*, para. 391.
[34] Ibid. para. 125.   [35] Ibid. para. 391.
[36] 'Pratica della scienza nuova', in *La scienza nuova seconda*, paras. 1405–11.

indicating that Vico intended the new science to take the place of that 'philosophy concerning things human' (*hē peri ta anthrōpina philosophia*) contained in Aristotle's *Nicomachean Ethics* (1181ᵇ15) and completed in the *Politics*.[37] Fisch holds that Vico wrote the *Pratica* because any science was expected to have both a 'theoric' and a 'practic', and the expected order was for the practic to follow the theoric as the conception of its application. Although Vico wrote the paragraphs of the *Pratica*, he never published them, and Fisch holds that Vico's reason for this was the realization that it was too short and, unless he were fully to develop it, it would detract from, rather than enchance, the achievement of the new science, with its full verification of the critical method.[38]

Fisch's explanation is quite persuasive and in a sense certainly correct, but there is another possibility. In introducing the idea of a diagnostic art and distinguishing it from the critical art, Vico calls both arts 'practical' (*due sono le pratiche*).[39] Both are 'practics' (to use Fisch's term). Vico's conclusion may have been that the new critical art is itself a diagnostic art, that in the end the critical art properly understood has the diagnostic as a dimension of it; that is, to determine the true within obscure and fabulous history is at the same time to have the power to diagnose the indubitable signs of the course of nations. A knowledge of the origin and of the common sense of the human race—the esoteric grounded in the vulgar wisdom—is itself a prudential wisdom that allows one always to perceive the natural course of events, to have, in Guicciardini's terms, the *buono occhio*, the 'good eye' for the true order of events. I think, in fact, that Vico collapses theoric and practic.

In my view, Vico's *New Science* contains the philosopher's wisdom, which is not the power to govern in the way of 'wise men and princes of the commonwealths' (as Vico puts it in the *Pratica*), but the power to act successfully within the events of human life. In this sense the *New Science* is a completion of Aristotle's *hē peri ta anthrōpina philosophia*. It is a guide to those who can grasp the *sapienza riposta* and read the indubitable signs of events for acting in the civil world of the moderns, a world of 'reflective barbarism',

---

[37] M. H. Fisch, 'Vico's *Pratica*', in *Vico's Science of Humanity*, 427.
[38] Ibid. 427–30.
[39] *La scienza nuova prima*, para. 391.

as Vico puts it in his portrait of the decline of the nations in the conclusion to the *New Science* (1106) which he allows to stand, a world suffering from the 'ultimate civil disease' of trying to live by logic instead of prudence and the false language of the self that produces only flattery and witticism. As Gianturco puts it in contemporary terms, 'We live in a Cartesian world, a world of scientific research, technology, and gadgets, which invade and condition our lives.'[40]

The new critical art reveals to us the providential order, the jurisprudence of history, which in its form as a narration produces the self-knowledge of humanity. The new critical art is an autobiographical art. It provides a narration of the truth of the things of the civil world of humanity by those who have made it. We can expect that Vico's understanding of self-knowledge, prudence, and this new critical art that have taken him to the new science of the life of nations will also provide him with an understanding of his own life—the life of the philosopher. His telling of his own life becomes a verification of the principles of his own philosophy. Vico's science of himself, like his science of the nations, is a true narration and a guide to philosophical wisdom.

---

[40] Gianturco, Introduction to *Study Methods*, p. xxi.

5

Vico's Fable of Himself

HIS FALL

Signor Giambattista Vico, he was born in Naples in the year 1670 of upright parents, who left behind them a very good reputation. The father was of cheerful humour, the mother of a quite melancholy temper; and both came together in the fair disposition of this little son of theirs. As a boy he was very lively and restless; but at the age of 7 he fell head-first from high on a ladder to the floor, and remained a good five hours motionless and senseless, fracturing the right side of the cranium without breaking the skin, hence from the fracture arose a shapeless tumour, and from the many deep lancings of it the child lost a great deal of blood; such that the surgeon, having observed the broken cranium and considering the long state of unconsciousness, made the prediction that either he would die of it or he would survive stolid. However, neither of the two parts of the judgement, by the grace of God, came true; but as a result of this illness and recovery he grew up, from then on, with a melancholy and acrid nature which necessarily belongs to ingenious and profound men, who through ingenuity flash like lightning in acuity, through reflection take no pleasure in witticism and falsity.

Vico begins his autobiography with this paragraph (given here in a literal translation). To the reader, opening Vico's work for the first time, this seems a natural enough beginning. Vico states his birth-date, mentions something about his parents, and describes the most traumatic incident of his childhood—his fall. The reader may hesitate at the end of the paragraph, wondering whether he has fully grasped Vico's sudden, sweeping conclusion about the formation of his character from this event, but in the next paragraph Vico moves smoothly into the details of his grammar-school education, and on into the rest of his story. The reader goes with him. Yet the image of his fall, especially its severity, sticks in the reader's mind. If the paragraph is read a second and third time, with a sense of Vico's other works in mind, and especially with a knowledge of the principles of his *New Science*, these lines can be seen to have a very specific intellectual structure, from which the rest of the autobiography is constructed.

In the *First New Science* Vico states: 'Mythos is [originally] defined as "true narration", and has remained to mean "fable" which has been held by everyone until now to mean "false narration".'[1] In the *Second New Science* Vico identifies not only *mythos* but also *logos* with fable: ' "logic" came from the word, *logos*, that first and properly meant "fable" [*favola*] that was carried over into Italian as "speech" [*favella*]—and fable in Greek was also called *mythos*, whence comes the Latin *mutus* [mute]' (401). Fable, in Vico's view, is the original form of articulate human speech. It is the language of the first gentile peoples, who organized their world in terms of poetic characters. These poetic characters are the elements of the fables or narrations by means of which the first peoples expressed interrelations between events. These narrations expressed truths about the world in imaginative form. They are to the poetic mind what the network of genera and species is to the rational-empirical mind that develops later in the course of a nation. Underlying the language of fable and prior to it in the course of the development of mind is gesture. Mute gestures directly represent the mute language of the world itself. The deed done, the gesture made is formed in the fable as a linguistic image, a metaphor. The world comes alive through metaphor.[2] And, as Vico says, 'every metaphor so formed is a fable in brief' (404).

Fable, in Vico's view, is the first true form of human speech, and it is the form in which any basic or first truth about the human world can be stated. The metaphor, not the proposition, the narration or fable, not the argument or theory, is the fountain-head from which human discourse can be generated. The fable is a 'true narration' (*vera narratio*) (403) because it is the form necessary to the expression of any true beginning. The language of beginnings is the metaphor or fable. Vico's conception of fable as the primordial form of language for the expression of any human

---

[1] *La scienza nuova prima, Opere di G. B. Vico*, ed. F. Nicolini, vol. iii (Bari: Laterza, 1931), para. 249.

[2] Vico's conception of language is a complex topic that has been much discussed. A great deal can be learned from Gianfranco Cantelli, *Mente corpo linguaggio: Saggio sull'interpretazione vichiana del mito* (Florence: Sansoni, 1986).

phenomenon illuminates Fubini's and De Mas's observations concerning the mythical character of Vico's autobiography. As mentioned in Chapter 1, Fubini says that Vico has given us a mythical story, 'almost the myth of himself'; De Mas says that the reader 'cannot fail to be struck powerfully by the mythical and prophetic tone that animates the narrative'.[3]

My central thesis in this chapter is that in his autobiography Vico has employed one of the fundamental conceptions of his philosophy for the presentation of himself. His autobiography is a fable of himself. This does not mean that what Vico has said of himself is false. Because we are moderns, and separated from the original power of the fable as the means for 'true narration', we are inclined (as Vico says in the passage quoted above from the *First New Science*) to think of fable as 'false narration'. It may be that all autobiographies, as Gusdorf and Olney hold, are myths of the author, metaphors of the self (as mentioned above in Chapter 2), but it is certainly true of Vico's autobiography. Given Vico's conception of language and of the life of the civil world as rooted in the fable, it is unnecessary for him explicitly to say, as Descartes does in the *Discourse*, that his text can be read as a fable. Descartes must say it because the reader does not know how to take what he says about himself. In fact, many readers have missed Descartes's claim about the fable entirely. The fable is the substructure of Vico's life of himself as it is the substructure of the life of the nation.

I do not mean that Vico has made a fable of himself in the same way that the first men made the first fables. The original power of *fantasia* from which the first fables are made is not as such available to the modern mind, which is not able literally to assume the mentality of its own origin. Vico's approach is Platonic in the general sense that Plato draws upon the myth to support and complete his dialectical exposition. Vico employs the faculty of *fantasia* as a basis for this philosophical narration. The *New Science* is not only based on a theory of 'poetic wisdom' (*sapienza poetica*), but the work itself, as many commentators have noted, has a poetic dimension. Vico's autobiography is a philosophical narration, just as he claims it is, but this narration draws upon the power of the fable for Vico to form and convey the basic truths of

[3] See above, Chapter 1, nn. 50 and 51.

his life as a philosopher. Vico does not feign a narration in order to introduce the perspective of his philosophy; instead he presents a narration that draws upon the very fundamentals of narration itself. Vico writes his work, as he says, as a historian. But history for Vico is never simply the story of events, nor even a developmental account of them. History for Vico is 'idea eternal', that is, history has a divine structure. Fables are the means by which the first men give form to the actions of the divine; in fables is captured the providential order of events. The prophetic and providential order Vico wishes to find in the events of his own life necessitates that the language of the fable runs through the narration or story of these events, with various of them being presented by Vico as signs of this order.

The place to begin to understand the *Autobiography* in the terms I have stated above is Vico's first paragraph, which I have translated in such a way as to bring out, so far as possible in English, how Vico says things in it. Not all paragraphs in the *Autobiography* are so closely constructed; most are not, and none equal it in establishing the structure of the work. I wish to go through this paragraph sentence by sentence, because from it a great deal about the rest of the work can be learned. My aim is not a full *explication de texte*. I wish to focus on certain passages about which I believe I have something to say and which will allow the reader to see how Vico's autobiography is a genuine part of his philosophy and not simply the story of his life. This is not to say that it is not the story of his life; it is of course at least that, as, in some sense, is any autobiography.

Within the *corso* of Vico's life three stages can be discerned that are analogous to the three ages of the life of any nation in the *New Science*. The divisions of this chapter are made according to this analogue. In the ideal eternal history of Vico's life the age of gods corresponds to his fall, early education, and self-teaching at Vatolla. In this period, as in the age of gods, Vico is articulating and making his world. On his return to Naples from Vatolla he enters a new world in which he is a stranger and in which he undergoes the trial of the loss of the university concourse. This corresponds to the age of heroes. Vico, the heroic mind, embodying certain virtues, endures the injustice of the failure of the concourse but, with a prudence that accords with providence, he surmounts the difficulty and achieves the great discovery of the *New Science*.

This corresponds to what in the Fisch and Bergin translation is called Part B of the original 1728 Venice text of the *Autobiography*.

Following this zenith of heroic mind Vico enters the age of humans, in which he is no longer making the meanings of a new world but living in *this* world of modern life. The age of humans is typified by a 'barbarism of reflection' (1106) which is accompanied by a solitude of spirit and will and the language of wit and flattery. This corresponds to Vico's 1731 continuation of his autobiography, in which he portrays himself as coping with the barbarism of the actual historical age of humans in which he lives. The retrospective account of his success with various commissioned works, etc., with which he begins his continuation, presents a rather unattractive portrait of Vico overcome by and attached to the superficialities of such a world of humans. His text closes with Vico, as a solitary ancient existing among moderns, ascending to his desk as if to a citadel. His life will continue this way, among barbarians, until his death.

Vico's account of his own life begins with his fall and with his establishment of the method by which he will tell it.

[Il] *signor Giambattista Vico, he* [egli] *was born in Naples in the year 1670 of upright parents* [onesti parenti], *who left behind them a very good reputation.* Jean Starobinski, in his conception of style in autobiography (as mentioned in Chapter 2), has suggested that an autobiography is a mixed entity that can be called 'discourse-history'.[4] By referring to himself in the third person Vico increases the sense that this is a history, not a discourse in the sense of a monologue, as Descartes creates with his abstract *I*. But Vico goes further than this and creates the sense of biography, of the telling of one of the great lives such as can be found in classical and humanist literature. In the first line Vico refers to himself by his full name and as *Il signor*. *Il* (literally, 'the') is used when talking about someone, not to refer to oneself. It is naturally used in writing about a historical person. *Il signor* is very formal, and Vico's addition of *egli* ('he') makes the construction even more formal. Vico puts himself at a great distance by this construction, as if he were talking about another person.

Vico gives his birth-date as 1670 rather than the actual date of

---

[4] J. Starobinski, 'The Style of Autobiography', in S. Chatman, ed., *Literary Style: A Symposium* (London: Oxford University Press, 1971), 288.

two years earlier, 1668. All modern editions of the *Autobiography* note this. It is a point that requires a great deal of consideration and I wish to delay my remarks on it for the moment. Vico's description of his parents as 'upright' (*onesti parenti*) is most probably intended to echo Petrarch's phrase in his *Epistle to Posterity* concerning his parents—*honestis parentibus.*[5] In making this reference Vico may also have meant to imply what Petrarch says about his parents, namely, that they were of 'middling means' (*fortuna mediocri*) and, as Petrarch adds, that to tell the truth they were on the edge of poverty. Vico's parents were certainly of this condition. Perhaps the reason that Vico violates that part of Porcìa's instructions, that authors were to begin by giving their parents' names, is that his parents' names meant nothing. His family could claim no status except that they were 'upright'. Although Vico, unlike Petrarch, was born not in exile but in his native city, he may have felt as though he were born in such conditions.

The father [il padre] *was of cheerful humour* [umore allegro], *the mother of a quite melancholy temper* [tempra assai malinconica]; *and both came together in the fair disposition* [naturalezza] *of this little son of theirs* [questo lor figliuolo]. Instead of saying simply 'his father' (*suo padre*) and 'his mother' (*sua madre*) Vico refers to his parents as 'the father' and 'the mother', which begins to read like a notary's record of the circumstances of his birth. Then Vico turns from this very formal statement to a description of himself as 'this little son of theirs'. This kind of tender statement, using the dimunitive *figliuolo* to describe himself, and speaking of his *naturalezza*, a word that carries a sense of balance and spontaneity, heightens the shock, for the reader, of the fall that literally takes Vico off balance and robs him of his *naturalezza*. Before his fall he is of a natural disposition, balancing within himself the *allegrezza* of his father and the *malinconia* of his mother. The fall eliminates the side of his character that he derives

---

[5] F. Petrarca, *Prose*, ed. G. Martellotti (Milan: Ricciardi, 1955), 6. See also A. Pons, *Vie de Giambattista Vico écrite par lui-même* (Paris: Grasset, 1981), 45 n. 13. Pons points out that the use of Petrarch's *honestis parentibus* had become a convention of Italian autobiographical writing. Giannone employs it in his autobiography. See *Opere di Pietro Giannone*, ed. S. Bertelli and G. Ricuperati (Milan: Ricciardi, 1971), 15.

from his father and emphasizes the side that he acquires from his mother.

As a boy he was very lively [spiritosissimo] and restless [impaziente di riposo]; but at the age of 7 he fell head-first [col capo in giù] from high on a ladder to the floor, and remained a good five hours motionless [senza moto] and senseless [privo di senso], fracturing the right side of the cranium without breaking the skin, hence from the fracture arose a shapeless tumour, and from the many deep lancings of it the child lost a great deal of blood; such that the surgeon, having observed the broken cranium and considering the long state of unconsciousness, made the prediction that either he would die of it or he would survive stolid [stolido]. In the first part of this compound sentence Vico adds another dualism to that of the characters of his father and mother by saying that he was 'very lively' and 'restless'; this also underscores the sense of himself as active and in motion before his fall. The sense of the Italian is that just in being a boy, just in the fact that he was a boy, he had these characteristics. Vico, like his first men, 'the children of the human race', is a natural being, full of spontaneity and active, running about in the world.

The sudden fall from the ladder is almost biblical, but it also has a Greek sense of *moira*, of establishing the conditions of his future fortune and fate. Just by exercising his natural human property of restlessness he falls, and is forever deprived of his childhood Eden. Yet his fall is part of a providential order that gives him the nature of a philosopher. The fall happens to him; it is not punishment for a transgression, and in this sense it is not fully biblical. His fall is a birth or rebirth sequence, as he falls 'head-first' (analogous to the position in the birth canal), and from the fall he is born as a different person. The surgeon makes the prediction, based on the human order of knowledge, that he will either die or survive 'stolid'.

Vico's term here is *stolido*, which is related to the Latin *stultus*, 'foolish'. It is not 'idiot', as in the Fisch and Bergin translation. To be stolid is to be slow-witted, dull, to be foolish due to mental thickness. Vico uses this as a contrasting term to his active character before the fall. He would either die or become slow-moving, slow-witted. Tommasèo, *Nuovo dizionario dei sinonimi della lingua italiana*, contrasts the stolid person and the fatuous person as two forms of human stupidity: *lo stolido* is rough, inept;

il fatuo is empty, airy. 'Stolidness', he says, is more *visibile*; 'fatuousness' is more ridiculous (*risibile*). In contrasting stolidity with imbecility, Tommasèo says the former tends to annoy and the latter invites compassion.[6] In the surgeon's prediction of death or surviving stolid, Vico has introduced another pair of opposites— the literal continuance of his motionless and senseless state as death, or its continuance as a kind of mental death, mental inactivity. As Tommasèo also points out, fatuousness can have the appearance of ingenuity, as can be present in the actions of fools (one thinks of Erasmus's encomium of folly), but stolidity can never involve ingenuity or its appearance.

However, neither of the two parts of this judgement [giudizio], *by the grace of God, came true; but as a result of this illness and recovery he grew up, from then on, with a melancholy and acrid nature* [una natura malinconica ed acre] *which necessarily belongs to ingenious and profound men* [uomini ingegnosi e profondi], *who through ingenuity flash like lightning in acuity* [che per l'ingegno balenino in acutezze], *through reflection* [riflessione] *take no pleasure in witticism and falsity* [dell'arguzie e del falso]. The surgeon's judgement, made from the human order of knowledge, is countermanded by the divine, providential order—God's grace. Vico's character, as a result of his fall and recovery, this second birth, is transformed from a balance between his father's *allegrezza* and his mother's *malinconia* to a new combination of melancholy and acrimony. Vico now adds several more pairs of terms to his dualistic construction of his fall: ingenious and profound; ingenuity and acuity versus witticism and falsity; and ingenuity versus reflection.

'Ingenuity' (Italian *ingegno*; Latin *ingenium*) is a term which runs throughout Vico's writings. In the *New Science* Vico describes *ingegno* as one of the aspects of memory which occurs when we give things a new turn or put things 'into proper arrangement and relationship' (819). *Ingegno*, in Vico's view, is a faculty different from intellect or from mind; *ingegno* is specifically a faculty of seeing relationships between things which can result, as Fisch puts it, 'on the one hand in analogy, simile, metaphor, and on the other

---

[6] N. Tommasèo, *Nuovo dizionario dei sinonimi della lingua italiana* (4th rev. edn., Milan, 1858), entries 2875 and 2877.

in scientific hypotheses'.[7] And as Fisch also points out: *'natura* and *ingenium* were synonyms. Elsewhere *(Opere*, i, 212) Vico had said that as nature of the divine *ingenium* generates physical things, so the human *ingenium* generates mechanical objects or artifacts.'[8] *Ingegno* is an original and originating power of mind that works together with *fantasia* (imagination) and *memoria* to make it possible for the first men to transpose what they sense and feel through their bodies into the orders and relationships they express in their fables. *Ingegno* is a faculty whereby thought attains to its beginning points or principles, its *archai*. *Ingegno* is a power to make in the human world what the divine makes in nature, and since it is presupposed by the fable, in Vico's view, it is the power whereby the divine order of nature is first apprehended.

Vico's connection of ingenuity or *ingegno* with lightning is a reference to the primordial phenomenon of Jove out of which the thought and life of any nation arises. In identifying himself with the class of 'ingenious and profound men', Vico uses the verb *balenare*, which is literally 'to flash with lightning'. When the giants that roam the earth after the biblical flood apprehend the thundering sky as Jove, they form the first human thought, as Vico elaborates in both the *First* and the *Second New Science*. Jove is the first poetic character or 'imaginative universal', the first name that is formed in the minds of the first men. Once the first men can form their perception of the sky full of thunder and lightning as the god Jove, they possess the power of the name and they can name all things as gods. Vico's epigraph for the *First New Science* is: *A Iove principium musae, Virgilio*. In his annotations to the *Second New Science* Vico says, 'If one does not begin from "a god who to all men is Jove" one cannot have any idea either of science or of virtue' (1212; cf. 415).[9] His theory of Jove runs throughout both the *First* and *Second New Science*.

The fear the first men experience, of Jove's thunder and lightning flashes, is the origin of man's senses of the divine and of virtue, which lead to the three principles of humanity—religion, marriage,

---

[7] *The Autobiography of Giambattista Vico*, trans. M. H. Fisch and T. G. Bergin (Ithaca, NY: Cornell University Press, 1983), 216 n. 141.

[8] Ibid. 218 n. 162.

[9] *La scienza nuova prima*, paras. 104–7. Vico's conception of Jove runs throughout the theory of 'poetic wisdom' of bk. 2 of the *New Science* (1730, 1744), see esp. 374–84.

and burial.[10] Jove's hurling of thunderbolts is the first act of divine acuity apprehended by the first men (who, as Vico claims, were all body, and thought with their bodies). This causes the first act of human acuity—the making of the first name—and remains as the power of acuity in the minds of ingenious men. Before his fall Vico is like the giants who roam the world after the deluge—a natural being, full of activity. As a result of his recovery from the fall Vico is reborn as a thinking being, with his character formed around his faculty of ingenuity.

The analogy is not perfect because Vico is reborn, not simply with the *fantasia* of the first poets, but with the melancholic and acrid temperament of the philosophical thinker. In his connection of ingenuity with melancholy Vico, I think, is echoing Cicero's statement in the *Tusculanae disputationes* concerning Aristotle's connection of these two properties of the thinker. Cicero says: 'Aristotle indeed affirms, all ingenious men to be melancholic' (*Aristoteles quidem ait, omnes ingeniosos melancholicos esse*) (*Tusc.* I. xxxiii. 80). Cicero has in mind Aristotle's first sentence in Book 30 of the *Problems:* 'Why is it that all men who have become outstanding in philosophy, statesmanship, poetry or the arts are melancholic?' (*Prob.* xxx. 1). It is very likely that Vico intends his statement to be a paraphrase of Cicero's paraphrase of Aristotle. As Vico is taking his ingenuity back to the Jove-experience of the first men, the poets of the human race, so he is taking its connection with melancholy back to the first philosophers, the Greeks.

Vico claims his melancholy to be the result of his fall. How is his fall a cause of this classic humour of the philosophical thinker and those who achieve greatness generally? The modern understanding of melancholy derives from Robert Burton's three-volume work, written in the early 1600s, *The Anatomy of Melancholy*, one of the great encyclopaedic works of Western thought. Burton's text draws together the classic views of the subject. In the first volume Burton discusses the causes of melancholy, beginning with its general causes, and in the final few pages of the volume he turns to 'particular causes' or specifically 'how the body works on the

---

[10] *La scienza nuova prima*, para. 59. Vico's phrase is *un dio ch'a tutti è Giove*, which paraphrases Tasso's *Gerusalemme liberata*, *Testimone e quel Dio ch'a tutti è Giove* (iv. 42) and Virgil's *Aeneid*, *rex Iuppiter omnibus idem* (x. 112).

mind'. He distinguishes three forms of such bodily caused melancholy—'head-melancholy', 'hypochondriacal or windy melancholy', and 'melancholy from the whole body'. Within each of these he distinguishes 'inward' from 'outward' causes, that is, causes from within the body as opposed to things that happen to the body from without it.

In discussing the brain as a cause Burton states: 'The brain is a familiar and frequent cause, too hot, or too cold, "through adust blood so caused", as Mercurialis will have it, "within or without the head", the brain itself being distempered.'[11] In this passage Burton appears to be establishing the brain as an 'inward' cause, and in the following section he proceeds to show that such a state of the brain can have an 'outward' cause. In this section titled 'Causes of Head-Melancholy' he states: 'As, for example, head-melancholy is commonly caused by a cold or hot distemperature of the brain, according to Laurentius, *Cap. 5, de melan.* but as Hercules de Saxoniâ contends, from that agitation of distemperature of the animal spirits alone. . . . It [melancholy] follows many times "frenzy, long disease, agues, long abode in hot places, or under the sun, a blow on the head", as Rhasis informeth us.'[12] The crucial phrase here is 'a blow on the head', as one of the classic outward causes of melancholy.

Burton's second volume is a discussion of the symptoms of melancholy. Under his discussion of general 'symptoms, or signs of melancholy in the body' he writes: 'Those usual signs appearing in the bodies of such as are melancholy, be these cold and dry, or they are hot and dry, as the humour is more or less adust. . . . Hippocrates in his book *de insania et melan.* reckons up these signs, that they are "lean, withered, hollow-eyed, look old, wrinkled, harsh. . . ."'[13] As mentioned earlier, Nicola Solla, a disciple and author of a brief biography of Vico, gives the following physical description of Vico: 'His stature was of medium height, his body tended to be adust [*l'abito del corpo adusto*] . . .'.[14] The key word is 'adust' (*adusto*)—a parched, tanned, wizened look (see

---

[11] R. Burton, *The Anatomy of Melancholy* (3 vols., London: John C. Nimmo, 1893), i. 493.
[12] Ibid. i. 496.
[13] Ibid. ii. 4.
[14] *L'autobiografia, il carteggio e le poesie varie*, 2nd rev. edn., *Opere di G. B. Vico*, ed. B. Croce and F. Nicolini, vol. v (Bari: Laterza, 1929), 133.

also the reference in the passage quoted from Burton to 'adust blood' as a cause). Solla is, of course, describing the mature Vico, who in fact has this 'adust' 'melancholic' appearance in the one portrait that survives of him. Solla mentions Vico's *ingegno* in the next sentence of his description, but he does not use the word *malinconica* for Vico's temperament. He does mention Vico's *collerico temperamento*, reflecting Vico's own attribution to himself of this characteristic at the end of the autobiography (199/86).

In saying that he was 'choleric to a fault' (*peccò nella collera*) Vico attributes to himself a second of the four humours. He is both melancholic and choleric (the other classic humours being sanguine and phlegmatic). Vico's claim to be choleric reflects his description of himself as *acre* at the end of the first paragraph of his autobiography. The choleric temperament is originally understood by Galen as producing keen perception and wit, but later it came to connote a kind of abrupt or acrimonious nature, that Vico says was combined with his melancholy as a result of his fall. This acrimoniousness may be a transformation or sublimation of the 'restlessness' that he claims was part of his childhood nature before his fall. Marsilio Ficino claims that adustion is common to both the melancholic and the choleric (*De vita*, I. v).

Vico's last words of his opening paragraph distinguish himself, as part of the class of ingenious and profound men, from those who employ reflection only to achieve 'witticism' and 'falsity'. With this statement about the misuse of reflection (*riflessione*) Vico is placing himself in the later stages of his cycle of ideal eternal history. In the *First New Science* Vico puts this in the following way: 'Men commonly first attend to necessity, thereafter to comfort, then to pleasure, beyond this to luxury or surplus, finally fall into a fury of excess and throw away their substance.'[15] Vico's comment about the misuse of reflection looks forward to the powerful passage in his conclusion to the *Second New Science*, where he describes the decline of society: 'Through long centuries of barbarism, rust will consume the misbegotten subtleties of malicious wits [*degl'ingegno maliziosi*] that have turned them into beasts made more inhuman by the barbarism of reflection [*la barbarie della riflessione*] than the first men had been made by the barbarism of sense' (1106). In the last stages of a nation's life

---

[15] *La scienza nuova prima*, para. 125.

ingenuity loses its connection with imagination and the insight that leads to the fable and turns in upon itself. Thought loses its original power of insight and becomes reflection on itself, dwelling on and displaying its powers of abstraction and criticism, the excesses of which parallel the excesses of social life in which modern men throw away their substance (cf. 241).

In the space of the first page of his autobiography Vico has brought himself through a whole course, from his birth to his adult character as a philosopher, ending with his conception of barbarity and falsity, which applies to the atmosphere he finds himself in with the injustice of the loss of the concourse, the need to sell his ring to publish the *First New Science*, etc. In his continuation of 1731 he ends with an explicit discussion of this theme, yet his original text of 1728 also ends with it, but not as explicitly.

If the beginning paragraph of the *Autobiography* is now looked at diagrammatically, it can be seen how Vico's two senses of motion that can be found within his philosophy are incorporated into this passage. The diagram (Fig. 5.1) is intended as a means whereby the reader can visualize this passage, not as a precise structure showing all its features. It does not show precisely how all the pairs of terms and opposites stand in relation to each other but it brings out how many of these Vico has used in such a short space. It shows that Vico takes on the melancholy of his mother, which may be parallel to his boyhood restlessness. In one place Burton, in his symptoms of melancholy, says: 'Inconstant they are in all their actions, vertigious, restless . . . restless, I say, fickle, fugitive, they may not abide to tarry in one place long.'[16]

Vico's restlessness (*impaziente di riposo*) may be the root of his melancholy in his state of *naturalezza*, but he loses the balance he had within his character with the cheerfulness he had inherited from his father. He physically loses his balance in the fall, and the balance of his spirit is also lost to the side of melancholy. This observation is not out of place given the body–mind parallel that runs throughout Vico's account of the development of humanity. Pairs of opposites run throughout Vico's work, between imaginative and intelligible universals, the barbarism of sense and that of reflection, the vulgar and esoteric wisdom, philosophy and philology, true and certain, giants and humans, gentiles and Hebrews,

---

[16] Burton, *Melancholy*, ii. 15–16.

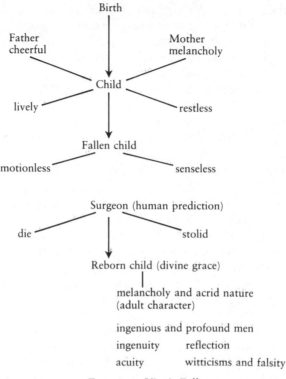

FIG. 5.1. Vico's Fall

gentile history and sacred history. A cyclic and oppositional structure (or at least a pairing of terms) is common to the *New Science* and the *Autobiography*.

The first paragraph has the organization of a Vichian cycle—there is Vico the natural child, Vico the fallen child who heroically survives, and Vico the reborn child with the nature of the adult philosopher. Each of these stages is dominated by a pair of terms: natural child—lively and restless; fallen child—die or stolid; reborn child—melancholic and ingenious.

HIS HEROIC MIND

In his oration of 1732, *De mente heroica*, delivered four years after the original publication of his autobiography, and in the year following his continuation of it, Vico advances the term 'heroic mind' as the summary term of his conception of human education. He urges the students in the audience to manifest the heroic mind 'through studies'. He says that he is not choosing his words lightly. Heroes, according to the poets, claim divine descent from Jove, and Vico says this symbolizes the fact that the mind has a near divine nature. The philosophers, Vico says, define 'hero' as 'one who seeks ever the sublime [*qui sublimia appetit*]'.[17] Vico connects this with Christian doctrine and concludes that to seek the sublime is to discover for the good of humanity all the marvels within nature. To do this is to discover the divine in nature and also to discover the full power of the divine element in each human, the power of mind.

Vico connects his conception of heroic mind with his earlier conception of wisdom (*sapientia*), which he equates with the idea of a university and which he says Plato defines 'as purge, curative, completion of the inner man'.[18] Wisdom, in Vico's view, is necessarily connected to piety because to cultivate wisdom is to pursue the sublime task of attempting to grasp the whole, which can never be grasped perfectly, but to the extent it can, the nature of the divine is revealed to the knower. Vico's last words in the *Second New Science* are an equation of piety and wisdom: 'that he who is not pious cannot be truly wise' (1112). In his oration Vico concludes: 'Cultivate knowledge as a whole. Celebrate the near divine nature of your minds. Take fire from the god who fills you . . . Undergo herculean trials, which, once passed, vindicate with perfect justice your divine descent from true Jove, Him the greatest and best. Prove yourselves to be heroes by enriching the human race with further giant benefits.'[19]

It has been said that Vico looks at history and never smiles, but that, of his three ages, the middle one, of the hero, is for him the best. The heroic stands between the 'barbarism of sense' of the first age and the 'barbarism of reflection' of the third. The hero has not lost the power of *fantasia* to form the things of the civil world, and

---

[17] 'On the Heroic Mind', trans. E. Sewell and A. C. Sirignano in G. Tagliacozzo, M. Mooney, and D. P. Verene, eds., *Vico and Contemporary Thought* (Atlantic Highlands, NJ: Humanities Press, 1979), 230. 'De mente heroica' in *Scritti vari e pagine sparse, Opere di G. B. Vico*, ed. F. Nicolini, vol. vii (Bari: Laterza, 1940), 9.
[18] 'On the Heroic Mind', 233.
[19] Ibid. 244.

yet his energies are directed to the formation of virtues which, with the coming of the philosophers, can be understood by reason. Understood within the principles of his philosophy, Vico's conception of 'heroic mind' is that form of mind wherein the philosopher directs his thought back toward virtue and that holistic and sublime sense of the world which is the theatre of the hero's deeds. The philosopher cannot act in the manner of the hero because he does not actually make the things of the civil world through virtuous deeds. The philosopher can think heroically by placing himself between the *fantasia* of bodily sense and the abstract reason of reflection. The philosopher, although always existing only in the third age of a nation's history, aims to think from the middle age. This piety to the wholeness of the origin in Jove and the heroic transformation of it into the imaginative articulation of human virtue determines the agenda for Vico's view of human education.

Vico does not use the term 'heroic mind' in the *Autobiography* but I wish to apply the term to two moments in it: to Vico's education of himself at Vatolla and to his discovery of the *New Science* in 1725. 'Heroic mind' is a term that can in fact be applied across the whole of Vico's account of his career because it describes Vico's own struggle and concept of himself, as suggested in the above-quoted passage—his 'herculean trials' and his vindication 'with perfect justice', his own enrichment of the human race with his discovery of his new science. 'Heroic mind' fits the portrait of himself seated at the altar of his desk that he gives at the end of the work. Vico intends his description of his own education to accord with his theory of education, and to emphasize this he quotes a very long passage from one of his later university orations, stating his themes of education in the model of his own description of his self-education at Vatolla (123–5/15–17). Vico's conception of heroic mind applied to his own case is his conception of himself as 'autodidact'.

Autobiographers and theorists of the nature of autobiography agree that the author of an autobiography must tell the truth or appear to the reader to tell the truth. What telling the truth about one's life means is problematic and divides various schools of autobiographical criticism, and even autobiographers themselves, but that an autobiography must make a truth claim is a point of general agreement. For example, Montaigne, Giannone, and Rousseau begin by emphasizing to the reader how much they are concerned to tell only the truth. But Vico's claim that he spent nine years at Vatolla, isolated in the Cilento, is what Nicolini calls Vico's *fictio*. And Fisch says of it: 'Now the *chief defect of detail in Vico's autobiography* is that it not only exaggerates his isolation from the new philosophy during his Vatolla years (1686–95), but represents him as having taken up a position against it when he did become acquainted with it, a position which in fact he did not approach until about 1708, and did not fully reach before 1720.'[20] Vico appears simply to lie, in the first part of his sentence, when he says of the end of his period at Vatolla: 'With this learning and erudition Vico returned to Naples a stranger in his own land, and found the physics of Descartes at the height of its renown among the established men of letters' (132/23). He returns to Ithaca to find that all the suitors to the queen of the sciences have assumed Cartesian guise.

But, as Fisch claims, 'Actually, moreover, Vico became a Cartesian and remained so until his own original doctrine began to emerge; that is, until about the age of forty. Indeed, the greatest critic of Descartes was himself the greatest Cartesian of Italy.'[21] Fisch holds that Vico has read his later position against Cartesianism into his early period. He does not say why he thinks Vico has done this, but he, and others, find it regrettable. I suggest that the situation is even worse. Vico's *fictio* involves more than the simple distortion that he lived in isolation at Vatolla only to return to Naples and experience the surprise that the Cartesian philosophy had taken over the intellectual climate. I believe that this is part of a larger pattern of Vico's text that he has deliberately engaged in, for reasons that I will try to discover. Vico's claim to have returned as a 'stranger in his own land' helps to reinforce his claim to have been an 'autodidact', a teacher of himself. In fact Vico at this time was pursuing studies in law at the University of Naples. This, however, can be considered as part of a pattern of altering the facts of his life that Vico has pursued in his narration from the beginning. It is connected with his alteration of his birth-date in the first sentence of his autobiography.

Vico gives his date of birth as 1670 instead of 1668. That Vico was born on 23 June 1668 there is no doubt. This is stated in the

---

[20] Fisch, Introduction to *Autobiography*, 35–6. My emphasis.
[21] Ibid. 36.

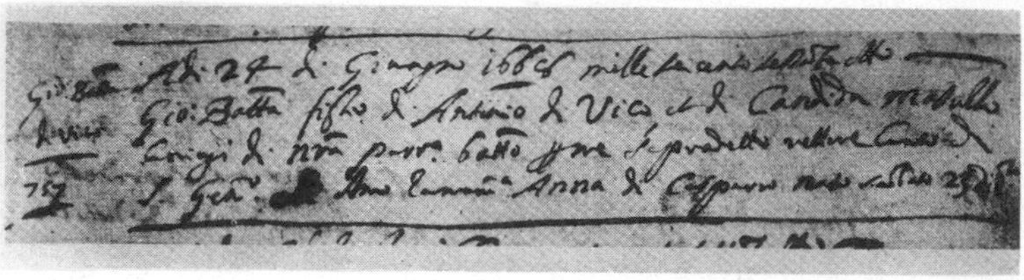

FIG. 5.2. Record of Vico's Baptism

parish book of S. Gennaro all'Olmo that records Vico's baptism, which took place the day after his birth (see Fig. 5.2).[22] Vico must have known the year of his own birth; his priest knew it and his family and friends knew it. It was a matter of local church record. The *atto di battesimo* of Vico was noted by Villarosa, and all critical editions of Vico's *Autobiography* carry a notation identifying Vico's birth-date as 1668 rather than 1670 (Pomodoro's edition of 1858 simply changes the date to 1668 in the text, giving the reader no indication that Vico's original states 1670). Editors make this as a simple correction for the reader; no editor knows what to say about it by way of explanation. In his early study of materials on Vico's life, Nicolini in *Per la biografia di Giambattista Vico* (1925) offers the following speculation: 'Neither would it be impossible that, at that moment precisely, in order not to make him appear too old in front of his fellow students, his parents might have introduced in his certificate of baptism a verbal retouching [*un ritocco verbale*], that induced him consequently to believe that he was born in 1670.'[23] Jacobelli takes this as the actual explanation, saying in her *G. B. Vico: La vita e le opere* (1960) that the father of Vico wished to spare his son 'the

---

[22] The lines in the parish book recording Vico's baptism, which are illustrated in Fig. 5.2, read: 'Gio Battā di Vico—A dì 24 di giugno 1668—milleseicentosessantotto—Gio Battā figlio di Antonio di Vico, et di Candida Masullo Coniugi di nra parrᵃ bātto per me sopradᵒ D. Giuseppe And. Campanile rettore Curato di S. Gennaro all'Olmo la Mámᵃ. Anna di Casparre nato sabbato 23 dᵒ.' In *Libro VIII (1656–1690) della Parrocchia di S. Gennaro all'Olmo*, fo. 64 n. 757.

[23] Nicolini, *Per la biografia di Giambattista Vico*, extracts from *Archivio storico italiano*, 2 parts (Florence: Olschki, 1925–6), i. 214.

humiliation of going to school several years late' because of the
long recovery from his fall.[24] Pons, in his authoritative notes to his
French translation of the *Autobiography*, says, 'We leave to others
the concern of explaining or interpreting this error.'[25]

Nicolini does not continue to push this early speculation on
Vico's birth-date in his later writings on Vico's life. No explanation
is offered in the notes to the Laterza edition of the *Autobiography*,
only the factual correction of the birth-date. Vico was in his fifties
in 1725, when he wrote the first part of his autobiography. Would
he, after all these years, decide to give his age according to this
ritocco verbale? Would he not ever have known his own birth-
date, even if his father had modified it to the school officials, when
all the mothers of other children, and the neighbours in his quarter
of the city in the close-knit society of Naples would have known
the year he was born? Mediterranean culture has always placed
importance on knowing the ages of everyone in one's family, and
of one's friends and associates, as part of the common wisdom
required for conducting human affairs.

What Nicolini says could be true, that a kind of family tradition
of Vico's birth-date of 1670 was established, and that Vico came
to hold this as the year of his birth. Gennaro appears to have more
or less followed the birth-date of the *Autobiography* in placing his
memorial inscription, as discussed in Chapter 1 above. Yet the
possibility Nicolini raises is problematic on the face of it. In the
Autobiography Vico says that he returned to the grammar school
(*restituitosi alla scuola della grammatica*) (111/3). In the notes to
the Laterza edition of the *Autobiography* Nicolini and Croce
comment that Vico returned, after his three years of convalescence,
to the school he had been attending before his fall.[26] Indeed, this is
the meaning of what Vico says; no commentator to my knowledge
has thought otherwise. How could his father hope to spare his son
any 'humiliation', by falsifying his age, when he returned after his
fall to a school which would have already known his age when he
was originally enrolled as a pupil, before his fall? Nicolini often
advances a homely explanation of puzzling or somewhat unpleas-
ant facts concerning Vico's life, such as his explanation of the

[24] A. M. Jacobelli Isoldi, *G. B. Vico: La vita e le opere* (Bologna: Cappelli,
1960), 95.
[25] Pons, *Vie de Giambattista Vico*, 44 n. 13.
[26] *L'autobiografia*, ed. Croce and Nicolini, 105.

reputation for laziness of Vico's wife by the hypothesis of a possible confusion of her with the wife of Ignazio.[27] Nicolini himself does not elaborate this speculation about Vico's birth-date, and Jacobelli is the only commentator I have found to repeat it.

A number of other possibilities may be considered. One hypothesis that must cross the reader's mind is whether Vico's birth-date could simply be a printer's error. Vico does complain, in his continuation of 1731, that the printer made many errors, 'even in important passages' (187/75). In fact, the second number of the *Raccolta* (1729) has at the end a page of elaborate apology by the printer for having made so many errors in the first number (perhaps this was the result of Vico's complaints).[28] Although the possibility of a printer's error seems plausible on first glance, it must be dismissed. In describing his defence of his father in the court case brought against him by another bookseller, Vico gives his age as 16 (*in età di sedici anni*) (117/9). Since this was a process of the public courts, its date can be established as 20 June 1686. This was three days before Vico's eighteenth birthday. Yet in his autobiography Vico reports this in accordance with his birth-date of 1670. This is the only place in the *Autobiography* where Vico gives his age precisely, and he gives it in relation to an event that can be independently dated.[29] Vico certainly intended to state his year of birth as 1670.

There is one other place where Vico mentions his age. In his continuation of 1731 he says he was 'an old man of 60' (*essendo vecchio di sessant'anni*) (189/77) when he heard of the unfavourable book notice in the Leipzig *Acta*, to which he wrote a reply, now known as *Vici vindiciae* (1729). The number of the *Acta* which carried this notice had the publication date of August 1727. Vico claims in the first sentence of his reply that a friend had brought this number of the *Acta* to his attention only in August 1729 (i.e. two years after its publication).[30] If we take seriously this date of his first awareness of the Leipzig review, Vico would just have completed his sixty-first year at his birthday two months earlier, according to his actual birth-date of 1668. Has Vico, in this

[27] See above, Chapter 1, esp. n. 38.

[28] *Raccolta d'opuscoli scientifici e filologici*, 2 (1729).

[29] One commentator who recognizes this is B. Donati, *Nuovi studi sulla filosofia civile di G. B. Vico* (Florence: Le Monnier, 1936), 37–9.

[30] *Vici vindiciae* in *Opere*, iii. 295.

continuation of his autobiography, deliberately gone back to his true birth-date, or does he mean the term in a kind of general sense of being 'in his sixties'? Reckoning by the 1670 birth-date, he would have just celebrated his fifty-ninth birthday and would be entering his sixtieth year of life, but he would not as yet have had his sixtieth birthday. Because of the variables of when Vico heard of the review and what he precisely means by sixty (as a precise age it does not fit either birth-date), this does not admit of as clear-cut interpretation as does the question of his age at the time of his father's court case.

How are we to understand Vico's alteration of his birth-date? Vico has errors in some of his dates throughout the *Autobiography* such as some of the years for his university orations; such errors Fisch simply corrects in the chronology at the end of his English translation. Battistini takes the view—and I am generally in sympathy with it—that Vico, and other autobiographers, by altering the actual chronology of the dates of events in their lives do not so much falsify the reality of them but, paradoxically, are thus able to express a deeper and more intimate structure that underlies the simple chronology of their life-events. Battistini refers to Starobinski's view of autobiography and especially to Olney's and Gusdorf's conception of autobiography as metaphor of the self.[31] Battistini discusses this view not as a specific explanation of the question of Vico's birth-date, but as a general view of the text. The one editor of Vico's *Autobiography*, V. F. Cassano, who attempts an explanation of Vico's birth-date in addition to his correction of it, employs an approach similar to the above: 'Vico was in reality born on 23 June 1668. The error, difficult to justify, might be explained only by considering the fact that he wrote the *Autobiography* more with the aim of showing the development of his thought than of narrating the events of his life.'[32] Although there is some general truth to this, it is hardly convincing as an explanation of why Vico altered this particular date and why by two years.

Vico's commentators generally accept that Vico, like any writer of

---

[31] A. Battistini, *La degnità della retorica: Studi su G. B. Vico* (Pisa: Pacini, 1975), 24 and 29. See also Battistini's 'L'autobiografia e i modelli narrativi settecenteschi', in P. Giannantonio, ed., *Cultura meridionale e letteratura italiana: I modeli narrativi dell'età moderna* (Naples: Loffredo, 1985), 145–90.

[32] V. F. Cassano, Introduction to *L'autobiografia* (Bologna: Cappelli, 1941), 3 n. 1.

his own life, has the liberty to present some events out of their actual sequence, and simply to misremember some of the dates and order of events, as long as this is done so the author can bring out certain features of his life, and so long as it is not done to excess or to create deliberate falsification. Such digressions from facts and dates are not usually seen as violations of the cardinal principle of the author's need to tell the truth. Certainly some discrepancies are due simply to errors of Vico's memory. But Vico's alteration of his own birth-date by two years is not of the same order of error as being off a year or more in citing the dates of some of his orations or other events.

Although the editors of the various editions of Vico's *Autobiography* have done their duty when they have informed the reader of the discrepancy in Vico's birth-date, the reader who wishes to understand the text cannot stop there. As readers of Vico's text we must at least entertain the hypothesis that Vico intends something for the reader by falsifying his birth-date. In so doing he violates one of the basic tenets of Aristotle's *Rhetoric*, that what the speaker says should be true and that the power of such is connected to the speaker's *ethos*. Vico consistently presents himself as the holder of virtue, the great truth-teller in the midst of 'witticism' and 'falsity'. The only specific model that Vico seems to be following in writing his autobiography is Descartes's *Discourse*, a text he is setting his own text against. As mentioned before, Vico says he will not 'feign' his account of himself as Descartes has done, but that he will make his narration (113/5) 'with ingenuousness fitting to a historian' (*con ingenuità dovuta da istorico*) Descartes's feigning is that of the logician—to produce his proof for inspection without any narration of how he arrived at it. Analogous to reciting a proof already discovered, Descartes presents the reader with just the tableau of himself in his chamber, making his discovery. He conceals the long process of thought and career that led to it. Although Descartes tells the reader that his work can be read as a fable or a history, the reader must imagine for himself the steps of Descartes's studies that led up to the discovery, as Leibniz, in his letter to Bourguet, says that we as readers must, when the author does not give them. Yet Descartes warns that historians do not tell the truth because they misrepresent, or exaggerate, or omit things.[33]

---

[33] Descartes, *Discours de la méthode*, chronology and preface by G. Rodis-Lewis (Paris: Garnier-Flammarion, 1966), 37.

Vico has a conception of history not as simple narration of the facts, but as narration of them in terms of their ideal eternal order as determined by providence. History forms its true story according to a structure that is already present in the construction of fables. Vico says: 'These fables are ideal truths suited to the merit of those of whom the vulgar tell them; and such falseness to fact as they contain consists simply in failure to give their subjects their due' (205). This gives priority to metaphysical truth: 'So that, if we consider the matter well, poetic truth is metaphysical truth, and physical truth which is not in conformity with it should be considered false' (ibid.). From this, Vico says, comes an important point in poetics: 'The true war chief, for example, is the Godfrey that Torquato Tasso imagines; and all the chiefs who do not conform throughout to Godfrey are not true chiefs of war' (ibid.).

The substructure of the fable of himself, the true thinker, upon which Vico builds the narration of the history of his own life, begins with him rounding off his own birth-date to the beginning of the decade—1670. Vico complains that Descartes has feigned the history of himself. Yet Vico has in the first sentence feigned his own birth-date. Descartes feigns the origin of his thought as being in the stove-heated chamber in Germany. Vico, with the 'ingenuousness' of the historian, feigns the date of his own origin. He does this as part of the philosophically formed history of the accidental series of events of his life. The truth of his life is not something given; it is something made in accordance with Vico's intention to display the providential structure of his own *corso*. Vico's historical 'candour' is not a simple frankness about historical facts.

Who is 'the signor Giambattista Vico' of the first sentence of Vico's *Autobiography*? Is he Vico giving the 'natural' history of his life? Or is he Vico shaping this history within a symbolic structure? Nicolini's suggestion of the *ritocco verbale* that Vico himself then came to believe presumes the first of these options—that Vico was simply writing his life-story. But Nicolini believes that later in his account Vico begins to formulate a *fictio* of himself. I suggest that Vico's *fictio* begins with the claim of his birth-date as 1670. Considered in this way, 1670 holds the possibility of a symbolic meaning connected to Vico's sense of the providential order of his life.

By placing the number seventy within his birth-date, Vico has placed his end in his beginning. Seventy years is the biblical life span allotted to humans. It is the figure which Dante plays upon in the first line of the *Divina commedia* and which is given in Psalms: 'The days of our years are three score years and ten' (Psalms 90:10) Vico is born at the end of the seventh decade of the century and he has seventy years to live. His birth is in biblical harmony with his death (in fact Vico lived past the age of 70, but these extra years, according to the Psalm, are not necessarily to be counted as an advantage). Writing this first line of his autobiography in his mid-fifties in 1725, Vico places within his own birthdate the number allotted by providence for the span of any human life.

In the *Dream of Scipio* with which he ends his *Republic*, Cicero says that the number seven is almost 'the key to the universe' (*De republica*, VI. xviii. 18). The number seven is associated with the World-Soul in Plato's *Timaeus* (35 B–C). Macrobius in his *Commentary* on Cicero's text of the *Dream of Scipio* says that this cosmological principle is the basis for why Scipio is told in the dream that at the age of 56, that is, at eight times seven, he will reach the perfection of his powers (*Comm.* I. vi. 3). Macrobius says that the number seven is made up of either one and six, two and five, or three and four. The first combination, that of one and six, he says, is called *monas* and is both male and female, odd and even, and is itself 'not a number but the source and origin of all numbers' (I. vi. 7). It is both beginning and ending of all things.

Philo of Alexandria cites a description of human life developed in terms of the number seven, attributed to Solon the lawgiver of the Athenians, which is also reflected in Hippocrates' conception of the nature of the child. This picture is built on the analogy of the infant becoming a full-fledged child in the period of seven years. This is the age at which the child is regarded to have attained the full power of language and at which the child has the reasoning faculty (*De opifico mundi*, 104–5; cf. *Legum allegoria* (i. 10). In Solon's account, in the eighth period of seven years, the man is 'strongest in insight and in powers of speech' (*De opifico mundi*, 104). He also affirms the tenth period of seven, or seventy years of age, to be the natural human life span. Philo says, echoing Pythagorean doctrine, that the number seven, unlike other numbers, is 'neither to beget nor to be begotten' (*De opifico mundi*,

99–100). Seven has a unique place within the decad. It is associated with the soul and with the idea of absolute beginning and with closure.

Macrobius, who summed up the Platonic account, had a great influence on medieval commentators, and views which he repeats from the ancient world emerge in various Renaissance works. There are two numerical streams of thought that come together in Renaissance thought—the biblical, and the divine arithmetic of Greek thought that is cosmologically based. The number seven occupies a similar position in both the Hebrew and pagan traditions and becomes Christianized in medieval and Renaissance traditions.

It is likely that Vico plays on the ancient character of the number seven in his act of making his own birth-date, a number which fits with his fall at 7 years of age and which, as a birth-date, contains one and six, then seven which, with the zero, symbolizes seventy— 1670. According to the birth-date he gives himself, he is just entering his fifty-sixth year in 1725 when he begins his autobiography (his fifty-fifth birthday being on 23 June of that year). This is the perfect age for the statesman's and hero's powers, according to the ancient text of Scipio's *Dream* (which features so strongly in the humanist and generally in the Italian historical and political imagination, especially as the subject of Petrarch's *Africa*). By his appropriated birth-date of 1670 Vico is just at the point in his life where, according to Solon, a man is at the greatest powers of insight and speech. This is when Vico writes the first part of his *Autobiography* and completes his first *New Science*. The number seven symbolizes the moment at which Vico finds himself presenting his own life. He is at this moment facing his intellectual enemies, as did Scipio his political ones.

Vico's fall when he was 7 (for which there is no independent verification) is connected with the symbolism of seventy in his birth-date. Since Vico presents this fall as a second birth sequence, then in the seven years before the fall he symbolically lives out a full life span (one year for each decade). In the fall he dies as a natural person; the natural temperament with which he was born vanishes. He is reborn with the nature of the philosophical thinker. His seven-year life as a child stands in relation to his full biblical life of three score and ten as microcosm to macrocosm. Providence has him complete a whole cycle as a child in order that he can acquire the nature that will govern the whole span of his life and account for his greatness.

Augustine, Vico's 'particular protector', was fascinated with the properties of number, and he discusses the importance of the number seven in a chapter of the *City of God* (xi. 31).[34] Augustine cites Proverbs 24: 16, 'For a righteous man falls seven times and rises again; but the wicked are overthrown by calamity'. Vico falls at the age of 7, but 'by the Grace of God' rises again, which is symbolic of his repeated 'falls' and 'risings again'—the discrimination against him in the 'diligences' for advancement in grammar school, the return from his sojourn in the Cilento as a 'stranger in his own land', the loss of the concourse for the chair of civil law, the withdrawal of financial support by Cardinal Corsini to publish the first *New Science*, the malicious notice of it in the Leipzig *Acta* by the *Ignotus erro*, the failure to employ the inscriptions commanded of him for the funeral rites of the Empress Eleanor, with those of another put up in their place, and the 'scheme' of the Venetian printers which caused Vico to withdraw the second *New Science* from their hands. After each of these calamities Vico rose again, and his detractors did not prevail. He could foresee, even when he wrote the first line of his autobiography, that his life would have these *ricorsi*. Misfortune would follow him even past that point at which he was writing his life. Offsetting misfortune was always the providential pattern of rising again that was established in the outcome of his original, physical fall. This pattern runs from the part of the autobiography published in 1728 through his continuation of it in 1731.

Vico's alteration of his date of birth to incorporate within it the number seventy is in accord with the practice of ancient historians. Alois Dreizehnter, in *Die rhetorische Zahl*, traces out how ancient writers used numbers, especially the number seven and variations on it.[35] The number of cities conquered, the size of groups, the number of years passed, the age of important figures, are often formed by ancient writers with regard to their rhetorical power rather than as an attempt to report actual fact. The number seven

[34] V. F. Hopper, *Medieval Number Symbolism: Its Sources, Meaning, and Influence on Thought and Expression* (New York: Cooper Square Publishers, 1969), 78–88.

[35] A. Dreizehnter, *Die rhetorische Zahl: Quellenkritische Untersuchungen anhand der Zahlen 70 und 700* (Munich: Beck, 1978).

multiplied by ten is particularly regarded as *numerus perfectionis* or *numerus universitatis*. A classic example in the use of number carrying rhetorical meaning is the use of seventy years as the maximum life span in reporting the age of Socrates. The primary sources for the age of Socrates at his death are Plato's *Crito* (52 E) and *Apology* (17 D). In the latter Socrates makes his famous statement that only now, at the age of 70, has he been brought into a law court for the first time. The date of Socrates' death is known, but not that of his birth. Diogenes Laertius reports that 'some say Socrates was 60 when he died' (2. 44).[36]

It is no accident that Vico concludes his fable of himself, in his continuation of 1731, with reference to the death of Socrates, whose life span of seventy years he had incorporated earlier into his own birth-date, in the first line of what he had published in 1728. Altering his own birth-date for rhetorical reasons, to give his beginning symbolic significance, is perfectly in accord with the sense of number in the ancient texts, upon which Vico always based his own work. If Vico does intend a symbolic significance in the alteration of his birth-date, then, in the first line of his work, he is deliberately employing a sense of number that stands in sharp contrast to the Cartesian view of numbers as ciphers in the process of right reasonings, and to numbers as indifferently representing historical facts.

Vico, like Roman and Renaissance writers before him, is deeply convinced of his own greatness and he intends his autobiography to demonstrate this. In response to Porcìa's proposal, Vico gives neither his correct birth-date nor his parents' names. His only true compliance with the first part of Porcìa's request is to give his correct place of birth, Naples, for whose glory, he later says, he was born. Because of Vico's themes of his isolation and poverty, the reader can easily forget that Vico is using these to demonstrate his own greatness and that he shares this aim with a long tradition of the writing of Latin lives.

Vico uses the description of his studies, from his return to grammar school after his fall to his return from Vatolla to Naples, to develop the central *topos* of his account of himself—what Battistini in his rhetorical analysis refers to as *l'isolamento del*

[36] Ibid. 70–81.

Vico, Vico's isolation, Vico as *isola*, as an island of himself.[37] Vico, who criticizes the solitude of the Stoics and of Descartes, presents himself as an isolated figure, and he does this first through his claim, which he proudly makes, of being an 'autodidact', a teacher of himself. He says that he was so called by Gregorio Caloprese, whom he describes as 'a great Cartesian philosopher' (130/22), and others; and Vico adds proudly, 'as Epicurus was called' (136/27). He earlier says that in his studies he took no pleasure in the moral philosophies of the Stoics or the Epicureans: 'For they are each a moral philosophy of solitaries: the Epicurean, of idlers enclosed in their own little gardens; the Stoic, of contemplatives who endeavor to feel no emotion' (122/14). Vico no doubt enjoys the irony of being like Epicurus, and, much more than is traditionally claimed, parts of the *New Science* are rooted in Italian Epicureanism and the *De rerum natura* of Lucretius, in particular his portrait of the development of language and society.

Vico's solitariness is typical of the melancholic thinker. When he returned to grammar school, he says that he began to work at night, sitting down to his desk at nightfall (112–13/4–5). His mother would wake and ask him to go to bed but would find, in the morning, that he had worked all night. Vico says this was a sign that he would become a scholar. It is also a sign of the melancholic. It is an example of the 'bat motif'. Klibansky, Panofsky, and Saxl, in *Saturn and Melancholy*, speak of the 'bat motif', which is a theme among Renaissance humanists: 'it served the Renaissance humanists (for better or for worse) as an example of night vigil or nightly work. According to Agrippa of Nettesheim its outstanding characteristic is "vigilantia" [wakefulness].'[38]

Melancholics are in astrological terms said to be children of Saturn, which Vico in the *New Science* many times reminds the reader has the Greek name Chronos and governs chronology or time (e.g. 73).[39] Raymond Lull held that the children of Saturn

---

[37] Battistini, *La degnità della retorica*, 32.

[38] R. Klibansky, E. Panofsky, and F. Saxl, *Saturn and Melancholy: Studies in the History of Natural Philosophy, Religion and Art* (London: Nelson, 1964), 323.

[39] The relationship between the four elements, earth, air, fire, and water, and the four humours, and the relation of the humours to the astrological interpretation of the planets is a vast subject which may have implications for Vico's portrayal of himself. I do not feel qualified to explore these. The astrological meanings of melancholy are expertly explained in *Saturn and Melancholy*. Vico certainly was a child of Saturn, but since Vico gives only his year of birth, and not even the day, he

'receive strong impressions from their imagination, which is more closely related to melancholy than to any other complexion'.[40] They were thought to have good memories and to lean toward *species fantasticas et matematicas*. In the melancholic the powers of memory and imagination were thought to combine with a strong interest in geometry because it depends upon image, i.e. figure and line. Vico, as I have discussed, makes this connection in his conception of education, always supporting education in geometry, as well as in the arts of memory and imagination, against algebra. He holds that his own science follows a geometric method, and at one point, in describing his studies at Vatolla, he says that he had discovered that the whole secret of geometric method comes to a particular way of defining terms and ordering thought, which he then spells out quite clearly (125/17).

Vico is first removed from the world by his fall. During his convalescence he studies on his own. When he re-enters grammar school he is prepared for a higher level than the one he is entered in. He asks to study on his own, and he says that then his teacher beheld 'a pupil acting as his own teacher' (*un fanciullo maestro di se medesimo*) (112/4) (his first appearance as autodidact). He then presents himself as moving in and out of the process of formal education, truly to educate himself, to read the grammar of Alvarez, to study the metaphysics of Suárez, to master civil and canon law. Finally, through a chance encounter with Monsignor Rocca and their conversation on the right method of teaching jurisprudence, he withdraws to Vatolla, where he depicts himself in isolation perfecting the course of his advanced studies. As various commentators have noted, Vico's period of nine years at Vatolla has a certain analogy with Descartes's nine years of wandering, that which he states, in the third part of the *Discourse*, he undertook to clear his mind of error.[41]

Was Vico really living the isolated existence at Vatolla that he claims? The portrait of his isolation at Vatolla is no more true to his actual existence during these years than is his birth-date of

---

does not appear interested in astrological interpretation as such, at least in the sense of a natal chart. This is in sharp contrast to Cardano, who gives precise astrological details of his birth.

[40] *Saturn and Melancholy*, 337.
[41] Descartes, *Discours*, 55–6.

1670 true to the actual date of his birth. Vico claims to have been at Vatolla between 1686 and 1695. During this period two events took place of which he gives no mention in his autobiography. The first of these concerned Vico's friends Giacinto De Cristofaro, Nicola Galizia, and Basilio Giannelli, who in 1692 were stigmatized by the Inquisition, and in the following year condemned and imprisoned. Vico himself underwent a religious crisis, and in 1692 wrote the poem, his first published work, 'Affetti di un disperato', which is Lucretian in its sentiments and, as Fisch says, could not have been written by a devout Christian.[42]

Vico's relationship to religion is a subtle question. He was very probably in deep sympathy with his friends who were brought before the Inquisition. Fisch is certainly right in his view that Vico's work cannot be understood without the awareness that the Inquisition functioned as an unofficial force in Naples throughout Vico's career. One conclusion Vico must have drawn from the events of 1692–3 was that to pursue philosophical ideas to their conclusion required a strategy to deal with religious and political power. In the *New Science* Vico affirms Lucretian themes such as the origin of religion in fear, but turns this from a critical principle to a principle of understanding religion as an institution necessary to social order.

As discussed in Chapter 1 above, Vico developed an art of writing his ideas and a system of personal relationships with the clergy that allowed him to make claims about the nature of history and society that in the hands of another would have provoked a reaction. This is a power he shares with Hobbes, who understood both personally and theoretically the nature of fear and the nature of power. Vico's personal relationship to the Catholic faith may not have been very different from that of any other member of Neapolitan society. But the early example of Vico's friends may have served as a guide for Vico concerning the position of the thinker in society throughout his career. It must have been a force in how he chose to present his 'rational civil theology' in his later work.

The second event which Vico omits to mention is that he

---

[42] Fisch, Introduction to *Autobiography*, 36. For a discussion of these conditions in Vico's time see G. L. C. Bedani, 'A Neglected Problem in Contemporary Vico Studies: Intellectual Freedom and Religious Constraints in Vico's Naples', *New Vico Studies*, 4 (1986), 57–72.

matriculated at the University of Naples and later received a
doctorate of laws, which modifies the picture of him as purely a
teacher of himself during these years and is more in agreement
with the picture of him as being in and out of formal study during
his early education. His participation in any system of formal
education throughout his youth was nominal.

In the *Rubriche delle matricole*, which is the record of those
matriculated at the University of Naples for these years, is the
following:

> 1688 – Giovanne de Vico   n. 1226
> 1689 – Gio. Batta de Vico   n. 830
> 1690 – Gio. Batta de Vico   n. 913
> 1691 – Gio. Batta de Vico   n. 1487

From this Benvenuto Donati concludes that Vico was registered, at
least for these four years, as a student at the University of Naples.[43]
The rules for pursuing a degree in jurisprudence at the University
of Naples at that time required that the candidate attend the
university for five years and that he have attained the age of 21.[44]
These dates raise some question of when Vico enrolled in the
university. Fisch in his chronology (agreeing with Nicolini) has
Vico enrolled for his first year in 1689, when he would have been
21 years old according to his actual birth-date of 1668 (by Vico's
date in his autobiography he would then have been only 19, and
the *Rubriche* show him perhaps even a year earlier, in 1688). It is
also not clear when Vico may have done his fifth year and when he
may have actually received his doctorate, because there are gaps in
the records. There is a strong question as to whether Vico had
received his doctorate at the time of his concourse for the chair of
rhetoric, which he competed for in 1698 and assumed in 1699.
According to Donati's research the records of the concourse do not
show the title of 'Dr' before his name, although in his later
candidacy for a university chair the title appears.[45]

[43] Donati, *Nuovi studi*, 33.   [44] Ibid. 31.
[45] Ibid. 53–5. In their annotations to the Laterza edition of *L'autobiografia* (2nd
rev. edn., 1925) Croce and Nicolini state that Vico received his degree in law before
12 Nov. 1694 (as reflected in Fisch's chronology in the English edition). Donati
points out that, given the lack of records confirming Vico's degree in the Archivio
Antico della Università di Napoli, Nicolini is inclined to think that Vico received

From either Nicolini or Donati's account of these dates it can be assumed not only that Vico accompanied the Rocca family in their movements between their residences in Vatolla and Naples during the years he was tutor, but also that he was engaged, at least officially, in formal study of some sort at the university. In fact, what Vico describes of his intellectual life before his departure for Vatolla in 1686 relates to events that took place during the Vatolla period. He reports his visit to the class of Don Felice Aquadia, head lecturer on law at the university, as prior to his nine-year period at Vatolla (115/7). Donati presents evidence that this lecture could not have occurred before the autumn of 1689 (at which time Vico was enrolled as a law student).[46] Vico also relates that for two months he attended lectures on the minutiae of civil and canonical practice by Don Francesco Verde (probably privately given) (ibid.). Vico might have attended these as early as he implies, but Donati advances the hypothesis that Vico may well have attended these in 1688, or at least in 1687, on the eve of his matriculation at the university, and within the Vatolla period.[47]

Vico says that at this time he returned to the study of philosophy, stimulated by the restoration of the Academy of the Infuriati (1683). This would be the same time that he returned to the Jesuit school to be taught by Father Giuseppe Ricci, as Vico reports (114/6). Vico is wrong about this, as Donati, Nicolini, and Fisch note. The Academy of the Investiganti was revived in 1683;[48] although Vico may have been invited to attend some of its meetings, he was only 15 (13, by his 1670 birth-date) at the time. The Academy of the Infuriati was in fact revived in 1692 as the Academy of Uniti, and Vico was elected to membership that year, on Valletta's motion, with the name 'Raccolto'. This was during the Vatolla years, when Vico was 24 (or 22). Given Vico's other displacements he may not have simply confused the restoration of the Infuriati with the Investiganti but may have made a deliberate alteration, to

---

his degree at the University of Naples (Salerno). Nicolini holds the 1694 date because of the existence of a legal document of Vatolla (*un rogito vatollese*) dated 12 Nov. 1694, which designates Vico as *utriusque iuris doctor* (Donatai, *Nuovi studi*, 50 n. 4).

⁴⁶ Donati, *Nuovi studi*, 43.   ⁴⁷ Ibid. 47–8.
⁴⁸ Ibid. 41–3 and 59. See also Fisch, *Autobiography*, 216 n. 133. Fisch describes this as a 'Freudian substitution', but given the pattern I have described, it may be part of Vico's deliberate fiction.

increase the power of his fable of himself as the autodidact, with the heroic character of his mind born in the isolation of Vatolla.

Vico emerges from this period of self-education to live in solitary fashion in his native city, not only as 'a stranger but quite unknown' (*da straniero nella sua patria, ma anche sconosciuto*) (134/26). There is a similarity to Descartes's solitude, which Descartes said he had within the continuing affairs of the city. Vico makes his isolation even more extreme that on his immediate return, when he says he was as a *forestiero*, an 'outsider'; now he says he lived as a *straniero*, a true foreigner, living unknown in Naples as if he were really a resident of another country (taking these two terms more in their older root meaning than in their contemporary, interchangeable sense).[49] This isolation is tempered by his success in obtaining the chair of rhetoric and by the inaugural orations he presents as part of its office. But it is reaffirmed in his unjust loss of the concourse for the morning chair of law.

As he states in his letter to Father Giacco, he regards himself as spared, by the loss of the chair of law, from becoming an ordinary professor, and is thus free to create the *New Science*, which he published two years later, at the same time as he drafted the first part of the autobiography.[50] Vico begins the last portion of his original text of the autobiography (what in the Fisch and Bergin translation is called Part B of the 1728 text) with the assertion that he was 'born for the glory of his native city [*patria*] and therefore of Italy since, being born there and not in Morocco, he became a scholar [*letterato*]' (165/55).[51] Vico now claims his own integration

---

[49] Tommasèo, *Nuovo dizionario dei sinonimi della lingua italiana*, makes the following distinction: 'per essere *forestiero* basta non essere nato dello stesso municipio; lo *straniero* ebbe i natali for della nazione . . . *Forestiero* è men di *straniero*, chiunque non altri in luogo che gli fu patria, ivi è forestiero . . . *straniero*, d'altro paese' (614, entry no. 2627).

[50] 'Letter to Father Giacco, 25 October 1725', in Fisch, Introduction to *Auto-biography*, 14–16. 'Al Padre Giacco', in *Autobiografia, seguita da una scelta di lettere, orazioni e rime*, ed. M. Fubini (Turin: Einaudi, 1970), 106–8.

[51] Battistini, *La degnità della retorica*, 26 n. 23, notes a possible relationship between Vico's opposition of Italy and Morocco and Descartes's statement in Part 3 of the *Discours* justifying his adherence to the maxims of his own country as against adopting those of the Persians or the Chinese. Vico also makes a contrast between ancient Greece and the Moors involving his theory of the origin of Ethiopia in the *New Science* (748–50). Cf. *Scienza nuova prima*, para. 448 and *Dissertationes*, in *Opere di G. B. Vico*, ed. F. Nicolini, vol. ii (Bari: Laterza, 1936), pt. 3, pp. 685–6.

into his native land, or at least its glory, and he ends the 1728 autobiography with the same point, quoting from Cardinal Corsini's praise: 'Therefore I congratulate upon it the fatherland [*patria*] that it so adorns' (173/62). Vico speaks almost like one of the conquerers of the New World, declaring the new world of the *New Science* he has discovered for the glory of his native Naples and for Italy.

In the 'Poetic Geography' of the *New Science* Vico holds that 'Within Greece itself, accordingly, lay the original East called Asia or India, the West called Europe or Hesperia, the North called Thrace or Scythia, and the South called Libya or Mauretania' (742). He claims that these names for the regions of Greece were later applied to the world at large; for example, 'They gave the name Hesperia to the western part of Greece, where the evening star Hesperus comes out in the fourth quarter of the horizon. Later they saw Italy in the same quarter much larger than the Hesperia of Greece, and they called it Hesperia Magna' (743). Vico's use of 'Morocco' in his claim of being born for the glory of his native city and Italy may be intended as a symbol for Africa as an opposite to Europe, *Mauretania* being the Roman term for Morocco and Libya in its transferred Latin meaning having the possibility of signifying Africa.

Tacitus, one of Vico's 'four authors', describes Mauretania and the Roman provinces of Africa as 'given to civil strife and sudden disturbances because of the fanaticism and superstition of its inhabitants, ignorant as they are of laws and unacquainted with civil magistrates' (*Hist.*, i. 9). Such conditions might allow for the emergence of a hero who would embody virtues in his deeds, but the emergence of a figure of 'heroic mind', a philosopher such as Vico, would not be possible. Vico 'becomes a scholar' because he is part of the third age of the particular *ricorso* of Western European history into which he was born.

The last pages of Vico's original text of the autobiography, ending with the judgement by Cardinal Corsini, are a summary of the ideas of the *First New Science*. In his letter to Father Giacco (1725) Vico says: 'This work has filled me with a certain heroic spirit.' He says that he is no longer troubled by any fear of death nor by the need to confront rivals. Vico has achieved the zenith of his heroic mind. The *New Science* is the ultimate product of his self-teaching, the result of the fact that he had 'no teacher whose words he had sworn by' (133/25). He was in fact unteachable. He was guided by his 'good genius' (*buon genio*), which he mentions several times in relation to his course of education (e.g. 114/6, 115/7, 133/25), almost as Socrates' famous light or genius, and certainly in opposition to the 'malignant demon' which Descartes uses in the *Meditations* to throw all his past education and beliefs into doubt. He has avoided the fashions of the city, where knowledge changes every two or three years, and is grateful for what he had learned in 'those woods' (*quelle selve*) of the Cilento (133/25). As teacher of himself in the actual woods of the Cilento, he had freed himself from the 'dark wood of error' of the city and, like Dante, had glimpsed the *dilettoso monte*. He had joined piety with wisdom and emerged from the trial of the concourse without the chair of law but with the discovery of the new law of nations. Vico, the isolated thinker, studying alone the laws and mythologies of the ancients, had discovered the key to the science of civil wisdom, and published it.

AMONG BARBARIANS

Vico's philosophy of history cannot be understood apart from his conception of barbarism, and his conception of his own life cannot be understood apart from the barbarity of his colleagues and the situation in which he found himself throughout his life. I am thinking not simply of Nicola Capasso, the coiner of 'mastro Tisicuzzo', and the formulators of the malicious Leipzig book notice, calculated to make his major work a laughing-stock to the scholars of northern Europe, but of the fact, as Isaiah Berlin and others have said, that even his friendly contemporaries had no real idea of what Vico was saying.[52] Vico knew that he lived in the third age of the recourse of Western history, the first *corso* having been completed with the fall of the Roman world and the heroic age of the second *corso* having been summed up by Dante. In the *Second New Science* Vico calls Dante the 'Tuscan Homer' (786, 817). As Homer brought together the elements of the Greek heroic age and was the great formulator of poetic wisdom before the

---

[52] I. Berlin, *Vico and Herder: Two Studies in the History of Ideas* (New York: Viking, 1976), 8.

arrival of the ancient philosophers and their pursuit of the 'intelligible universal' (34, 209, 934–5), Dante was the great summary poet of the heroic world of the Middle Ages, after which came the philosophy and science of the Renaissance, from which by Vico's day had developed the concern for method in the 'sciences' and metaphysics and the delight in witticism in the arts of speech and society. However, this was not a view of Dante to which Vico had fully come in the *First New Science*.[53]

In his *First Discourse* (1750), in response to the Academy of Dijon's question, 'Has the restoration of the sciences and the arts contributed to purifying morals?', Rousseau affixed an epigraph from Ovid's *Tristia* (v. x. 37): *Barbarus hic ego sum, qui non intelligor illis* ('Here I am the barbarian because no one understands me'). This is a motto Vico could also have used. Ovid in his *Tristia* describes his exile to Tomis, on the Danube near the Black Sea, where he must live among the Scythians—he, the master of Latin, sees passing him each day people bearded, with uncut hair, armed, dressed in skins, and speaking in barbarous tongues, which he himself must try to speak (*Tristia*, v. vii). But in this world he is the barbarian, who can only wave his arms and is not understood. Vico, like Rousseau, stands as an outsider to his own time; his words are no more than mute gestures, which few if any can grasp.

Vico does not reply on Ovid as he does on some Latin authors, but his statement in the above-quoted passage from the *Heroic Mind* to 'take fire from the god who fills you' is a paraphrase of Ovid's *Est deus in nobis, agitante calescimus illo* (*Fasti*, vi. v). One of Vico's themes in his conception of education, as he states in *De mente heroica* and which goes back to the *De nostri* or *Study Methods*, is that wisdom or *sapientia* is, in Platonic terms, a 'purge, curative, completion of the inner man'.[54] As Gianturco says, '*De mente heroica* (*The Heroic Mind*) may be considered the logical prolongation of the *De nostri*. It is one of the most inspired

---

[53] Vico did not hold this view of Dante as a truly heroic poet, parallel to Homer, in the *Scienza nuova prima*, para. 314. He comes to it in the *Scienza nuova seconda* (1730, 1744). See also, 'Discoverta del vero Dante; overo, Nuovi principi di critica dantesca', in *Scritti vari e pagine sparse*, *Opere di G. B. Vico*, ed. F. Nicolini, vol. vii (Bari: Laterza, 1940), 79–82. 'Discovery of the True Dante', trans. I. Brandeis, in *Discussions of the Divine Comedy*, ed. I. Brandeis (Boston: Heath, 1961), 11–12.

[54] 'On the Heroic Mind', 233.

"invitations to learning" ever penned.'[55] In beginning his own education in the Vatolla period Vico was 'still wedded to the corrupt style of poetry' (*vivendo egli ancora pregiudicato nel poetare*) (119/11). As Nicolini points out, this was a form of *barocchismo*.[56]

To cure himself of this corrupt style Vico devised a special method of reading the masters of the Tuscan tongue against the Latin. He made the following pairs, which he read as a cycle, studying each pair of authors on successive days:

Latin	Tuscan
Cicero	Boccaccio
Virgil	Dante
Horace	Petrarch

His aim was to discover the differences between the Latin and the Tuscan tongue by reading their most cultivated authors. To do this he always read each three times, according to the following plan: 'The first time to grasp each composition as a whole, the second to see the transitions and sequence of things, the third in greater detail to collect the fine turns of thought and expression' (120/12). Vico's process of reading recapitulates as an act of comprehension the classical and humanist rhetorical principles of composition of *inventio* (discovery of material), *dispositio* (its arrangement), and *elocutio* (its formulation in language).

In his 1730 edition of the *Second New Science* Vico adds a series of points of conclusion to his introduction to the idea of the work, addressing these points to whatever 'young reader' may wish to profit from the work (1131). He says that the ideas in the work are of 'a wholly new kind' and he asks such a reader to read this work 'at least three times' (1137). If in Vico's view the civil world is a book to be read, analogous to the 'book of nature' that as Galileo says can only be read in mathematical characters, then in his

---

[55] E. Gianturco, Introduction to *On the Study Methods of Our Time*, trans. E. Gianturco, reissued with a preface by D. P. Verene (Ithaca, NY: Cornell University Press, 1990; orig. pub. 1965), p. xxii.

[56] Nicolini, ed., *Opere* (Milan: Ricciardi, 1953), 13 n. 4. See also F. Lanza, 'Linguaggio barocco e filosofia vichiana', in *Saggi di poetica vichiana* (Varese: Magenta, 1961), 169–86.

threefold method of reading described in the *Autobiography*, Vico may have given the clue to how his new science is to be meditated so that the reader may prove it for himself by its narration to himself.

Vico's threefold plan of reading parallels his threefold conception of memory that he later states in the *Second New Science* (819). He says that memory has 'three different aspects': memory (*memoria*) when it 'remembers things' (this is parallel to grasping the composition as a whole, i.e. holding the whole work in mind); imagination (*fantasia*) when it 'alters or imitates them' (the reader closely follows, but alters into his own mind the connections and sequence of things in the text); and ingenuity (*ingegno*) when it 'gives them a new turn or puts them into proper arrangement and relationship' (by collecting the fine turns of thought and expression the reader obtains those particular moments of perception or insight that are distinctive to the author and through which he can activate his own power of *ingegno*). Reading is always a memorial act, an act of recovery and repetition in which the reader attempts to make for himself what is true and present in the text. The act of reading, whether it is the reading of the book of the civil world of the nations or the reading of particular texts, fits Vico's principle of the convertibility of the true and the made. To read is to make for oneself the truth that has already been made in the text.

In reading these pairs of classical and Tuscan authors, Vico is comparing the founding poets of the modern world, of the *ricorso* of Western culture, against the fruits of the *corso* of the ancient world. The Tuscans, who are themselves the rediscoverers of the ancients, are the means of Vico's own rediscovery and poetic cure. According to Vico's thesis in the *Most Ancient Wisdom of the Italians*, the Latin poets are the inheritors of the meanings embedded in the Latin language that go back to the earliest wisdom of the Ionian philosophers and the Etruscans. Vico concludes in his programme of reading that 'in all three cases the Latin tongue surpasses the Italian' (120/12). Vico is able to cure himself of modern poetry, which is more wit than wisdom, that is, which does not contain the features of poetic wisdom (*sapienza poetica*), by going back through the poetry of the Tuscans to the poetic wisdom of the Latin classics which conserve, through the root meanings of the Latin language itself, elements of original human wisdom. Vico says that because of his reading of Horace's *Art of*

Poetry (probably lines 309–16, which Vico quotes in his address to the Academy of Oziosi in 1737) he was led to read the ancient philosophers, especially Aristotle and Plato. Such study of the ancients, over the course of the Vatolla period, is the curative of Vico's propensity to embrace the modern physics and metaphysics of Cartesianism or the modern versions of Stoic philosophy and Epicurean atomism.

Vico's reading programme to overcome his corrupt style of poetry is certainly part of the Arcadian themes that run throughout his *Autobiography*, as is Vico's pastoral image of his education in the 'woods' of Vatolla for which he is thankful for making it necessary for him to be his own teacher. The aim of the Academy of Arcadia was the restoration of classical taste in poetry. It should be remembered that when Vico was elected to membership of the Arcadia in 1710, his invitation to membership was based on his activity as a poet. Vico has, in fact, presented an analogue in philosophy to this Arcadian theme in poetry. His aim is to restore the genius of the ancients in philosophy as a counter to the abstractions of Cartesianism. As the Arcadians are concerned to oppose Marinism in poetry (named after the Neapolitan, Giambattista Marino, 1569–1625), with its devices and artifices designed to produce surprise in the reader, Vico is concerned to oppose the new metaphysics that pursues truth only in terms of a single method.

In the face of the new critical philosophy, Vico wishes to restore confidence in the classical belief in the importance of topical philosophy. Gabriello Chiabrera's (1552–1638) Horatian odes and satires were of importance to the Arcadians because he was an opposing source to the 'corrupt' poetry of Marino. Ironically, Queen Christina of Sweden is both the cause of the founding of the Academy of Arcadia by *letterati*, who had met in her house during the last period of her life in Rome, before her death in 1689, and who wished to carry on their association, and also a cause of Descartes's death. In 1649 Christina summoned Descartes to her court in Stockholm, where he was required to rise at such an early hour, to meet with her in the mornings of the Swedish winter, that he caught pneumonia and died in February 1650.

Seen in its broadest terms, what Vico has accomplished in the Vatolla period is to teach himself the wisdom of the ancients, to have taken his mind back to original forms of poetry and to *phronēsis* or *prudentia*, an original wisdom of human affairs in which the ancients excelled, and the *scienza in divinità*, the wisdom of things divine, in which the Etruscans excelled (365). This forms Vico, the inner man, and isolates him from the fashions of modern methodological and metaphysical thought. Because he has understood what is at the origin, his thought is not really intelligible to those around him who have embraced a modern, logical conception of knowledge and who are cut off from the origin. To speak of, and even more, actually to think from a world of poetic wisdom, a primordial *fantasia*, in a world that has married thought to the kind of intelligibility acquired through step-by-step reasoning, is not only to live as a stranger, but to appear a fool. One of Vico's detractors, as mentioned earlier, said that it was first thought he was just a learned man, but when he published the *New Science* then everyone considered him quite unstable.[57]

When Vico had published the *First New Science* and, as he says in letters to friends, no one took any notice of it, he knew he was living not merely as a stranger in his own land, and quite unknown, he was living among the barbarity of modern man that he describes in the work itself. Vico paints a vivid picture of this in his letter to Father de Vitry of 20 January 1726, in which he describes the sorry state of learning in Naples as he then perceives it.[58]

The first portion of his continuation of his autobiography of 1731 is a retrospective presentation of the years 1702 to 1727 that he had already presented in the original Venice text of his life. He now goes back over the years from within the period of his university orations almost to the publication of his original autobiography. Yet in this retrospective we are presented with a rather different picture of Vico's development. Gone is Vico's presentation of the causes of his intellectual progress, the generation of his ideas described as he moved from one level of understanding to the next. Instead the reader is faced with a parade of Vico's minor and even totally insignificant achievements and writings. They are passed to the reader one after another, and Vico exhorts the reader to realize how important they are, and how fortunate Vico found himself to

---

[57] See my discussion of Finetti's remark in Chapter 1.
[58] Letter to Father Eduardo de Vitry, 20 Jan. 1726 ('Al Padre de Vitry', in *Autobiografia*, ed. Fubini, 113–16). Vico's letter to de Vitry is the major source for reflecting the intellectual climate of Naples of the time in G. Galasso, *Storia di Napoli*, vol. vi, pt. 1 (Naples: Società editrice Storia de Napoli, 1970), 485–514.

be associated with the persons who brought the commissions to
him for such works, etc. The commentators who have remarked
upon this part of the autobiography have usually found it a rather
unattractive portrait of Vico and have attributed it to the many
disappointments he suffered, and perhaps also to be the result of
his difficult temperament.

Although Giannone said it of Vico's original 1728 portion of the
Autobiography, his comment that it was 'both the most insipid and
the most braggadocian thing one could ever read' has some truth
in application to the first portion of Vico's 1731 continuation.[59] In
these pages (173–81/63–70) he describes how he was commanded
by the Duke of Escalona, then governor of Naples, through
Serafino Biscardi, etc., to compose his 'Panegyric to Philip V' on
his visit to Naples, and had only eight days to do it. He describes
how later, with Naples under Austrian rule, the commander of the
Imperial armies, Count Wierich von Daun, wrote to him requesting
inscriptions for the funerals of Don Giuseppe Capece and Don
Carlo di Sangro. Vico reprints the whole of Count von Daun's
letter, apparently taking seriously such comments as 'admiring
your lofty style' and 'I shall keep a lively memory of your noble
labours'.

Even within the series of such commissions Vico was subject to
misfortune. As mentioned above, he was commanded, by Cardinal
Wolfgang von Schrottenbach, then viceroy, to compose the inscriptions for the funeral of the Empress Eleanor, which were not put
up, but Vico reprints them in full in his text! He then relates in
detail the apology he received from an agent of the viceroy. He
tells of how he wrote 'Juno in Dance' for the nuptial rites of Don
Giambattista Filomarino, how he dedicated his study on the history
of Italian poetry to Donna Marina della Torre, and how he
composed his oration on the death of Anna d'Aspermont. He
describes in elaborate detail how he came to the honour of writing
the *History of the War of the Spanish Succession*. He records the
writing of his oration on the death of Donna Angiola Cimmino.
This latter oration is a work worthy of Vico, and does honour to a
patroness of letters, but Vico tells the reader of his autobiography
how excellent it was, how excellently it was printed (a detail he
includes about other works as well), and mentions that the

---

[59] Pons, *Vie de Giambattista Vico*, 45 n. 18.

introduction was written by Father Don Roberto Sostegni. To demonstrate what a fine scholar this author of the introduction was, Vico spends the rest of the page within his own autobiography presenting a eulogy to him.

I have related some of these details to remind the reader how tedious they really are. Vico is a great thinker. He has made the greatest discovery in thought of his time, has discovered the modern philosophy of history and the science of mythology, and much else, all of which he is well aware of. Why does he devote this part of his autobiography to a description of these hollow distinctions? Even granted that such projects and honours had more sense of weight at the time, Vico was a mind and spirit of the first order, who even had a specific conception of the luxury and shallowness of modern life in which 'men waste their substance'. My question is not why Vico does these things, accepts these commissions, etc., but why he reports them in his autobiography as part of his achievement, and in such braggadocian fashion.

One answer is that Vico, unlike Descartes, wished to present all sides of his career, and there is some truth to this. But as has been shown, Vico has no difficulty in suppressing certain aspects of his career, such as the condemnation of his friends by the Inquisition, his own religious crisis, and his university studies. The psychological hypothesis of Vico's personal need for some type of recognition, no matter how superficial, can be advanced, but such explanations never do explain the motives of great thinkers, who, although subject to such forces personally, ultimately think from the true principles of their thought.

Whatever Vico's motivations, his 1731 continuation gives us a picture of Vico among the barbarians. Here is Vico, the philosopher, the heroic autodidact, in concourse with the political world of viceroys, cardinals, aristocrats, and those in power of all kinds. Vico knows that such funeral inscriptions, orations, and histories have no comparison with his philosophical works and the discovery of the *New Science*. He must have intended the reader to see the irony between the ease in which such works as these come to print, and their immediate recognition, and the struggles he has with the publication of both the 1725 and the 1730 *New Sciences*, and the slowness of their recognition.

What a contrast between the 'Funeral Rites of Carlo di Sangro and Giuseppe Capece', which 'were published in an illustrated volume, magnificently printed in folio at the expense of the royal treasury' (175/65) and the almost unreadable, pocket-size publication in duodecimo of the *First New Science*, made possible only because Vico sold his family ring, after financial support was withdrawn by Cardinal Corsini. Consider the difference between this poorly published volume, which contains the principles of human history itself, and the minor 'official' (although intelligently written) history of the war of Spanish succession, 'bound in a great volume on white paper' (180/69), which has a limited significance, useful to scholars of the particular period, and which is of essay length.

The theme of Vico's continuation of his autobiography is the philosopher dealing with the modern world, using the skills of poetry and rhetoric that he has learned from the ancients, to survive in a world of which he is not really a part. As he says at one point, his youthful study of good writers of the vulgar tongue allows him in his old age to accomplish such poems and orations (178/68). This theme, of Vico dealing with the modern world of luxury, witticism, and falsity, is developed, from his recounting of these commissions, orations, poems, and histories, to his problems with the Venetian attempt to capture his works, to the final paragraph describing how he was received in his native city after becoming the author of the *New Science*. Part of this account is ironic and part of it is so much in earnest that Vico shows himself to be partially drawn into the shallow distinctions bestowed on him. He is himself part barbarian. But his final paragraph puts to rest any doubts as to how he understood his relation to the *polis*.

Vico's final paragraph of his autobiography is fashioned almost as finely as his first. But I do not think it warrants a sentence by sentence analysis for its comprehension, and I have already said a good deal about it in Chapter 1. Vico presents himself as, above all, a teacher who adheres to his own conception of education and rhetoric, as he did in his teaching of himself. He has never separated wisdom and eloquence and he understands eloquence as *la sapienza che parla*, as 'wisdom speaking'.[60] Knowledge is a whole and eloquence is that power to present it as a whole—to speak in a way such that this whole is produced for the hearer and thus becomes wisdom.

---

[60] See also Vico's letter to Estevan, *Autobiografia*, ed. Fubini, 117.

Vico continues his *topos* of isolation to the end, saying that he lectured as if great men came to attend his classes (but none ever did). He refers to the constant misconduct and misunderstandings of those around him, saying, 'among the caitiff semi-learned or pseudo-learned, the more shameless called him a fool, or in somewhat more courteous terms they said that he was obscure or eccentric and had odd ideas' (199–200/87). He says the even more malicious damned him with compliments. In response to this, he says, he withdrew to his desk as to a 'high impregnable citadel'. Here the reader may be reminded of Machiavelli, who during a certain period of his career withdrew in the evenings to his desk, and became even more clever concerning the true workings of nations and the empirical science of the civil world. Vico said he called his own works so written 'so many noble acts of vengeance against his detractors'. Presumably his autobiography is among these acts. As I have said earlier, I believe that the cause of all true autobiography is the adversity the author has experienced at the hands of the world. Vico's autobiography is certainly not born out of happiness, and it is in many respects ironic.

Vico ends his autobiography with an understanding of his own death and, indirectly, with a final affirmation of his own melancholy. As mentioned variously above, in describing his natural response to his adversaries he says he was 'choleric to a fault'. Burton, in describing symptoms of 'head-melancholy', says: 'The symptoms of the mind are superfluous and continual cogitations; "for when the head is heated, it scorcheth the blood, and from thence proceed melancholy fumes, which trouble the mind", Avicenna. They are very choleric, and soon hot, solitary, sad, often silent, watchful, discontent, Montaltus, *cap.* 24.'[61] This list of symptoms is very nearly the list of characteristics that Vico attributes to himself, directly and indirectly, in his final description of himself in his last paragraph. The melancholic and acrid temperament comes full circle from his fall to his projected end.

In his quotation from Phaedrus' *Fabulae* concerning Socrates, Vico concludes with the theme of his own solitariness, which is that of the philosopher alone in the world: 'If I were consigned his fame, I would not shun to die as he, and because I would be acquitted when I became ashes, I would endure the inequity of the

---

[61] Burton, *Melancholy*, ii. 40.

sentence.' As I have said earlier, Vico's point is not a comparison of himself with Socrates, any more than any philosopher is comparable with the spirit of the original philosopher. The theme of this fable of Phaedrus is friendship (*Socrates ad amicos*) and this comment occurs parenthetically, with Socrates being questioned about the smallness of the house he is building and his reply that his wish would be to fill even it with friends. Thus in context, Vico's final words, put in the mouth of Phaedrus, put in the mouth of Socrates, are of his isolation, despite his heroic discovery and his union of piety and wisdom. The divine order of things which Vico has grasped prevents him from ever entering the human order, or the human order from ever understanding him. This was the third possibility that was left out of the surgeon's original prediction of Vico's future.

What is the overall structure of Vico's autobiography? In what form is he telling the fable of himself? As stated previously, no specific model for his text has been identified beyond Vico's own identification of his opposition to Descartes's *Discourse* and beyond St Augustine's *Confessions* as a source which, perhaps, stands behind the telling of any philosophical life, but, as I have maintained, has some specific parallels with Vico's work. Vico's autobiography, I think, is not based on any one model. I think rather that it is based on the general form of writing one's life that has emerged from the rhetorical tradition of humanism itself. The first representative of this is Petrarch's *Epistle to Posterity*, which has already been mentioned as the basis for Vico's phrase *onesti parenti* in the first sentence of the *Autobiography*. Josef IJsewijn has analysed this tradition in an essay, 'Humanistic Autobiography', and has shown that besides Cicero, which was standard reading for any humanist, the first and foremost example followed by the humanist writers of their own lives was Ovid's autobiography in the fourth book of his *Tristia* (IV. x).[62]

---

[62] J. IJsewijn, 'Humanistic Autobiography', in E. Hora and E. Kessler, eds., *Studi Humanitatis: Ernesto Grassi zum 70. Geburstag* (Munich: Fink, 1973), 210–11. T. C. P. Zimmerman, 'Confession and Autobiography', in A. Molho and J. A. Tedeschi, eds., *Renaissance Studies in Honor of Hans Baron* (Florence: Sansoni, 1971), has argued that the confessional of the Middle Ages leads to the art of autobiography in the Renaissance through a connection with ancient literature and the practice of history. From this perspective he sees Augustine as an influence on Petrarch. If this thesis can be sustained, it makes an interesting addition to that of IJsewijn and provides support for the general views I have espoused above.

IJsewijn points out that the humanist autobiographers, who generally wrote their lives in fairly brief form, of 100–200 verses (although Petrarch wrote his *Epistle* in prose), rarely specified their model.[63] And with this tradition Vico is in accord. IJsewijn shows that humanist autobiography follows the rhetorically prescribed *topoi* of the panegyric. I believe that the form of Vico's autobiography is that of the panegyric, derived from the classical writers and employed by humanist autobiography. The established themes of the panegyric, following IJsewijn's statement of them, are as follows.[64] The reader will immediately see the similarity with Vico's work.

1. A fitting introductory formula.
2. Remarks on the theme of *genus*, wherein mention can be made of fatherland, parents, and origins.
3. *Educatio* or one's upbringing. Here there may commonly be discussion as to whether one studied law and the extent to which one was attracted toward poetry.
4. *Res gestae* or a relation of one's deeds and adventures, employing key themes of *animus* or mind (qualities of character, wisdom), *corpus* or body (in Vico's case, his statements on his health), and *fortuna* (offices, friends, etc.).
5. *Comparatio* or comparison with others, which may result in praise of others or complaint.
6. Epilogue.

IJsewijn points out that unlike eulogies which follow this pattern rather strictly, humanistic autobiographies allow for a fair amount of variation, especially on how the fourth point is treated. He also points out that 'the humanist writes his autobiography not so much with the intention of providing factual data on his life or insight into his inner life, but with the intention of immortalizing his own name'.[65] This was of course the purpose of the writing of Romans lives generally, which, as I suggested earlier, strongly contrasts with St Augustine's conception of confession. The panegyric used as autobiography is a document or speech of self-praise. This way of speaking certainly runs through Vico's text. Vico both praises himself and, using the well-known rhetorical device of having an

---

[63] IJsewijn, 'Humanistic Autobiography', 211–12.
[64] Ibid. 214.   [65] Ibid. 212.

authority speak for him, he quotes, for example, Le Clerc's or Corsini's views of his work. Vico's concern is with posterity, as is also that of the humanist autobiographers from Petrarch forward. But Vico is concerned with immortalizing his name in a particular way—that appropriate to a historian and a philosopher.

Vico's self-panegyric is carefully built on his principles for understanding a historical *corso*, that he takes from the *New Science*. Unlike other writers of their own lives, statesmen or poets, Vico forms the meaning of his own humanity from the principles he has discovered whereby humanity in general forms itself. In forming his own life in this way, Vico gives a vivid demonstration of the truth of his own metaphysics of history and the new art of criticism by which such truth can be reached. Any philosopher is in some way his own philosophy. Vico, faced with the opportunity to show this, having mastered the ancient rhetorical and humanist traditions, found a new way to reveal himself as the agent of his philosophy. There are in the end two ways to Vico's wisdom, and both are needed; one is to meditate and narrate the course of the *New Science* itself, the other is to meditate and narrate the *sapienza riposta* of the panegyric of Vico, the melancholic and ingenious thinker.

6

Conclusion: Vico's Art

With the candor proper to a historian, we shall narrate plainly and step by step the entire series of Vico's studies, in order that the proper and natural causes of his particular development as a man of letters may be known (1728; 113/5).

And, as may be seen, he wrote it as a philosopher, meditating the causes, natural and moral, and the occasions of fortune; why even from childhood he had felt an inclination for certain studies and an aversion from others; what opportunities and obstacles had advanced or retarded his progress; and lastly the effect of his own exertions in right directions, which were destined later to bear fruit in those reflections on which he built his final work, the *New Science*, which was to demonstrate that his life of letters had to be such as it was and not otherwise (1731; 182/71).

In response to Porcìa's proposal, Vico devised a new art to write his own life. That has been my theme. In his introduction to the *New Science* (1730, 1744) Vico very frankly tells the reader what the 'master key' to the work is—the 'poetic character' or 'imaginative universal' (34). In like manner of frankness in the *Autobiography* (1728, 1731) Vico tells the reader what the master key to his conception of it is, the standpoint from which he wrote it—as a historian and a philosopher.

In order to understand humanity, the world of civil things, Vico invented philosophical history, which he called 'the new science concerning the common nature of nations'. By the principles of this new science Vico was able to describe the life of any nation as a cycle following an eternal pattern of origin, maturity, and fall. History, governed by this eternal pattern or providence, is a theatre of nations undergoing their respective *corsi* and *ricorsi*. Their 'common nature' is their adherence to this providential order present in their separate and interlocking individual lives. This providential order of beginning, middle, and end is within the life of any particular nation and it is also that element which it shares with the particular life of any other nation.

Vico says that this science depends upon a 'new critical art', that is, upon a special manner of analysing the details of the life of any nation so that they can be seen as governed by and embodying the principles of all nations that Vico has discovered in his science. Vico's 'science' refers to the 'principles of humanity' that he has articulated. His 'new art of criticism' refers to the kind of memory, imagination, and ingenuity that are required to perceive and express these principles, these 'trues', as part of the particular 'certainties', the customs, laws, deeds, and language of each nation's life.

Vico's new science depends upon a kind of meditation that unites a logical, metaphysical (that is, philosophical understanding of these principles), with an etymological, historical (that is, philological) comprehension of the languages and institutions of the civil world. The reflective combination of principle with civil certainty results in narrative truth. The meditative grasp of the human universal in the human particular does not take a deductive or logistic form; it does not take the form of an argument or sorites. It is expressed as a narration. Logical form is suited to a timeless and finished sense of truth. Narration is suited to what develops in time, what is tied to Saturn or Chronos. The primordial form of narration is the fable, which is the product of the 'making' imagination (*fantasia*), that type of imagination that can make a human truth, that can narrate a universal principle of the human condition in the form of a specific story. The fable relates a universal meaning in terms of particular events and figures and it constructs this relation as a plot, something that develops in time, that has beginning, middle, and end.

The fables by which humanity originally constitutes itself, by which man originally makes intelligible to himself the human, natural, and divine, become the abiding ground, the touchstone, for the later pursuit of human wisdom, the pursuit of wisdom that takes place after the origin of a nation has been passed and its fables have ceased to govern its life. This is the point at which its perceptions of virtue are embodied no longer in its heroes, but in moral systems; at which its social bonds are held together no longer by the immediate bonds of custom, but by written law; at which its language is no longer based on metaphor, but its metaphors have generated logical analogies; at which wisdom is no longer simply there in the patterns of life and speech, but must be pursued intellectually, so that it becomes the subject of philosophy.

Philosophical history is governed by the example of the fable, specifically by its power to relate a human truth as a story, and by its eloquence—its comprehensiveness, its power to bring into thought the whole of a human reality. Logic abstracts from life. Narrations puts life into words.

Vico's aim in his *New Science* is not to produce a special kind of knowledge, which would be to make something partial. His aim is to produce a complete speech about the human world, one that, with Demosthenes, can go into the farthest corners of what is human, and yet, like Demosthenes' mighty enthymeme, can bring the reader back to the most powerful maxims of humanity and history. Vico's aim for the *New Science*, as he says was his aim in his own teaching, is to be 'wisdom speaking'. The love of wisdom is a kind of speaking; it can be expressed only in language. Philosophy is a form of literature and as such it is governed not only by the logical sense of thought that unites its ideas but also by the principles of rhetoric that govern speech. Seen in this way, philosophy is a kind of speech in which all of the human world is comprehended; philosophy becomes self-knowledge based on a grasp of the totality of 'civil things'. Because of its grasp of the totality of human affairs, being wisdom in this sense, philosophy has natural ties to prudence, to *phronēsis, prudentia*, to the sense of wisdom required actually to function in the world of human affairs.

Self-knowledge understood in this way is not a kind of introspective truth, but a kind of human wisdom that is required for human action. A wisdom of the civil world, that is, a comprehension of it in its totality, is also a civil wisdom, because it is from such a comprehension that the philosopher can guide his own actions in the world. Philosophy as a practical wisdom is based on the philosopher's comprehension of the principles of humanity itself, and these principles in rhetorical terms are like *topoi* from which the philosopher can draw forth what is needed to speak and act successfully. From them he can draw forth the understanding needed for his conduct of life. The philosopher's understanding of the 'jurisprudence of the human race' is the basis of his own prudence in human affairs. In Vico's view of prudence the philosopher's model for wise action is not the study of the lives of specific historical figures but the study of the 'jurisprudence' of the human race itself, derived from his own meditation and narration of its courses.

Vico says that the proof of his science, that which 'reigns in this science', is for the reader to make it for himself, to meditate and narrate it to himself by that power (which in fact is the power attributed to the Muses), to grasp events as being 'what had, has, and will have to be'. The reader is then to think of the human world in terms of a cycle of past, present, and future that holds the events of a nation together in such a way that once grasped as a whole it is evident that these events must have been so and not otherwise. The narration, with its order of beginning, middle and end, is a way to master time. The reader will be convinced of the truth of Vico's science only if he does what Vico has done, if he meditates on the materials of human history and finds in them the principles of Vico's narration. In this way the reader would make it his own narration. By repeating it he would prove it for himself. Vico's conception of human history is a conception of the repetition of patterns. His proof of it is also based on the idea of repetition. The reader is invited to make his own repetition of it and so to realize the truth for himself. No philosophical proof is ever truly a proof for us unless we can make it for ourselves.

In introducing the principles of the *New Science*, Vico says that 'the conceits of nations and of scholars' act against our understanding the principles of humanity because both of these reduce all to the familiar. The conceit or arrogance (*boria*) of nations is for each nation to think that it is as old as the world, and that of scholars is to think that their form of learning is also as ancient. Both of these cut us off from any sense of origin and from the future as in any fundamental way different from the present. Both scholars and nations, in their respective ways, think they have mastered time rather than finding the eternal in time as the providential, which is itself not of their making. Vico says: 'So, for purposes of this inquiry, we must reckon as if there were no books in the world' (330). This may be surprising to the reader because Vico's *New Science*, if it is anything, is a book about other books. This assertion itself may be a reference to Descartes's assertion in the *Discourse* that as soon as possible he abandoned entirely the study of letters and 'resolved no longer to search for any other science than that which could be found in myself or in the great book of the world'.[1]

---

[1] Descartes, *Discours de la méthode*, chronology and preface by G. Rodis-Lewis (Paris: Garnier-Flammarion, 1966), 38.

This statement reminds one of Montaigne's claim, in his essay 'On Experience', that the only business he has is with himself, that this self-study is both his physics and his metaphysics.

Vico's sweeping assertion that we must reckon as if there were no books in the world means, I think, that no books before the *New Science* can be pointed to that practise his particular art of narration. We must look beyond all books that purport to give us the truth of the civil world, to the book of the civil world itself, in which they are rooted, and discover from this master book the meaning of the partial views of the principles of humanity that these conceited books contain. But this may also be applied to the book of the *New Science* itself, in relationship to Vico's invitation to the reader to make the proof of this science for himself. The truth of Vico's narration of the ideal eternal history of nations can be had by mastering not Vico's book as such, but by mastering its principles so that the reader can read the book of the world for himself and fully realize the meaning of Vico's science. Vico's aim, like Plato's, is to make the reader a practitioner.

The proof of Vico's new science, understood as a whole process, then, is the mastery of the principles of his science coupled with his new art of criticism, which is in its one moment the meditation or analysis of the certainties of the human world in terms of these principles and in its other moment the narration of the results of this meditation as a series of cycles or stories of humanity, intellectually told, showing the course or life of the nations. Vico says that this new critical art is a metaphysics. Seen in metaphysical terms it essentially means that anything in the civil world has a life and its life can be formed as a narration; it can be understood in narrative terms. One way to put this is to say that every nation is a life, and conversely every life is a 'nation', in the sense that its being can be understood in narrative terms, based on the application to it of the new critical art.

Vico's metaphysics of history, his union of metaphysics and historical life, has within it the great Renaissance principle of macrocosm and microcosm, held by Bruno and others. We as humans can understand the collective life of humanity as historical and as cyclic because we in fact apprehend our own individual life as a cycle and even the episodes within it as composed of cycles, or like cycles, that is, as having beginnings, middles, and ends. The whole of our life has this natural course. Viewed from this perspective there is a metaphysics of the self that is microcosmic of the metaphysics of history. The divisions or ages of ideal eternal history that show its providential pattern have validity for us as individuals because if we meditate on the 'certainties' that make up the particular character of our own life in its course we can perceive it as having an analogy to ideal eternal history. We can understand our own being metaphysically as having an eternal pattern and as governed by Chronos.

The panegyric as a rhetorical form sees the individual life as a cycle that goes from conditions of birth and origin, to heroic achievement deserving of praise, to epilogue. The terms of Porcìa's proposal to the scholars of Italy are essentially that the author formulate a panegyric of himself. All lives can be spoken of in this form of a cycle. But this is not to say that the idea of panegyric contains within it Vico's idea of an ideal eternal history of a self. The one can be adapted to the other, and that is what I have claimed Vico has done in order to construct his autobiography, his narration of the truth of his own life.

In narrating the truth of his life Vico claims he will give the causes both 'natural and moral, and the occasions of fortune'. A 'natural' cause that operates throughout Vico's autobiography is his acrid and melancholic nature which is determined as a result of his childhood fall. This nature is not a matter of choice or intent any more than is the fall itself. In the *New Science* Vico says there are three kinds of natures which correspond to the three ages of a nation's cycle (916–18). These cause each age to be what it is and not another.

A 'moral' cause in Vico's life is his cultivation of his 'heroic mind' and pursuit of piety and wisdom which allow him to respond to the loss of the concourse by the creation of the new science and enable him to overcome the adversities he faced in its publication. In the *New Science* virtues are born out of severity and necessity and are lost as the life of a nation becomes more luxurious. The heroes, as opposed to the plebeians, are those who are able to surmount the severity of existence and rise above the ordinary social structures upon which the plebs depend (one place to see this is Vico's 'Corollary Concerning the Heroism of the First Peoples', 666 ff.). The causes of the actions of Achilles or Ulysses are due not to the ordinary forces of society but to their ability to embody virtues (valour and wisdom) which are beyond the reach of the plebs.

An 'occasion of fortune' is Vico's chance meeting with Monsignor Rocca in a bookstore, resulting in his offer to Vico to become a tutor to the Rocca family. This is a force that comes to Vico from without and lifts him from the conditions of his poverty and the low station of his family, as well as from the threat of destruction by consumption, and puts his life on a new course. Without this fortunate turn of events, Vico would have remained struggling and sickly. The good climate of the Cilento, the convent library (another occasion of fortune), and the leisure gave him a future. In the *New Science* Vico says that when a nation is in a state of 'ultimate civil disease' one possibility is that it can be conquered by a better nation and preserved from without (1106). This would not remove the cycle of ages from any nation but it would alter the pace.

The life of a nation, like Vico's life cycle, is governed by providence. An 'ideal eternal history' operates in both. Thus the causes both natural and moral and the occasions of fortune that can be identified in Vico's narrative operate within a larger sense of causality—the notion of an overall providential order to human events, whether individual or collective. The fact that Vico 'meditated' these causes 'as a philosopher' means that the specific natural and moral causes and the occasions of fortune which he relates all occur within a total order represented by the coherence of the narrative. Vico's narrative is an attempt to realize this providence in language. Providence is a metaphysical principle which allows Vico to give specific causes for events. They neither occur simply by chance nor are they ordained by fate. None of these causes or occasions of fortune are just free-standing, independent of the total. That Vico can construct a narrative of himself in accordance with the idea of providence is proof of its validity as a principle. As with the *New Science*, the reader will have to meditate it for himself to see this. There is no 'logical' proof of such a coherence apart from Vico's ability to give the story of his life as an ideal eternal history.

The two portions of Vico's *Autobiography*, the Venice text of 1728 and his continuation of 1731, interlock with the two versions of the *New Science* of 1725 and 1730. Vico's invitation to the reader to make the science for himself is meant to apply directly to the subject-matter of the work—the world of nations. But when Vico turns to the task of making a book of himself, he must also reckon as if there are no books in the world. There is no book of himself or of anyone's self apart from the self. Like the book of the world, the book of the self is there to be read. In what terms is Vico to read it? He meditates the certainties of his own existence and narrates them as an extension of the principles of his own new science. Now in full possession of his own understanding of any human thing, having arrived at this through his new science, Vico turns to himself, with this general wisdom at his disposal, to find the particular wisdom of his own life course.

The philosopher, unlike the ordinary writer of an autobiography, can, if he chooses, draw upon his whole philosophy as a basis. Vico does not write his autobiography as a mechanical application of the principles of his philosophy to the events of his life. No true narrative could result from this, but, as I have tried to show, he writes his life from its centre points, not as a work separate from its great truths. In this way Vico's text of his own life is a verification of his reading of the book of the world. The *New Science* could certainly stand without Vico's 'proof of himself'. But Vico's ability to apply the meanings of his own philosophy to himself as an actual philosophical life gives proof of his new science as a genuine human wisdom. Vico can, with Socrates, claim to possess human wisdom (*Apology*, 20 D).

The *Autobiography* demonstrates to us the prudential character of the *sapienza filosofica* that the *New Science* contains. In this way it verifies that Vico, beginning from his analysis of *sapienza poetica*, has derived a kind of civil wisdom for modern man that is not unlike that sought in ancient texts, in Cicero, Plato, and Aristotle. However, in ancient texts this is not done in terms of the metaphysics of history that Vico has sought in his attempt to comprehend the elements of the Judaeo-Christian and Graeco-Roman world that come together in the *ricorso* of modern Western man, the cycle in which Vico himself is living.

As I have said, Vico's *New Science* could stand on its own without Vico's *Autobiography* as an underlying or accompanying text. We can easily say with Adams that 'it is difficult to imagine what one's studies of Vico would have been like had one not possessed the autobiography.'[2] Once written, his autobiography

---

[2] H. P. Adams, *The Life and Writings of Giambattista Vico* (London: Allen and Unwin, 1935), 176.

serves as a special guide to the meaning of Vico's ideas and as a kind of proof for Vico and for the reader of these ideas. Like a pioneering scientist in need of an experimental subject for his discovery, Vico uses himself. The source and the ground for the truth of any philosopher's ideas is the sense he can make of them in terms of his own reality. This is especially true of the modern thinker who is cut off from a continuum with the *polis* and is always thrown back on himself as individual. If nature and the civil world are like books to be read, as Galileo and the humanists thought, the life of the thinker is also like a book. It can, in fact, be ordered as a book and read. Vico can read the providential text that underlies the life of a nation and the common world of nations. He can read the text that underlies the pattern of natural and moral causes that have led him to his philosophical ideas.

If Vico can give a genetic account of his own life, a true philosophical history of himself, it will show that the self can be understood in a manner different from Descartes's conception of it. It will show that Vico's way of thinking about the human world is rooted in the only way we can truly make a knowledge of ourselves. Vico's aim is to show how the self is governed by both Chronos and the 'true Jove'. The transference of the spirit of the *New Science* on to the understanding of himself is not simply a theoretical project, because the providential order that Vico depicts as present in his life-events has implicit in it a prudence. Here, too, *providentia* is interlocked with *prudentia*.

Vico's life becomes not simply his own particular life but also a universal. It is a model of the philosophical life. The way in which Vico presents himself as acting and reacting within the providential order becomes a model of instruction in practical wisdom for those who can read the signs of his actions. As writer of his life in this manner, Vico has the power of the Muses over it; he can grasp it as a continually repeating sequence of 'had, has, and will have to be'. The key to successful human action, to acquiring practical wisdom or prudence, is memory. *Memoria* is the faculty that, being presented with a particular situation, allows us to derive it from its origin—to treat it in our minds as having had a past and to attempt to reconstruct for ourselves that past, and place ourselves within or without its course. Furthermore it is to remember that events in the human order are repetitive, that all things undergo courses. *Fantasia* enters into this memorial approach to the world as our ability to internalize the course of an event and to project it against the future it may have. *Ingegno* allows us, within the framework of the present, to see the particular connections between the past and future of an event's life course and provides a basis for prudent action.

To comprehend this sense of human events in autobiographical terms is the key to comprehending it at large in the civil world. Vico's power to see his early life as a series of signs of what is to come is crucial to demonstrating the meaning of his idea of a cycle, as is also his ability to show how out of the negative is born the positive good—the injustice of the loss of the concourse, the justice of the discovery of the new science. The *summum bonum* is born upside-down in history and in Vico's own life cycle. If the reader allows the events of the *Autobiography* to speak to him in this way, it becomes a text that is of a piece with the *New Science*, which, although not necessary to its truth, is an enrichment of it. In a sense Vico has told his philosophical truth in two ways, as the story of humanity, and as the story of his own particular humanity: the melancholic course of history, the melancholic course of Vico. Beyond this world is the divine order as such, the life of which is partially realized in history. Within this world is the philosopher's prudence.

In Chapter 1 the first two of the three questions I raised concerned the sense in which Vico's *Autobiography* was the application and the verification of his *New Science*. The foregoing comments are intended to highlight my answers to these two questions. My third question concerned the sense in which Vico's autobiography is unique in the history of the development of the writing of autobiography and the sense in which Vico's work may suggest something about the nature of autobiography itself, in particular, intellectual autobiography and the nature of autobiographical truth. It is to these concerns that I wish now to turn.

Fisch's judgement that Vico's autobiography 'has the unique interest of being the first application of the genetic method by an original thinker to his own writings'[3] is certainly correct. Ancient autobiographies are devoted, especially in the case of the Romans,

---

[3] Fisch, Preface to *The Autobiography of Giambattista Vico*, trans. M. H. Fisch and T. G. Bergin (Ithaca, NY: Cornell University Press, 1983), p. v.

largely to immortalizing the name of the author and are accounts of *res gestae* more than pictures of the author's mental development, although there are works of greater purpose, such as the *Meditations* of Marcus Aurelius, upon which Cardano claims his *Vita* is based. The three great lives of the Renaissance, those of Montaigne, Cellini, and Cardano, although in many ways quite modern, in no sense employ a genetic method. Montaigne is concerned to record eloquently his impressions and thoughts of himself, Cellini to record his exploits, and Cardano offers an ahistorical analysis of himself, a self-diagnosis of the unique symptoms of his personality. The self-panegyrics of the Renaissance humanists, stemming from Petrarch's *Epistle to Posterity*, like the Roman autobiographies which were their model, were brief works designed to immortalize their own names.

Vico's transformation of this rhetorical form by infusing it with the concept of historical narration, guided by the philosophical idea that such a narration can show that the course of his life was determined to be as it was and not otherwise, is something absolutely new in the art of writing one's own life. It is possible for Vico to approach his own life in these terms only because he has approached history itself in philosophical terms. Vico is generally, and rightly, regarded as the founder of the philosophy of history, and because he can see history in this way, he is the first to comprehend the history of his own life in philosophical-historical terms.

There is certainly a sense in which Descartes and Vico combined are the co-authors of modern autobiography; modern autobiographies are often a combination of a filled-out Cartesian *I* and a version of the genetic method, plus or minus something like Vico's sense of providence. Behind all philosophical autobiography is Augustine's *Confessions*. I have suggested ways in which this work contains specific elements that parallel those Vico employs in the construction of his own text. But the central point which may have influenced Vico is the parallel that exists between Augustine's *City of God* and his *Confessions,* the former being the unfolding of God's action in the progress of the world's history and the latter being the revelation of God's action in man. Vico saw the *New Science* in Augustinian terms as the 'great city of the human race'. In writing his life Vico was completing the other part of the Augustinian project.

Autobiography is the basis of history. It is no accident that the founder of modern philosophy of history is also the founder of the modern art of intellectual autobiography. The self makes itself through its actions, as humanity collectively makes itself through the actions of its cultural life. The coherence of the world of the human self can be formed or 'told' as a story, as the world of nations can be formed as a story. The single human has a history, a *storia*, just as humanity has a history, a *storia*. The reality of both the self and humanity is subject to expression in the word, *logos*. Always near to *logos* and presupposed by it is *mythos*. There is always a coherence in human reality, whether individual or collective, that can be felt and first expressed in the image or metaphor. This felt coherence can then become the basis for an intellectual coherence expressed in terms of principles. Plato's method in the *Republic* of expressing the nature of the state first in large letters and then finding the individual writ small in the same letters is Vico's procedure. Vico's announced topic in the *New Science* is the 'principles of humanity', but his unannounced topic is an understanding of the reality of the modern individual who exists among the barbarians of the third age of any nation. Vico's sense of the principles of the life of collective humanity becomes the unstated means for the construction of the story of his own life—his own humanity.

In the *New Science* 'ideal eternal history' is a kind of intellectually formed imaginative universal that gives us as thinkers access to Vico's principles of the life of nations. 'Ideal eternal history' is not itself a principle and it is never called such nor proved by Vico. He employs it as part of his explanation of various axioms, but he never names 'ideal eternal history' itself as one of the axioms. It is an analogue to the primordial universal of 'Jove' which initially gives the first men access to thought and to speech. 'Ideal eternal history' is an image of history as a totality; this image has intellectual and empirical content only when it is employed as a guiding insight for organizing the details of historical life into coherent patterns. But history would not make sense to us in these philosophical terms unless we can presuppose all along the Platonic analogy of the large and small letters. Humanity in its individual form, not simply its collective form, must be capable of autobiographical or historical coherence.

The image of 'ideal eternal history' is in essence the grasp of the life of nations and of any single nation's reality as 'heroic'. The nation rises to its point of greatness and falls. This fall, whether it happens from within or by conquest from without, is due to its failure to maintain itself as a perfect poem. As a nation develops its life, it becomes progressively unwise; that is, it loses the sense of the whole that should guide its specific actions and thoughts. It loses that completeness of form which is sought in the eloquence of a speech. This rise and decline is due to the imperfections in the nation's origin and is simply what it means to live *in* history, to be one of the gentile nations in Vico's terms. Vico's metaphor for himself is that of the 'hero'. His story of himself is of his rise to the heroic moment of his discovery of his new science and then he forecasts his potential decline, saying that he could ask for nothing more in the world. This great discovery was complete in itself and could lead to nothing further. He portrays himself as totally spent.

'Vico Hero' the heroic autodidact, runs the course of a nation. The events of his life are analogues to the events of the life of humanity; both are governed by providence. Vico's life is a series of symbolic and providential turns that give content to the overriding metaphor or 'imaginative universal' of Vico as hero or, more specifically, 'heroic mind'. Vico's heroism is only as a thinker and is not truly heroic because he lives in an age governed by the barbarism of reflection. He is not the summation of his age as he would be if he were a hero of deeds, actually forming the meaning of human virtues by his own actions in society, as with heroes in the heroic age of nations. Vico instead occupies his own island. His heroic mind is portrayed by him through his *topos* of isolation.

Mary B. Hesse, in an aptly titled essay, 'Vico's Heroic Metaphor', has pointed to 'the *ideal* or *normative* character of imaginative universals. Metaphors are "ideal portraits"'; and she has argued that 'without this feature of idealization it is difficult to understand how Vico could claim "truth" (almost by definition) for the first imaginative class concepts drawn pre-linguistically from experience'.[4] I believe her view is quite correct and, as she points out, it is not something which I have emphasized in my own previous discussion of imaginative universals. Because imaginative

---

[4] M. B. Hesse, 'Vico's Heroic Metaphor', in R. S. Woolhouse, ed., *Metaphysics and Philosophy of Science in the Seventeenth and Eighteenth Centuries* (Dordrecht: Kluwer, 1988), 198. Hesse's claim is made about the role of imaginative universals in primitive mentality.

universals are ideal portraits as well as forms of thought through which objects in the world are known, Vico's employment of *fantasia* to make a fable of himself is normative. Vico's deliberate creation of a symbolic substructure to his autobiography based on his conception of primitive *fantasia*, his transformation of himself into a metaphor, allows him the power not simply to form a concept of himself but to present himself as an ideal of philosophical life, an embodiment of 'heroic mind' which unites wisdom and piety (as he concludes in the *New Science*, 1112). Imaginative universals in their original state in primitive mind and life are not only ways to think about the world, they are ways to act in the world. The recollective *fantasia* whereby Vico makes his modern fable of himself plays upon both of these sides of the imaginative universal, its joint metaphysical and ethical power.

The fact that we can make sense of history is evidence that we can make sense of ourselves and the reverse. The principles by which we can make sense of history have some commonality with the principles by which we can make sense of our own autobiographies. For Vico, as for the ancients, history, biography, and finally autobiography are interlocking forms of thought. To write an autobiography is to put the self of the author together in some specific way so that the author's reality is generated from his own specific origin, and this is exactly what is required to write the history of something in modern terms. This is not to say that history, biography, and autobiography are all the same art. It is to say that all three are part of a general art of remaking human reality in words, and that it is an art in which the subject attempts to tell the truth about itself. In other words, the object of its account is perceived in one manner or another as its *alter ego*. But to tell the truth about itself is not a simple matter of the relation of the chronology of life-events. Truth is truth only in relation to some theoretical or narrative stance that the author takes toward his own reality, a stance that is often simply implicit in the work itself. These assertions take us to the threshold of a complex of problems that cannot be pursued here, concerning the relation of such an art to that of the novel, the poet, and literature in general. I mention them here only to underscore the point that history, biography, and autobiography are part of the human project of self-knowledge. The many languages of self-knowledge constitute the humanities or rhetorics of the human.

As mentioned above, the third question raised in Chapter 1 of this work concerned the implication Vico's autobiography might have for understanding the art of autobiography generally. Does Vico's autobiography, as the first example of the application of the genetic method by an original thinker to his thought, contain any clues to the general process of autobiographical narration and the kind of truth that can be achieved through it? These are questions that concern the reader of Vico, but they are also questions that concern the general interpreter of autobiographical literature. The reader has no doubt already drawn out various implications from what has been said about Vico's autobiography according to what the reader's own general interest in questions about autobiography may be. But several things may be fairly simply and directly said. They should be considered especially in relation to my discussion of the idea of autobiography in Chapter 2.

Any work of philosophy is both a work about that particular philosophy and a work about what philosophy is, just as any works of literature (in particular any major work of literature) is both a particular work and a conception of what that form of literature truly is. The same can be said about autobiography. Any autobiography is not only the life of its author, but, implicitly or explicitly, it contains a conception of how such a life can be expressed, a conception of what autobiography is. It is not my intention to generalize about all autobiographies here. But it is possible to bring forth some features from Vico's autobiography as the first of its kind that may illuminate the form of modern intellectual autobiography.

Some modern intellectual autobiographies, including ones by philosophers, for example, those of Russell or Quine, are works in which the author attempts to tell the story of his life without any apparent special conception of what autobiography is. Even in such 'naturally' told stories of an author's life, the tale is guided by some *topoi* and the writer builds for himself a persona. This is to say that even the most straightforwardly told life story is subject to the techniques of rhetorical and literary analysis. No text can be written without such conventions even if the author makes no deliberate use of them. On one level Vico's autobiography reads like this. Vico presents a story line that appears to be the 'natural' history of himself. Its details are basically correct and in sequence, and the reader learns what the course of Vico's life, at least his intellectual life, was up to the point where the text ends in 1731.

But in Vico's autobiography there are two Vicos, the Vico who is the subject of the basic story line, and a second Vico. The second Vico is the figure the author is forming through his text to convey a certain narrative truth. This is the figure that Vico makes of himself out of the details of the course of his life. This figure is Vico the heroic thinker, who embodies the ancient theme of the philosophical life. This is Vico the philosopher, who is constructed from the principles of his own philosophy and who remains as an expression of their truth in particular form. Crucial to this is Vico's grand *topos* of himself as isolated and because of this in touch with a divine providential order that allows him to understand things, including his own existence, in ways others cannot.

There is a third Vico, the one who actually writes the autobiography, who is the maker of himself as *alter ego*. The self that exists through his actions as he has them in his memory is now made as a true or intelligible self that shows the reality that informs or is claimed to have informed these recalled actions through which Vico's self has lived. The two Vicos of the text suggest Vico's distinction between the philological and the philosophical, the certain and the true. The third Vico, the author, is the power to convert what is done (*factum*) with the true (*verum*), that is, to move from what is there as a set of remembered actions of the self to the formation of a sense of the self that makes them intelligible in a transcendental sense. Vico accomplishes this, not as a series of factual observations about himself or a set of true propositions, but as a narration which presents his life, to the point he has written it, as a whole; that is, as an eloquent speech about himself that is also in fact a self-made panegyric.

What I have called the 'three Vicos' (the 'Vico' who is directly being written about, the 'Vico' who emerges as the overall figure, and the 'Vico' who is writing) could be extrapolated as elements from a number of modern intellectual autobiographies. They are not unique to Vico's work, but they are in fact there in this work and are thus there in the founding example of the modern art of autobiography. They are part of what supports the claim that Vico's autobiography is the first work of modern intellectual autobiography. These three elements correspond to principles in Vico's epistemology and metaphysics. Vico's ability to take these principles and make the kind of narrative of his life that he has made shows the validity of these principles to bring forth a knowledge of the human.

The two hallmarks of autobiography, things which no autobiography can dispense with, are that the author must tell the truth (or at least the reader must be convinced that the truth in general is being told) and that the author must formulate his life *as* something (even if it is as detached as Cardano's attempt to analyse himself as a kind of unique 'species'). The author is always in the position of both telling the truth and making the truth. In this the author is at the epicentre of self-knowledge. How profoundly he can do this depends upon how profound a thinker the author actually is. The principles of Vico's philosophy are susceptible to this double sense of truth because his approach to humanity is essentially autobiographical; his new science, as I have called it, is the autobiography of humanity. Because such principles guide Vico in writing his own autobiography and devising the new art of autobiography, his work may serve as a model for the writing of autobiography just as Porcìa and the group of scholars working from Leibniz's letter envisioned. Leibniz's claim that it is important for thinkers to show us the steps by which they arrived at their discoveries so that we do not have to discover them ourselves in order better to benefit from their work is still valid and valuable.

But more than acting as a model for writing intellectual autobiography, Vico's conception of knowledge and of narrative suggests a way in which autobiographies that show the mental development of their authors can be read. All autobiographies in which the author attempts to apply a genetic method to his own development to discover its nature and truth, to make the memory of himself a truth in this way, are Vichian and subject to forms of thinking first formulated by Vico. Although a Vichian history of autobiography is yet to be written and a theory of literary interpretation of autobiography based on the specifics of Vichian principles is yet to be formulated, both are there to be done. No other philosophy offers a more fruitful base.

Vico is certainly not the first to think philosophically about his own life; that is an ancient project. But he is the first to think both philosophically and historically about his life, to merge the two such that his *animus* is understood in genetic terms, governed by causes which can be philosophically comprehended. No one can approach his own life in these terms earlier than Vico because no one is in possession of the 'genetic method' of which Vico is the discoverer and master. Vico has discovered this method in the *New Science* and it is only because of this that he naturally turns to the study of his life in these terms. He may have done this so naturally that he did not himself realize that he was formulating a new art of writing one's own life. Vico was never slow to praise himself for the newness of the new science, and had he fully realized how different from earlier traditions was his approach to understanding his own life and self, he would have had no difficulty in saying so.

There is no specific model for Vico's *Autobiography* in the sense of a single work which he imitated. Instead, I believe Vico assembled his text out of three elements. First, the content of Vico's text in the sense of his conception of himself is constructed against the anti-model of Descartes's *Discourse*. On the positive side, Vico's conception of his own reality is derived from the genetic understanding of human events that he has developed in his philosophy. Secondly, the method of Vico's text, that is, the general form of the organization of his presentation, is taken from the rhetorical device of the panegyric as developed in the tradition of humanist autobiographies from Petrarch onwards. Thirdly, the style Vico employs, in the sense of the way in which he actually expresses his narrative—his use of the third person, his often detailed quotations of the praise given him by others—has a source in the Arcadian literary tradition that saw the sixteenth-century autobiography of the poet Gabriello Chiabrera as a model of perfection. Vico combines these two traditions, rhetorical and literary, with his new conception of genetic understanding of a subject to make a new form of autobiography. It is a form based on a new way of thinking, but a way of thinking that embodies and modifies these established traditions of expression.

Writers on the history of autobiography have had little or no understanding of Vico's place in the development of the idea of autobiography. They have realized that there is a break between the Renaissance writing of lives and the way in which modern authors look at themselves, but they have not faced the issue in theoretical terms. Misch's history of the writing of autobiography is an enormous compendium that categorizes shifts in the development it describes in broad terms, with only a few comments about their meaning. Although a great work, it is a large and indecisive work. It is burdened by the size of its own project and this contributes to its indecision.

The causes of the lack of proper attention to the significance of Vico's autobiography by those specifically interested in autobiography as a literary subject are not difficult to ascertain. First, the investigation of autobiography as a literary form is quite new, the term itself having been in widespread use for little more than a century. The study of autobiography as a topic of critical literature has been pursued for no more than a generation.

Secondly, Vico as a thinker has been little known in general, and only during this last generation has he undergone a renaissance of wide and varied critical study. Moreover, to understand the way in which Vico has written his autobiography, the principles of his philosophy must be understood, which is not an easy task. The connection between these principles and the way he has written his own life must be seen, which is in itself a new subject in Vico studies.

Thirdly, Vico's autobiography is thoroughly modern in its use of the genetic method. That is, its form of narration is, in general terms, what we have come to expect in reading an intellectual autobiography. Vico explains his thought as a development. The idea of the developmental understanding of the human self or of culture or the mind, since the Romantics, and especially since Hegel's *Bildungsroman* of Spirit in the *Phänomenologie des Geistes* (1807), comes to us as the natural way to understand what seems to have organic form or that exists as a process, or that is self-creative. Thus to the modern Vico scholar who does not pause to reflect, Vico's autobiography appears as the story of Vico's life told in much the same way that we in an age of autobiographies have come to expect. In the fully articulated history of autobiography, Vico is without doubt the archetype. Because so little interpretation has been done on his autobiography by Vico's commentators, and because literary investigators are largely uninformed about Vico, works in the history of autobiography naturally focus on the widely known *Confessions* of Rousseau as the first modern philosophical autobiography.

The one great 'commentary' on Vico's autobiography is James Joyce's *Finnegans Wake*. It has been clear to Joyce scholars and readers who know the background of his works that Joyce was a lifelong reader of Vico and that he based *Finnegans Wake* on

Vico's *Scienza nuova*. This is to say that he deliberately used Vico's text as a grid for the construction of *Finnegans Wake*, as he had used Homer's text as a basis for *Ulysses*. Very early in his career, Joyce told his pupil, the Triestine lawyer Paolo Cuzzi (to whom he gave English lessons between 1911 and 1913), that Freud had been anticipated by Vico.[5] Writing to Harriet Weaver in 1925, from Paris, suffering from his increasing eye trouble, Joyce said: 'I should like to hear Vico read to me again', and he advertised in a Paris newspaper for an Italian to read it to him.[6] He recommended Vico to his friends who had difficulty understanding the instalments of *Work in Progress* that was to become *Finnegans Wake*. That was his advice to the Danish writer Tom Kristensen, who asked, 'But do you believe in the *Scienza Nuova*?' Joyce's now well-known reply was: 'I don't believe in any science, but my imagination grows when I read Vico as it doesn't when I read Freud or Jung.'[7]

To my knowledge, Joyce never mentioned Vico's *Autobiography*. The first volume of the Laterza edition of Vico's works to appear was the *Autobiography*, in 1911 (although volume v of the edition)—about the same time that Joyce discussed Vico with his pupil Cuzzi. Joyce knew Italian well from his early years in Trieste; he even at one time qualified for a certificate to be a teacher in the Italian public schools. The elements of Vico's *New Science* run throughout *Finnegans Wake*,[8] from 'Ordovico or viricordo' (215) to Joyce's four-term combinations such as 'thunderburst, ravishment, dissolution and providentiality' (362), to the straightforward assertion, 'The Vico road goes round and round to meet where terms begin' (452), to the unforgettable 'Our wholemole millwheeling vicociclometer' and 'eggburst, eggblend, eggburial and hatch-as-hatch can' (614) and other references to Vico's cyclic sense of time. But what also runs throughout *Finnegans Wake* is Vico himself. He arrives in the first page 'by a commodius vicus of recirculation'. The first page of *Finnegans Wake* is modelled on the

---

[5] R. Ellmann, *James Joyce* (rev. edn., New York: Oxford University Press, 1982), 340.

[6] *Letters of James Joyce*, ed. R. Ellmann, vol. iii (New York: Viking Press, 1966), 117–18.

[7] Ellmann, *James Joyce*, 693.

[8] J. Joyce, *Finnegans Wake* (London: Faber and Faber, 1939). Hereafter cited in the text by page number.

first page of Vico's *Autobiography*. Finnegan, the giant of the human race, falls on his head from a ladder, his fall issuing in the hundred-letter thunder word Joyce coins, and which recurs in various spellings throughout the work. The parents, 'Eve and Adam', are introduced in the first sentence.

At one point in *Finnegans Wake* Vico is introduced by name, 'the producer (Mr John Baptister Vickar)' (255); in the schoolday section appears 'Old Vico Roundpoint' (260), next to which is the marginal comment 'IMAGINABLE ITINERARY THROUGH THE PARTICULAR UNIVERSAL', a reference to Vico's conception of heroes as 'imaginative universals'. The Vichian giant, Finnegan, is reborn as the modern family man, 'Harold or Humphrey Chimpden' Earwicker (30) or H.C.E., 'Here Comes Everybody!' Vico, Vickar, Earwicker, the modern family man, the virtuous pagan who yet has an ear for the ancient thunder through which his ancestors, the 'Chimpden', like the children of the human race, or giants, experienced the thunderburst as Jove, and became humans. Joyce turns Vico himself into one of his own imaginative universals. Finnegan is '*fine* again'—like Vico's own name, *vicus*, the road that goes round and round Vico's point. *Finnegans Wake* in a sense becomes Vico's wake.

Seen in this way, it is not only a rewriting of the *New Science*, it is the story of Vico, who is reborn along with Finnegan in his fall on the first page. No more complicated a commentary is likely to be written on Vico, who in Joyce's hands becomes himself the symbol for the complete speech of the human world. I do not mean that Joyce intends his work as simply a commentary on Vico. Joyce did what he wished with all books at the wake. But Joyce's work stands as an ingenious commentary on Vico. Other than such possibilities with Joyce there seems to be no clearly identifiable effect of Vico's autobiography on other works of literature or autobiography.[9]

An autobiography is certainly a form of knowledge. It is a knowledge that the self makes of the self, and in this way it is an instance of Vico's principle of *verum ipsum factum*, a type of knowing that is not possible for the subject or knower to have of the object, but only of itself. Autobiography is also based on Vico's

---

[9] Another use of Vico as a literary theme is J. L. Borges, 'The Immortal', in D. A. Yates and J. E. Irby, eds., *Labyrinths* (New York: New Directions, 1962).

principle of *certum est pars veri*, in that we are told the story of a particular life, but a life so told embodies human universals. It is itself a kind of particularized universal.

Any autobiography is a rational document in the sense that it is open to reason, and it is a product of reason in the sense that reason is the faculty that typifies the human. But autobiography is an act of the intellect only to the degree that the intellect can form itself in terms of memory. Autobiographical knowledge is the subject's memorial ordering of itself. Vico, in a line in the *New Science* which much interested Joyce, says 'memory is the same as imagination' (*la memoria è la stessa che la fantasia*) (819).[10] The image and the structuring of images into an order is the natural language of memory. To imagine or to make what is true through the formative powers of the imagination (*fantasia*) is not the creation of novelty. It is, instead, the counter to 'forgetting'; that is, the tendency to live in the present apart from any course of awareness that runs back to the origin. Forgetting works away at the subject's life and at cultural memory, continually threatening to leave us living only in the present without the past, without a sense of the connection of the present to our own origins, or worse, to be constantly fascinated with the future.

In Vico's view autobiographical knowledge is imaginative in form. The wholeness of the self and the wholeness of culture are always in some way presupposed in order than any form of knowing can take place. Autobiography is an articulation of this whole that the knower presumes in any act of knowing. In this sense autobiography always involves a metaphysics of the self as an analogue to the traditional conception of a metaphysics of the whole of experience. The intellect, although neither memory nor imagination, enters into autobiographical thinking in terms of the 'causes both natural and moral'. The images of the self that are narrated, and narrated perhaps around a central image, must be intellectually satisfying. Connections within what is remembered must be perceived with *ingegno* and attain an intellectual validity when expressed as part of the coherence of the subject's life story.

In Vico's view autobiography is not simply introspection, nor is it reflective knowledge in the sense of critical understanding of the

---

[10] Joyce told his friend, Frank Budgen, 'Imagination is memory' (Ellmann, *James Joyce*, 661 n.). Among the last words in *Finnegans Wake* is 'mememormee!'

connections between concepts and phenomena. Autobiographical thinking, in Vico's view, is *speculative* or, to put it in his own terms, it is meditative-narrative thinking. In this kind of knowing the knower repeats or 'imitates' in language the actions of his own being until the knower holds that he has attained the true *speculum* of himself. The autobiographer's task of self-knowledge is complete when he judges to have placed, within the theatre of the world, the theatre of himself.

His complete speech, never fully complete because it cannot include the fact of his own death, has as its constant aim this act of self-recognition. Autobiography is self-recognition. In this act the author has made the truth of himself by imitating his own reality in language—his linguistic double. The motivation for this form of knowledge is the knower's awareness of his own mortality, whether it be in the Roman sense of immortalizing his own name, the Greek philosophers' sense of learning to die, the modern man's sense of setting the record straight against his detractors, or all of these.

I would point to one final thing that Vico's conception of the world of 'civil things' and his own life as part of that world suggests about the nature of philosophical autobiography and the philosopher's natural interest in self-knowledge. In terms of Vico's vision every human event has its own narration that is appropriate to it. Each thing has a life lived out in terms of beginning, middle and end, which in Vico's terms of ideal eternal history means that it has a divine moment of origin in which its potentialities exist in their fullest reality, and that this solidifies into the moment of heroic achievement when the creative forces of its origin are most focused and mature.

Past this zenith the event becomes problematic for itself. What lies ahead is the dispersal of the *fantasia* of its origin and the concentration of its power in its heroic moment. The event enters a phase wherein its momentum may succumb to forces from without, and it is at the same time threatened from within by things that were not properly accounted for in its origin and not allowed their proper development. In the end this human reality will come apart and will cease to have its unity. It will end in its death. From the perspective of Vico's thought we can say with Socrates that the profession of philosophers is to learn to die. It is a melancholic wisdom, but why should we have expected otherwise?

Autobiography, then, is a species of moral philosophy. Morals has its origin in literature, in the transformation of the Greek myths, with their sense of tragic flaw, into the plays of the Greek theatre and into the questions of Socrates. The theatre of the world, on to the stage of which both Descartes, in his comic mask, and Vico, in his melancholic mask, step forth is a play of morals or customs. Philosophy is our guide in the human world as Virgil is Dante's guide in the script of the divine comedy.

The point of this threefold cycle at which narration can and frequently does enter is just past the moment of heroic achievement, just after its heroism is realized. Now the heroism must be recorded and understood as connected to its origin in order to stand against the external conditions that are forces to barbarize it, to make it into an abstraction of thought instead of a reality of action and deed. This is the Homeric moment; it was Homer who summed up the age of heroes in the first *corso* of Western life. Homer, the first narrator of the heroic, represents the moment of narration that is there in all events and in all human lives. The Vichian sense of the human event involves a sense of when narration is possible and appropriate.

I have said that I think that the motive for the writing of autobiography, at least the kind I have been describing, is the author's dissatisfaction with the world. He must proclaim what is rightfully his to the world which has not truly recognized it, or which has in fact abused him. This claim cannot be meaningfully made until the author has accomplished the heroic moment, has made his great discovery or great achievement. This is the turning-point at which he can narrate his own genesis for the world to see.

Vico's Venice text of 1728 ends with his description of the publication of the *First New Science*. His continuation of 1731 reaffirms this with a description of the publication of the *Second New Science*. True to his principles, Vico discusses as his theme the external forces that now exist in a barbaric ring around this achievement. He forecasts his own death, saying, through the quotation of Phaedrus, how he will regard it: once the new science had been achieved there was nothing left to do.

Bibliography

I. EDITIONS OF VICO'S AUTOBIOGRAPHY

Original title:
Vita di Giambattista Vico scritta da se medesimo (Life of Giambattista
Vico written by himself). The title given to the work by Vico; written in
1725–8 and continued in 1731.

First publication:
Raccolta d'opuscoli scientifici e filologici, vol. i, ed. Angelo Calogerà
(Venice: Cristoforo Zane, 1728), pp. 145–256. First publication of Vico's
1725–8 manuscript, including a catalogue of his writings. Corresponds to
parts A and B of the Fisch and Bergin English translation. Vico's text was
published as one of several studies in the first number of this journal.

First full publication:
Opuscoli di Giambattista Vico, vol. i, ed. Villarosa (Naples: Porcelli,
1818), *Vita*, pp. 1–231. Republication of the 1728 text of Venice with
Vico's continuation of 1731, left in manuscript at his death. Includes
Villarosa's addition on 'Vico's Last Years'. Part of a four-volume edition
of Vico's 'minor works' by the Marquis of Villarosa.

A nineteenth-century edition:
Raccolta di vite e memorie d'uomini illustri scritte da loro medesimi (2
vols. in 1, Milan: Sonzogno, 1821). Vol. i contains the autobiographies of
the first-century Jewish historian Flavius Josephus, Vico, and the early
modern Italian poet Gabriello Chiabrera. Vol. ii is the autobiography of
the Renaissance physician and philosopher Gerolamo Cardano. It reprints
only Vico's Venice text of 1728. This edition enjoyed a wide circulation;
copies of it remain in a number of libraries, including the Gabinetto
Scientifico Letterario G. P. Vieusseux in Florence and the British Library.

The Laterza edition:
L'autobiografia, il carteggio e le poesie varie, ed. B. Croce and F. Nicolini
(2nd rev. edn., Bari: Laterza, 1929; orig. pub. 1911). Vol. v of the
standard edition of Vico's works: *Opere di G. B. Vico* (8 vols. in 11, Bari:
Laterza, 1911–41). The first critical edition of Vico's autobiography and
the basis of all subsequent editions; reprints the 1728 catalogue of Vico's
writings and contains substantial annotations to Vico's text.

Fubini's and other Italian editions:
Autobiografia, seguita da una scelta di lettere, orazioni e rime, ed. Mario
Fubini (2nd edn., Turin: Einaudi, 1965, with subsequent reprintings; orig.

pub. 1947). One of the most widely available editions of Vico's autobiography; follows the text of the Laterza edition. Vico's autobiography is included in the early editions of Vico's collected works: the Ferrari (1852–4) and the Pomodoro (1858–69). Vico's autobiography has been reprinted in many modern editions and included in many anthologies of his works. Among these are those edited by V. F. Cassano (1941), E. Paci (1952), N. Abbagnano (1952), E. De Falco (1954), P. Rossi (1959), M. F. Sciacca (1969), P. Cristofolini (1971), R. Parenti (1972), and P. Soccio (1983). Notable is Nicolini's one-volume *Opere* (Milan: Ricciardi, 1953) which includes Vico's autobiography with extensive notes, some of which add to those of the earlier Laterza edition. There is also Nicolini's particular edition of the *Autobiografia* (Milan: Bompiani, 1947) containing fourteen 'medaglioni illustrativi', his own sketches of each phase of Vico's career.

The Fisch and Bergin English translation:
The Autobiography of Giambattista Vico, trans. Max Harold Fisch and Thomas Goddard Bergin (Ithaca, NY: Cornell University Press, 1983; orig. pub. 1944). The only, but extremely reliable, English translation; includes Fisch's valuable introduction, notes, and chronological table. Follows the 1929 Laterza edition of Croce and Nicolini.

Pons's French translation:
Vie de Giambattista Vico écrite par lui-même, trans. Alain Pons (Paris: Grasset, 1981). Especially useful for its introduction and notes. There is an earlier French translation by J. Chaix-Ruy (1943) and Michelet's *Œuvres choisies de Vico* (1835) contains a translation of the autobiography.

Other translations:
There is a nineteenth-century German translation of the 1728 Venice text of Vico's autobiography which is part of W. E. Weber's translation of the *Scienza nuova* (1822); more recently there is *Autobiographie, mit einer Einführung in Vicos philosophische Bedeutung* by V. Rüfner (Zurich: Occident, 1948).

Translations into other languages include: Russian (abridged) (1940), Spanish (Buenos Aires) (1970), Polish (1971), Romanian (1972), Chinese (1985), and Japanese (1990).

II. SOME WORKS ON AND BY VICO RELEVANT TO HIS AUTOBIOGRAPHY

The standard guide to critical literature on Vico is the revised edition of Croce and Nicolini's *Bibliografia vichiana* (2 vols., Naples: Ricciardi, 1947–8) and its updatings by M. Donzelli (Naples: Guida, 1973) and

A. Battistini (Naples: Guida, 1983). Also relevant are the issues of the *Bollettino del Centro di Studi Vichiani*, 1971–. For English-language publications in particular see G. Tagliacozzo, D. P. Verene, and V. Rumble, *A Bibliography of Vico in English (1884–1984)* (Bowling Green, Ohio: Philosophy Documentation Center, 1985) and its supplements in *New Vico Studies*, 1985–.

The works listed below were specifically consulted in the preparation of this volume. Not all works related to Vico cited in the footnotes appear here, e.g. some studies of the period, of Naples, and works of general culture and philosophy. Under 'Vico' are listed those writings of particular importance for themes in this study. For each of these I have indicated whether an English translation or partial translation exists.

ABBAGNANO, N., Introduction to *La scienza nuova e altri scritti di Giambattista Vico*, ed. N. Abbagnano (Turin: Unione Tipografico-Editrice Torinese, 1976).

ADAMS, H. P., *The Life and Writings of Giambattista Vico* (London: Allen and Unwin, 1935).

AGRIMI, M. 'Presenza di Vico nella cultura veneziana del primo settecento (La "politicità" del *De ratione*)', in C. De Michelis and G. Pizzamiglio, eds., *Vico e Venezia* (Florence: Olschki, 1982).

—— 'La formazione di Vico e l'Accademia di Medinaceli', in M. Agrimi, *Ricerche e discussioni vichiane* (Rome: Itinerari, 1984).

ALTAMURA, A., 'Giambattista Vico, "Homo Neapolitanus"', *Forum Italicum*, 2 (1968), 494–502.

AMERIO, F., *Introduzione allo studio di G. B. Vico* (Turin: Società editrice internazionale, 1947).

BADALONI, N., *Introduzione a G. B. Vico* (Milan: Feltrinelli, 1961).

—— Introductions to *Opere filosofiche* and *Opere giuridiche*, ed. with translations of the Latin texts by P. Cristofolini (Florence: Sansoni, 1971 and 1974).

—— 'La cultura', in *Storia d'Italia*, vol. iii: *Dal primo Settecento all'Unità* (Milan: Einaudi, 1973).

BATTISTINI, A., 'Il traslato autobiografico', in *La degnità della retorica: Studi su G. B. Vico* (Pisa: Pacini, 1975).

—— 'L'autobiografia e i modelli narrativi settecenteschi', in P. Giannantonio, ed., *Cultura meridionale e letteratura italiana: I modelli narrativi dell'età moderna* (Naples: Loffredo, 1985).

BEDANI, G. L. C., 'A Neglected Problem in Contemporary Vico Studies: Intellectual Freedom and Religious Constraints in Vico's Naples', *New Vico Studies*, 4 (1986), 57–72.

—— *Vico Revisited: Orthodoxy, Naturalism and Science in the 'Scienza Nuova'* (Oxford: Berg; New York: St Martin's Press, 1989).

BELAVAL, Y., 'Vico and Anti-Cartesianism', in G. Tagliacozzo and H. V. White, eds., *Giambattista Vico: An International Symposium* (Baltimore: Johns Hopkins University Press, 1969).

BERLIN, I., *Vico and Herder: Two Studies in the History of Ideas* (New York: Viking, 1976).

BORGES, J. L., 'The Immortal', in D. A. Yates and J. E. Irby, eds., *Labyrinths* (New York: New Directions, 1962).

BURKE, P., *Vico* (Oxford: Oxford University Press, 1985).

CANTELLI, G., *Mente corpo linguaggio: Saggio sull'interpretazione vichiana del mito* (Florence: Sansoni, 1986).

CARPANETTO, D., and RICUPERATI, G., 'The *veteres* against the *moderni*: Paolo Mattia Doria (1662–1746) and Giambattista Vico (1668–1744)', *Italy in the Age of Reason 1685–1789*, trans. C. Higgitt (London: Longman, 1987), ch. 7.

CASSIRER, E., 'Descartes, Leibniz, and Vico', in D. P. Verene, ed., *Symbol, Myth, and Culture: Essays and Lectures of Ernst Cassirer 1935–1945* (New Haven, Conn.: Yale University Press, 1979).

CHAIX-RUY, J., *La Formation de la pensée philosophique de G.-B. Vico* (Gap: L. Jean, 1943).

—— *J.–B. Vico et illuminisme athée* (Paris: Editions Mondiales, 1968).

CORSANO, A. *Umanesimo e religione in G. B. Vico* (Bari: Laterza, 1935).

—— *G. B. Vico* (Bari: Laterza, 1956).

COSPITO, A., 'Intorno all'*Autobiografia* di G. B. Vico', *Sophia*, 31 (1953), 115–18.

COSTA, G., 'An Enduring Venetian Accomplishment: The Autobiography of G. B. Vico', *Italian Quarterly*, 21 (1980), 45–54.

—— 'La posizione di Vico nella storia dell'autobiografismo europeo', *Bollettino del Centro di Studi Vichiani*, 10 (1980), 143–6.

COTTINO-JONES, M., 'L'*autobiografia* vichiana: Il rapporto vita-scrittura', in C. De Michelis and G. Pizzamiglio, eds., *Vico e Venezia* (Florence: Olschki, 1982).

COTUGNO, R., *La sorte di Giovan Battista Vico* (Bari: Laterza, 1914).

CROCE, B., *La filosofia di Giambattista Vico* (Bari: Laterza, 1962; orig. pub. 1911), trans. R. G. Collingwood, *The Philosophy of Giambattista Vico* (New York: Russell and Russell, 1964; orig. pub. 1913).

—— 'On the Life and Character of G. B. Vico', *The Philosophy of Giambattista Vico*, Appendix 1, trans. R. G. Collingwood (New York: Russell and Russell, 1964; orig. pub. 1913).

—— 'Giambattista Vico e la famiglia Rocca', in *Nuove curiosità storiche* (Naples: Ricciardi, 1922).

D'AMARO, A. V. A., *L'adamantina rocca di G. B. Vico* (Naples: Loffredo, 1986).

DAUS, H.-J., *Selbstverständnis und Menschenbild in den Selbstdarstellungen Giambattista Vicos und Pietro Giannones: Ein Beitrag zur Geschichte der italienischen Autobiographie* (Geneva: Droz, 1962).

DE FALCO, E., *La biografia di G. B. Vico* (Rome: Crianna, 1968).

DE MAS, E., 'Vico's Four Authors', in G. Tagliacozzo and H. V. White, eds., *Giambattista Vico: An International Symposium* (Baltimore: Johns Hopkins University Press, 1969).

—— 'On the New Method of a New Science: A Study of Giambattista Vico', *Journal of the History of Ideas*, 32 (1971), 85–94.

—— 'Vico e la cultura veneta', in C. De Michelis and G. Pizzamiglio, eds., *Vico e Venezia* (Florence: Olschki, 1982).

DE MICHELIS, C., 'L'autobiografia intellettuale e il "progetto" di Giovanartico di Porcìa', in C. De Michelis and G. Pizzamiglio, eds., *Vico e Venezia* (Florence: Olschki, 1982).

DE SANTILLANA, G., 'Vico and Descartes', *Osiris*, 21 (1950), 565–80.

DONATI, B., *Nuovi studi sulla filosofia civile di G. B. Vico* (Florence: Le Monnier, 1936).

DONZELLI, M., *Natura e humanitas nel giovane Vico* (Naples: Istituto italiano per gli studi storici, 1970).

ENGELL, J., 'Leading Out Into the World: Vico's New Education', *New Vico Studies*, 3 (1985), 33–47.

FABBRI, M. DEL S., 'Eredità e kenosi tematica della "confessio" cristiana negli scritti autobiografici di Vico', *Sapienza*, 33 (1980), 186–99.

FAÇON, N., 'Sur la vie passionée de Jean-Baptiste Vico', *Archives de Philosophie*, 40 (1977), 127–37.

FASSÒ, G., *I 'quattro autori' del Vico: Saggio sulla genesi della 'Scienza nuova'* (Milan: Giuffrè, 1949).

—— *Vico e Grozio* (Naples: Guida, 1971).

—— 'The Problem of Law and the Historical Origin of the *New Science*', in G. Tagliacozzo and D. P. Verene, eds., *Giambattista Vico's Science of Humanity* (Baltimore: Johns Hopkins University Press, 1976).

FAUCCI, D., 'Vico and Grotius: Jurisconsults of Mankind', in G. Tagliacozzo and H. V. White, eds., *Giambattista Vico: An International Symposium* (Baltimore: Johns Hopkins University Press, 1969).

FINETTI, G. F., *Difesa dell'autorità della sacra scrittura: Contro G. B. Vico* (Bari: Laterza, 1936; orig. pub. 1768).

FISCH, M. H., 'Vico on Roman Law', in M. R. Konvitz and A. E. Murphy, eds., *Essays on Political Theory: Presented to George H. Sabine* (Ithaca, NY: Cornell University Press, 1948).

—— 'The Academy of the Investigators', in E. A. Underwood, ed., *Science Medicine, and History: Essays on the Evolution of Scientific Thought and Medical Practice Written in Honour of Charles Singer*, vol. i (2 vols., London: Oxford University Press, 1953).

FISCH, M. H., 'Vico and Pragmatism', in G. Tagliacozzo and H. V. White, eds., *Giambattista Vico: An International Symposium* (Baltimore: Johns Hopkins University Press, 1969).

—— 'Vico's *Pratica*', in G. Tagliacozzo and D. P. Verene, eds., *Giambattista Vico's Science of Humanity* (Baltimore: Johns Hopkins University Press, 1976).

—— Introduction to *The Autobiography of Giambattista Vico*, trans. M. H. Fisch and T. G. Bergin (Ithaca, NY: Cornell University Press, 1983; orig. pub. 1944).

FLINT, R., *Vico* (Edinburgh and London: Blackwood, 1884).

FUBINI, M., review of Vico's *L'autobiografia*, ed. F. Nicolini (Milan: Bompiani, 1947), *Giornale storico della letteratura italiana*, 127 (1950), 203–14.

—— *Stile e umanità di Giambattista Vico* (2nd edn., Naples: Ricciardi, 1965; orig. pub. 1946).

—— Introduction to *Autobiografia, seguita da una scelta di lettere, orazioni e rime*, 2nd edn., ed. M. Fubini (Turin: Einaudi, 1970).

GALASSO, G., 'G. B. Vico nella cultura napoletana', in *Storia di Napoli*, vol. vi, pt. 1 (Naples: Società editrice Storia di Napoli, 1970).

—— 'Napoli ai tempi del Vico', in *Giambattista Vico nel terzo centenario della nascita* (Naples: Edizioni scientifiche italiane, 1971).

GARDINER-JANIK, L., 'A Renaissance Quarrel: The Origin of Vico's Anti-Cartesianism', *New Vico Studies*, 1 (1983), 39–50.

GARIN, E., 'Cartesio e l'Italia', *Giornale critico della filosofia italiana*, 4 (1950), 385–405.

—— 'A proposito del rapporto fra Vico e Rousseau', *Bollettino del Centro di Studi Vichiani*, 2 (1972), 61–3.

—— 'Vico and the Heritage of Renaissance Thought', in G. Tagliacozzo, ed., *Vico: Past and Present* (Atlantic Highlands, NJ: Humanities Press, 1979).

GASPARDO, P. G., and PIZZAMIGLIO, G., 'La pubblicazione dell'autobiografia vichiana nella corrispondenza di Giovan Artico di Porcìa con il Muratori e il Vallisnieri', in C. De Michelis and G. Pizzamiglio, eds., *Vico e Venezia* (Florence: Olschki, 1982).

GENTILE, G., 'Il figlio di G. B. Vico e gl'inizi dell'insegnamento di letteratura italiana nella Università di Napoli', in *Studi vichiani* (2nd rev. edn., Florence: Le Monnier, 1927).

GIANTURCO, E., 'Character, Essence, Origin and Content of the *Jus Gentium* According to Vico and Suárez', *Revue de littérature comparée*, 10 (1936), 167–72.

—— 'Vico's Significance in the History of Legal Thought', in G. Tagliacozzo and H. V. White, eds., *Giambattista Vico: An International Symposium* (Baltimore: Johns Hopkins University Press, 1969).

GIANTURCO, E., Introduction to *On the Study Methods of Our Time*, trans. E. Gianturco, reissued with a preface by D. P. Verene (Ithaca, NY: Cornell University Press, 1990; orig. pub. 1965).

GIARIZZO, G., *Vico, la politica e la storia* (Naples: Guida, 1983).

GIORDANO, P., *Vico filosofo del suo tempo* (Padua: CEDAM, 1974).

GRASSI, E., 'Critical Philosophy or Topical Philosophy? Meditations on the *De nostri temporis studiorum ratione*', in G. Tagliacozzo and H. V. White, eds., *Giambattista Vico: An International Symposium* (Baltimore: Johns Hopkins University Press, 1969).

—— *Rhetoric as Philosophy: The Humanist Tradition* (University Park, Pa.: Pennsylvania State University Press, 1980).

—— *Vico and Humanism: Essays on Vico, Heidegger, and Rhetoric* (New York: Peter Lang, 1990).

GUERRIERI, G., ed., *Mostra bibliografica e documentaria: Catalogo* (Naples: L'arte Tipografica, 1968).

HADDOCK, B. A., *Vico's Political Thought* (Swansea: Mortlake Press, 1986).

HESSE, M. B., 'Vico's Heroic Metaphor', in R. S. Woolhouse, ed., *Metaphysics and Philosophy of Science in the Seventeenth and Eighteenth Centuries* (Dordrecht: Kluwer, 1988).

JACOBELLI ISOLDI, A. M., *G. B. Vico: La vita e le opere* (Bologna: Cappelli, 1960).

—— 'The Role of the Intellectual in Giambattista Vico', in G. Tagliacozzo and D. P. Verene, eds., *Giambattista Vico's Science of Humanity* (Baltimore: Johns Hopkins University Press, 1976).

KELLEY, D. R., 'Vico's Road: From Philology to Jurisprudence and Back', in G. Tagliacozzo and D. P. Verene, eds., *Giambattista Vico's Science of Humanity* (Baltimore: Johns Hopkins University Press, 1976).

—— 'Vico and Gaianism: Perspective on a Paradigm', in G. Tagliacozzo, ed., *Vico: Past and Present* (2 vols. in 1, Atlantic Highlands, NJ: Humanities Press, 1981).

KUNZE, D. E., *Thought and Place: The Architecture of Eternal Places in the Philosophy of Giambattista Vico* (New York: Peter Lang, 1987).

LANZA, F., 'Linguaggio barocco e filosofia vichiana', in *Saggi di poetica vichiana* (Varese: Magenta, 1961).

LAURO, A., 'Vico, Nicolò Capasso e Vincenzo d'Ippolito', *Bollettino del Centro di Studi Vichiani*, 2 (1972), 65–9.

LEVINE, J. M., 'Collingwood, Vico and the *Autobiography*', *Clio*, 9 (1980), 379–92.

LOVEKIN, D., 'Giambattista Vico and Jacques Ellul: The Intelligible Universal and the Technical Phenomenon', *Man and World*, 15 (1982), 407–16.

MAKKREEL, R. A., 'Vico and Some Kantian Reflections on Historical Judgment', in G. Tagliacozzo, ed., *Vico: Past and Present* (2 vols. in 1, Atlantic Highlands, NJ: Humanities Press, 1981).

MATHIEU, V., 'Truth as the Mother of History', in G. Tagliacozzo and D. P. Verene, eds., *Giambattista Vico's Science of Humanity* (Baltimore: Johns Hopkins University Press, 1976).

MICHELET, J., 'Vico', in *Biographie universelle ancienne et moderne*, vol. xliii (new edn., 45 vols., Paris and Leipzig: Desplaces and Brockhaus, 1854–65).

MODICA, G., *La filosofia del 'senso comune' in Giambattista Vico* (Caltanissetta: Sciascia, 1983).

MOONEY, M., *Vico in the Tradition of Rhetoric* (Princeton, NJ: Princeton University Press, 1985).

NICOLINI, F., *Per la biografia di Giambattista Vico*, extracts from *Archivio storico italiano*, 2 parts (Florence: Olschki, 1925–6).

—— *Giambattista Vico nella vita domestica: la moglie, i figli, la casa* (Naples: Ricciardi, 1927); repr. without archival extracts in Giambattista Vico, *Opere*, ed. F. Nicolini (Milan: Ricciardi, 1953).

—— 'La teoria del linguaggio in Giambattista Vico e Giangiacomo Rousseau', *Revue de littérature comparée*, 10 (1930), 292–8.

—— *La giovinezza di Giambattista Vico (1668–1700): Saggio biografico* (2nd rev. edn., Bari: Laterza, 1932).

—— 'Di alcuni amici e conoscenti di Giambattista Vico', in *Atti della reale accademia pontaniana di scienze morali e politiche* (Naples, 1941).

—— *Uomini di spada, di chiesa, di toga, di studio ai tempi di Giambattista Vico* (Milan: Hoepli, 1942).

—— 'Medaglioni illustrativi', in *Autobiografia di Giambattista Vico*, ed. F. Nicolini (Milan: Bompiani, 1947).

—— *La religiosità di Giambattista Vico: Quattro saggi* (Bari: Laterza, 1949).

—— Introduction and notes to Giambattista Vico, *Opere*, ed. F. Nicolini (Milan: Ricciardi, 1953).

—— *Saggi vichiani* (Naples: Giannini, 1955).

—— *Vico storico*, ed. F. Tessitore (Naples: Morano, 1967).

O'NEILL, J., 'Vico on the Natural Workings of the Mind', *Phenomenology and the Human Sciences*, supplement to *Philosophical Topics*, 12 (1981), 117–25.

PETERS, R., 'Aurelius Augustinus und Giambattista Vico', *Geist und Gesellschaft*, 3 (1928), 1–37.

POMPA, L., *Vico: A Study of the 'New Science'* (Cambridge: Cambridge University Press, 1975; 2nd edn., 1990).

PONS, A., 'Prudence and Providence: The *Pratica della Scienza nuova* and the Problem of Theory and Practice in Vico', in G. Tagliacozzo and

D. P. Verene, eds., *Giambattista Vico's Science of Humanity* (Baltimore: Johns Hopkins University Press, 1976).

—— Introduction to *Vie de Giambattista Vico écrite par lui-même; Lettres; La méthode des études de notre temps*, ed. A. Pons (Paris: Grasset, 1981).

RAK, M., *Letture vichiana* (Naples: Liguori, 1971).

—— 'Vico in "Tel Quel"', *Bollettino del Centro di Studi Vichiani*, 1 (1971), 53–7.

RIGHI, G., ed., *Il pensiero del Vico nella sua continuità*, vol. i: *La preparazione e meditazione giovanile*, published from a manuscript of Antonio Bernardini (Bologna: Tipografia militare già delle scienze, 1931).

ROSSI, P., *Le sterminate antichità: Studi vichiani* (Pisa: Nistri-Lischi, 1969).

SAID, E., 'Vico: Autodidact and Humanist', *Centennial Review*, 11 (1967), 336–52.

—— *Beginnings: Intention and Method* (New York: Basic Books, 1975).

SCHAEFFER, J. D., *Sensus Communis: Vico, Rhetoric, and the Limits of Relativism* (Durham, NC: Duke University Press, 1990).

SCIACCA, G. M., 'Vico e le filosofie del suo tempo', *Nuovi Quaderni del meridione*, 6 (June 1968), 11–34.

SEMERARI, G., 'Intorno all'anticartesianesimo di Vico', in *Omaggio a Vico* (Naples: Morano, 1968).

SINA, M., *Vico e Le Clerc: Tra filosofia e filologia* (Naples: Guida, 1978).

SORRENTINO, A., *La retorica e la poetica di Vico* (Turin: Bocca, 1927).

STONE, H., 'Vico and Doria: The Beginnings of Their Friendship', *New Vico Studies*, 2 (1984), 83–91.

STRUEVER, N. S., 'Vico, Valla, and the Logic of Humanist Inquiry', in G. Tagliacozzo and D. P. Verene, eds., *Giambattista Vico's Science of Humanity* (Baltimore: Johns Hopkins University Press, 1976).

—— 'Vico, Foucault, and the Strategy of Intimate Investigation', *New Vico Studies*, 2 (1984), 41–70.

TAGLIACOZZO, G., 'Epilogue', in G. Tagliacozzo and H. V. White, eds., *An International Symposium* (Baltimore: Johns Hopkins University Press, 1969).

—— 'Toward a History of Recent Anglo-American Vico Scholarship,' series in five parts, *New Vico Studies*, 1–5 (1983–7).

VASOLI, C., 'Vico sul "metodo"', in E. Riverso, ed., *Leggere Vico* (Milan: Spirali, 1982).

—— 'Note sul "metodo" e la "struttura" della *Scienza nuova prima*', *Bollettino del Centro di Studi Vichiani*, 24–5 (1984–5), 21–37.

VAUGHAN, F., *The Political Philosophy of Giambattista Vico: An Introduction to 'La Scienza Nuova'* (The Hague: Nijhoff, 1972).

VERENE, D. P., *Vico's Science of Imagination* (Ithaca, NY: Cornell University Press, 1981).

—— 'The New Art of Narration: Vico and the Muses,' *New Vico Studies*, 1 (1983), 21–38.

—— 'Vico as Reader of Joyce', in D. P. Verene, ed., *Vico and Joyce* (Albany, NY: State University of New York Press, 1987).

VERRI, A., 'Vico e Rousseau filosofi del linguaggio', *Bollettino del Centro di Studi Vichiani*, 4 (1974), 83–104.

—— 'Vico, Rousseau e Venezia', in C. De Michelis and G. Pizzamiglio, eds., *Vico e Venezia* (Florence: Olschki, 1982).

VICO, G. B., *Opere di G. B. Vico* (8 vols. in 11, Bari: Laterza, 1911–41).

—— 'Affeti di un disperato' (1692), in *Opere*, vol. v; trans. H. P. Adams, *The Life and Writings of Giambattista Vico* (London: Allen and Unwin, 1935), 223–6, and T. G. Bergin, *Forum Italicum*, 2 (1968), 305–9.

—— Six Inaugural Orations (1699–1707), in *Opere*, vol. i, trans. G. A. Pinton (privately issued, 1988).

—— *De nostri temporis studiorum ratione* (1709), in *Opere*, vol. i; trans. E. Gianturco as *On the Study Methods of Our Time*, reissued with a preface by D. P. Verene (Ithaca, NY: Cornell University Press, 1990); orig. pub. 1965).

—— *De antiquissima Italorum sapientia ex linguae latinae originibus eruenda* (1710) and *Risposte* (1711–12), in *Opere*, vol. i; trans. L. M. Palmer as *On the Most Ancient Wisdom of the Italians Unearthed from the Origins of the Latin Language*, including the Disputation with the *Giornale de' letterati d'Italia* (Ithaca, NY: Cornell University Press, 1988).

—— *Il diritto universale* (1720–2), in *Opere*, vol. ii; consists of *Sinopsi del diritto universale* (1720), *De universi iuris uno principio et fine uno liber unus* (1720), *De constantia iurisprudentis liber alter* (1721), *Notae in duos libros* (1722).

—— *Scienza nuova prima* (1725), in *Opere*, vol. iii; partial trans. by Leon Pompa, *Vico: Selected Writings* (Cambridge: Cambridge University Press, 1982), which also contains partial translations of *De studiorum ratione*, *De Italorum sapientia*, and *Scienza nuova seconda*.

—— Letter to Father Bernardo Maria Giacco (25 Oct. 1725), in *Opere*, vol. v; trans. M. H. Fisch in the Introduction to M. H. Fisch and T. G. Bergin, *The Autobiography of Giambattista Vico* (Ithaca, NY: Cornell University Press, 1983; orig. pub. 1944).

—— *Vita di Giambattista Vico scritta da se medesimo* (1728 and 1731), in *Opere*, vol. v; trans. M. H. Fisch and T. G. Bergin as *The Autobiography of Giambattista Vico* (Ithaca, NY: Cornell University Press, 1983; orig. pub. 1944).

—— Letter to Abbot Giuseppe Luigi Esperti (1726), in *Opere*, vol. v.

Vico, G. B., Letter to Father Eduardo de Vitry (20 Jan. 1726), in *Opere*, vol. v.

—— Letter to Francesco Saverio Estevan (12 Jan. 1729), in *Opere*, vol. v.

—— 'Discoverta del vero Dante' (1728 or 1729), in *Opere*, vol. vii; trans. I. Brandeis as 'Discovery of the True Dante', in I. Brandeis, ed., *Discussions of the Divine Comedy* (Boston: Heath, 1961).

—— *Vici vindiciae* (1729), in *Opere*, vol. iii; partial trans. by A. Illiano, J. D. Tedder, and P. Treves as 'A Factual Digression on Human Genius, Sharp Witty Remarks, and Laughter' [sect. 16: 'De humano ingenio, acute arguteque dictis et de risu e re nata digressio'], *Forum Italicum*, 2 (1968), 310–14.

—— *Scienza nuova seconda* (1730, 1744), in *Opere*, vol. iv; trans. T. G. Bergin and M. H. Fisch as *The New Science of Giambattista Vico* (Ithaca, NY: Cornell University Press, 1984; orig. pub. 1948).

—— 'Pratica della scienza nuova' (1731), paras. 1405–11 of *Correzioni, miglioramenti e aggiunte terze* to the *Scienza nuova seconda*, in *Opere*, vol. iv; trans. T. G. Bergin and M. H. Fisch as 'Practic of the New Science', in G. Tagliacozzo and D. P. Verene, eds., *Giambattista Vico's Science of Humanity* (Baltimore: Johns Hopkins University Press, 1976); repr. in the paperback edition of *The New Science of Giambattista Vico* (Ithaca, NY: Cornell University Press, 1984).

—— 'Riprensione delle metafisiche di Renato delle Carte, di Benedetto Spinosa e di Giovanni Locke' (1731), paras, 1212–17 of *Correzioni, miglioramenti e aggiunte terze* to the *Scienza nuova seconda*, in *Opere*, vol. iv; trans. D. P. Verene as 'Reprehension of the Metaphysics of René Descartes, Benedict Spinoza, and John Locke', *New Vico Studies*, 8 (1990), 2–18.

—— *De mente heroica* (1732), in *Opere*, vol. vii; trans. by E. Sewell and A. C. Sirignano as 'On the Heroic Mind', in G. Tagliacozzo, M. Mooney, and D. P. Verene, eds., *Vico and Contemporary Thought* (Atlantic Highlands, NJ: Humanities Press, 1979).

—— 'Le accademie e i rapporti tra la filosofia e l'eloquenza' (1737), in *Opere*, vol. vii; trans. D. P. Verene as 'The Academies and the Relation between Philosophy and Eloquence', in *On the Study Methods of Our Time*, trans. E. Gianturco, reissued with a preface by D. P. Verene (Ithaca, NY: Cornell University Press, 1990; orig. pub. 1965).

Vismara, S., 'Vita e pensiero del Vico nella sua autobiografia', in P. A. Gemelli, ed., *G. B. Vico, volume commemorativo nel secondo centenario della pubblicazione della 'Scienza nuova' (1725–1925)* (Milan: Società Editrice 'Vita e Pensiero', 1926).

Werner, K., *Giambattista Vico als Philosoph und gelehrter Forscher* (New York: Burt Franklin, 1962; repr. of orig. edn., Vienna, 1879).

III. SOME AUTOBIOGRAPHIES AND WORKS ON AUTOBIOGRAPHY

The list below includes all critical studies on autobiography cited in footnotes and others specifically consulted in the preparation of this volume. It does not list all critical literature in general that is cited, e.g. some studies on Descartes cited in Chapter 3. It attempts to list most ancient 'lives' and modern 'autobiographies' worth special attention in considering the significance of Vico's autobiography in the general history of intellectual autobiography, including autobiographical works by figures in modern and contemporary philosophy. These autobiographies are mentioned or discussed at various places in the text, especially in Chapter 2.

ABELARD, P., *The Story of Abelard's Adversities: A Translation with Notes of the Historia Calamitatum*, ed. J. T. Muckle (Toronto: Pontifical Institute of Medieval Studies, 1964).

ADAMS, G. P., and MONTAGUE, W. P., eds., *Contemporary American Philosophy: Personal Statements* (2 vols., New York: Macmillan, 1930).

AUGUSTINUS, A. *St Augustine's Confessions*, with an English trans. by W. Watts, ed. W. H. D. Rouse (Loeb Classical Library, 2 vols., Cambridge, Mass.: Harvard University Press; London: Heinemann, 1977–9).

AYER, A. J., *Part of My Life* (London: Collins, 1977).

—— *More of My Life* (London: Collins, 1984).

BARTHES, R., 'To Write: An Intransitive Verb?', in R. Macksey and E. Donato, eds., *The Structuralist Controversy: The Languages of Criticism and the Sciences of Man* (Baltimore: Johns Hopkins University Press, 1972).

BATTISTINI, A., *Lo specchio di Dedalo: Autobiografia e biografia* (Bologna: Mulino, 1990).

BERDYAEV, N., *Dream and Reality: An Essay in Autobiography*, trans. K. Lampert (London: Bles, 1950).

BRUSS, E. W., *Autobiograhical Acts: The Changing Situation of a Literary Genre* (Baltimore: Johns Hopkins University Press, 1976).

BUCK, A., 'Das Lebensgefühl der Renaissance im Spiegel der Selbstdarstellungen Petrarcas und Cardanos', in G. Reichenkorn and E. Haase, eds., *Formen der Selbstdarstellungen: Analekten zu einer Geschichte des literarischen Selbstporträts. Festgabe für Fritz Neubert* (Berlin: Duncker and Humblot, 1956).

BURR, A. R., *The Autobiography: A Critical and Comparative Study* (Boston: Houghton Mifflin, 1909).

BUTLER, LORD R., *The Difficult Art of Autobiography* (Oxford: Clarendon Press, 1968).

CAMERON, J. M., 'Autobiography and Philosophical Perplexity', in E. Schaper, ed., *Pleasure, Preference and Value: Studies in Philosophical Aesthetics* (Cambridge: Cambridge University Press, 1983).

CARDANO, G. (Jerome Cardan), *The Book of My Life*, trans. J. Stoner (London: Dent and Sons, 1931).

—— (Hieronymus Cardanus), *De vita propria liber*, in *Opera omnia*, vol. i, ed. A. Buck (facsimile edn. of the Lyon edn. of 1663; Stuttgart: Frommann, 1966).

CELLINI, B., *The Life of Benvenuto Cellini Written by Himself*, trans. J. Addington Symonds (2 vols., New York: Brentano, 1906).

CHIABRERA, G., 'Vita di Gabriello Chiabrera scritta da lui medesimo', in *Canzonette, rime varie, dialoghi di Gabriello Chiabrera*, ed. L. Negri (Turin: Unione Tipografico-Editrice Torinese, 1952).

CICERO, *Letters to Atticus*, with an English trans. by E. O. Winstedt (Loeb Classical Library, 3 vols., London: Heinemann; New York: Macmillan, 1912–18).

CLARK, A. M., *Autobiography: Its Genesis and Phases* (Edinburgh: Oliver and Boyd, 1935).

COCKSHUT, A. O. J., *The Art of Autobiography in Nineteenth and Twentieth Century England* (New Haven, Conn.: Yale University Press, 1984).

COLLINGWOOD, R. G., *An Autobiography* (London: Oxford University Press, 1939).

COURCELLE, P., *Les Confessions de Saint-Augustin dans la tradition littéraire: antécédents et postérité* (Paris: Études Augustiniennes, 1963).

COX, P., *Biography in Late Antiquity: A Quest for the Holy Man* (Berkeley, Calif.: University of California Press, 1983).

CRANSTON, M., *Jean-Jacques: The Early Life and Work of Jean-Jacques Rousseau 1712–1754* (New York: Norton, 1983).

CROCE, B., *An Autobiography*, trans. R. G. Collingwood (Oxford: Clarendon Press, 1927).

—— *Memorie della mia vita*, ed. Istituto italiano per gli studi storici (Naples, 1966).

CURTIN, J. C., 'Autobiography and the Dialectic of Consciousness', *International Philosophical Quarterly*, 14 (1974), 343–6.

DANTE, *Vita nuova*, ed. D. De Robertis (Milan: Ricciardi, 1980).

DERRIDA, J., *Otobiographies, l'enseignement de Nietzsche et la politique du nom propre* (Paris: Gallilée, 1984).

—— 'Roundtable on Autobiography', in C. V. McDonald, ed., *The Ear of the Other: Otobiography, Transference, Translation* (New York: Shocken Books, 1985).

DESCARTES, R., 'Balzac à Descartes (Paris, 30 mars 1628)', in *Œuvres de Descartes*, vol. i: *Correspondance*, ed. C. Adam and P. Tannery (Paris: Cerf, 1897).

—— *Cogitationes privatae*, in *Œuvres de Descartes*, vol. x, ed. C. Adam and P. Tannery (Paris: Cerf, 1908).

DESCARTES, R., *Discours de la méthode*, chronology and preface by G. Rodis-Lewis (Paris: Garnier-Flammarion, 1966).

DILTHEY, W., *Entwürfe zur Kritik der historischen Vernunft*, in *Gesammelte Schriften*, vol. vii: *Der Aufbau der geschichtlichen Welt in den Geisteswissenschaften* (Stuttgart: Teubner; Göttingen: Vandenhoeck and Ruprecht, 1979).

EAKIN, P. J., *Fictions in Autobiography: Studies in the Art of Self-Invention* (Princeton, NJ: Princeton University Press, 1985).

EARLE, W., *The Autobiographical Consciousness* (Chicago: Quadrangle Books, 1972).

EGAN, S., *Patterns of Experience in Autobiography* (Chapel Hill, NC: University of North Carolina Press, 1984).

ELBAZ, R., *The Changing Nature of the Self: A Critical Study of the Autobiographic Discourse* (Iowa City, Ia.: University of Iowa Press, 1987).

ELIADE, M., *No Souvenirs: Journal 1957–1969*, trans. F. H. Johnson, Jr. (London and Henley: Routledge and Kegan Paul, 1978).

—— *Autobiography*, vol. i, trans. M. L. Ricketts (New York: Harper and Row, 1981).

FINDLAY, J. N., 'My Life: 1903–1973', in R. S. Cohen, R. M. Martin, and M. Westphal, eds., *Studies in the Philosophy of J. N. Findlay* (Albany, NY: State University of New York Press, 1985).

FIRPO, L., MASOERO, M., ZACCARIA, G., eds., *Autobiografie di filosofi: Cardano, Bruno, Campanella* (Turin: Giappichelli, 1982).

FLEISHMAN, A., *Figures of Autobiography: The Language of Self-Writing in Victorian and Modern England* (Berkeley, Calif.: University of California Press, 1983).

FORTI-LEWIS, A., *Italia autobiografica* (Rome: Bulzoni, 1986).

FOUCAULT, M., 'What is an Author?', trans. J. Venit, *Partisan Review*, 42 (1975), 603–14.

FRANKLIN, B., *The Autobiography of Benjamin Franklin*, ed. L. W. Labree *et al* (New Haven, Conn.: Yale University Press, 1964).

FREUD, S., *An Autobiographical Study*, in *The Standard Edition of the Complete Psychological Works of Sigmund Freud*, vol. xx, trans. and ed. J. Strachey (London: Hogarth Press and the Institute of Psycho-Analysis, 1959).

GIANNONE, P., *Vita*, in *Opere di Pietro Giannone*, ed. S. Bertelli and G. Ricuperati (Milan: Ricciardi, 1971).

GIBBON, E., *The Autobiography of Edward Gibbon*, ed. D. A. Saunders (New York: Meridian Books, 1961).

GOETHE, J. W. VON, *The Autobiography*, trans. J. Oxenford (Chicago: University of Chicago Press, 1974).

GREENE, D., 'The Uses of Autobiography in the Eighteenth Century', in P. B. Daghlian, ed., *Essays in Eighteenth-Century Biography* (Blooming-ton, Ind.: University of Indiana Press, 1968).

GUICCIARDINI, F., *Maxims and Reflections of a Renaissance Statesman* (*Ricordi*), trans. M. Domandi (New York: Harper Torchbooks, 1965).

GUNN, J. V., *Autobiography: Toward a Poetics of Experience* (Philadelphia: University of Pennsylvania Press, 1982).

GUSDORF, G., *La découverte de soi* (Paris: Presses Universitaires de France, 1948).

—— 'Conditions and Limits of Autobiography', trans. J. Olney, in J. Olney, ed., *Autobiography: Essays Theoretical and Critical* (Princeton, NJ: Princeton University Press, 1980).

HART, F. R., 'Notes for an Anatomy of Modern Autobiography', *New Literary History*, 1 (1970), 485–511.

HARTLE, A., *The Modern Self in Rousseau's Confessions: A Reply to St. Augustine* (Notre Dame, Ind.: University of Notre Dame Press, 1983).

—— *Death and the Disinterested Spectator: An Inquiry into the Nature of Philosophy* (Albany, NY: State University of New York Press, 1986).

HERBERT of CHERBURY, LORD, *The Life of Edward, First Lord Herbert of Cherbury Written by Himself*, ed. J. M. Shuttleworth (London: Oxford University Press, 1976).

HOBBES, T., *Vita*, in *Opera philosophica*, vol. i, ed. G. Molesworth (5 vols., London: Bohn, 1839–45).

HOWARTH, W. L., 'Some Principles of Autobiography', in J. Olney, ed., *Autobiography: Essays Theoretical and Critical* (Princeton, NJ: Princeton University Press, 1980).

HUME, D. *The Life of David Hume Esq. Written by Himself* (London: W. Strahan, 1777).

IJSEWIJN, J., 'Humanistic Autobiography', in E. Hora and E. Kessler, eds., *Studia Humanitatis: Ernesto Grassi zum 70. Geburtstag* (Munich: Fink, 1973).

JOSEPHUS, F., *Bios*, in *Josephus*, vol. i, with an English trans. by H. St J. Thackeray (Loeb Classical Library, Cambridge, Mass.: Harvard University Press; London: Heinemann, 1926).

KAZIN, A., 'Autobiography as Narrative', *Michigan Quarterly Review*, 3 (1964), 210–16.

KESSLER, E., 'Autobiographie als philosophisches Argument? Ein Aspekt des Philosophierens bei Cicero und die gegenwärtige Praxis der Philosophie', in E. Hora and E. Kessler, eds., *Studia Humanitatis: Ernesto Grassi zum 70. Geburtstag* (Munich: Fink, 1973).

KIERKEGAARD, S., *Autobiographical, Søren Kierkegaard's Journals and Papers*, vols. v and vi, ed. H. V. Hong and E. H. Hong (Bloomington, Ind.: Indiana University Press, 1978).

LACHTERMAN, D. R., 'Descartes and the Philosophy of History', *Independent Journal of Philosophy*, 4 (1983), 31–46.

LEIBNIZ, G. W. F., 'Leibniz an Bourguet (22 mars 1714)', in *Die philosophischen Schriften von G. W. Leibniz*, vol. iii, ed. C. J. Gerhardt (Hildesheim: Olms, 1960; orig. pub. 1887).

LEJEUNE, P., *Le Pacte autobiographique* (Paris: Éditions du Seuil, 1975).

—— 'Autobiography in the Third Person', *New Literary History*, 9 (1977), 27–50.

—— *On Autobiography*, ed. P. J. Eakin, trans. K. Leary (Minneapolis: University of Minnesota Press, 1989).

LLOYD, G., 'The Self as Fiction: Philosophy and Autobiography', *Philosophy and Literature*, 10 (1986), 168–85.

MANDEL, B. J., 'The Autobiographer's Art', *Journal of Aesthetics and Art Criticism*, 27 (1968), 215–26.

MARTELLO, P. J., 'Vita di Pier Jacopo Martello scritta da lui stesso fino l'anno 1718 e consegrata al signor Giovanartico Conte di Porcìa, secondo il di lui progetto', *Raccolta d'opuscoli scientifici e filologici*, vol. ii (Venice: Cristoforo Zane, 1729), 273–92.

MAUROIS, A., *Aspects of Biography*, trans. S. C. Roberts (New York: Appleton, 1929).

MAY, G., *L'Autobiographie* (2nd edn., Paris: Presses Universitaires de France, 1984; orig. pub. 1979).

MEHLMAN, J., *A Structural Study of Autobiography: Proust, Leiris, Sartre, Lévi-Strauss* (Ithaca, NY: Cornell University Press, 1974).

MILL, J. S., *Autobiography*, in *Collected Works of John Stuart Mill*, vol. i: *Autobiography and Literary Essays*, ed. J. M. Robson and J. Stillinger (Toronto: University of Toronto Press, 1981).

MISCH, G., *Geschichte der Autobiographie*, vol. i (3rd edn. Bern: Francke, 1949–50; orig. pub. 1907), vols. ii–iv (Frankfurt-on-Main: Schulte-Bulmke, 1955–69).

—— *A History of Autobiography in Antiquity*, trans. E. W. Dickes (2 vols., Cambridge, Mass.: Harvard University Press, 1951).

MOMIGLIANO, A., *The Development of Greek Biography* (Cambridge, Mass.: Harvard University Press, 1971).

—— *Second Thoughts on Greek Biography*, lecture text of 14 June 1971, 'Nieuwe Reeks', NS 34: 7 (Amsterdam: North Holland Publishing Co., 1971).

MONTAIGNE, M. DE, *The Complete Essays of Montaigne*, trans. D. M. Frame (Stanford, Calif.: Stanford University Press, 1958).

—— *Les essais de Michel de Montaigne*, ed. P. Villey (Paris: Presses Universitaires de France, 1965).

MUIRHEAD, J. H., ed., *Contemporary British Philosophy: Personal Statements* (3 vols., New York: Macmillan, 1924).

MURATORI, I. A., *Intorno al metodo seguito ne' suoi studi: Lettera all'illustrissimo signore Giovanni Artico Conte di Porcìa*, in *Opere di L. A. Muratori*, vol. i, ed. G. Falco and F. Forti (Milan: Ricciardi, 1964).

NEUMANN, B., *Identität und Rollenzwang: Zur theorie der Autobiographie* (Frankfurt-on-Main: Athenäum, 1970).

NIETZSCHE, F., *Ecce Homo: How One Becomes What One Is*, trans. R. J. Hollingdale (Harmondsworth, Middlesex: Penguin, 1979).

NORTH, R., 'General Prcface' [eighteenth-century theory of the nature of biography], in R. North, *General Preface and Life of Dr John North*, ed. P. Millard (Toronto: University of Toronto Press, 1984).

O'CONNELL, R., *Saint Augustine's Confessions: The Odyssey of a Soul* (Cambridge, Mass.: The Belknap Press of Harvard University Press, 1969).

OLNEY, J., *Metaphors of Self: The Meaning of Autobiography* (Princeton, NJ: Princeton University Press, 1972).

—— ed., *Autobiography: Essays Theoretical and Critical* (Princeton, NJ: Princeton University Press, 1980).

—— ed., *Studies in Autobiography* (New York: Oxford University Press, 1988).

OTTO, S., 'Zum Desiderat einer Kritik der historischen Vernunft und zur Theorie der Autobiographie', in E. Hora and E. Kessler, eds., *Studia Humanitatis: Ernesto Grassi zum 70. Geburtstag* (Munich: Fink, 1973).

OVID, *Tristia*, with an English trans. by A. L. Wheeler (Loeb Classical Library, London: Heinemann, 1924).

PASCAL, R., *Design and Truth in Autobiography* (London: Routledge and Kegan Paul, 1960).

PETRARCA, F., *Epistola ad posteros*, in *Prose*, ed. G. Martellotti (Milan: Ricciardi, 1955).

—— *Epistle to Posterity*, in *Letters from Petrarch*, selected and trans. M. Bishop (Bloomington, Ind.: Indiana University Press, 1966).

PILLING, J., *Autobiography and Imagination: Studies in Self-Scrutiny* (London: Routledge and Kegan Paul, 1981).

PLINY (the Younger), *Pliny: A Self-Portrait in Letters*, trans. B. Radice (London: The Folio Society, 1978).

POPKIN, R. H., 'Intellectual Autobiography: Warts and All', in R. A. Watson and J. E. Force, eds., *The Sceptical Mode in Modern Philosophy* (Dordrecht: Martinus Nijhoff, 1988).

PORCÌA, COUNT G. A. DI, 'Progetto ai letterati d'Italia per scrivere le loro Vite', *Raccolta d'opuscoli scientifici e filologici*, 1 (1728), 127–43.

PRINI, P. 'Autobiografia, storia del mondo e escatologia', *Archivio di Filosofia*, 2 (1971), 81–6.

QUINE, W. V., *The Time of My Life: An Autobiography* (Cambridge, Mass.: MIT Press, 1985).

R E S C H E R, N., *Mid-Journey: An Unfinished Autobiography* (Washington, DC: University Press of America, 1983).

R I C O E U R, P., *Time and Narrative*, vol. i, trans. K. McLaughlin and D. Pellauer (Chicago: University of Chicago Press, 1984).

R O B I N S O N, P., 'Jean-Jacques Rousseau and the Autobiographical Dimension', *Journal of European Studies*, 8 (1978), 77–92.

R O U S S E A U, J.-J., *Les Confessions et autre textes autobiographiques*, *Œuvres complètes*, vol. i, ed. B. Gagnebin, M. Raymond *et al.* (Paris: Pleïade, 1959).

—— *The Confessions*, trans. J. M. Cohen (London: Penguin, 1988).

R U B I N, D. C., ed., *Autobiographical Memory* (Cambridge: Cambridge University Press, 1986).

R U S S E L L, B., *My Philosophical Development* (London: Allen and Unwin, 1959).

—— *Autobiography of Bertrand Russell* (3 vols., London: Allen and Unwin, 1967–9).

R Y C R O F T, C., 'On Autobiography', in P. Fuller, ed., *Psychoanalysis and Beyond* (London: Hogarth, 1985).

S A N T A Y A N A, G., *Persons and Places: Fragments of Autobiography*, critical edn., ed. W. G. Holzberger and H. J. Saatkamp, Jr., *The Works of George Santayana*, vol. i (Cambridge, Mass.: MIT Press, 1986).

S A R T R E, J.-P., *Les Mots* (Paris: Gallimard, 1964).

S C H I L P P, P. A., ed.: see the autobiographical essays in the various volumes of *The Library of Living Philosophers* beginning with that of John Dewey. Published by the Library of Living Philosophers, Inc., in connection with various publishers from 1939 to the present. Recent volumes coedited by Lewis Edwin Hahn.

S H U M A K E R, W., *English Autobiography: Its Emergence, Materials and Forms* (University of California English Studies, 8; Berkeley, Calif.: University of California Press, 1954).

S I M P S O N, D., 'Putting One's House in Order: The Career of the Self in Descartes' Method', *New Literary History*, 9 (1977), 83–101.

S P E N C E R, H., *An Autobiography* (London: Williams and Norgate, 1904).

S P E N D E R, S., 'Confessions and Autobiography', in J. Olney, ed., *Autobiography: Essays Theoretical and Critical* (Princeton, NJ: Princeton University Press, 1980).

S P E N G E M A N N, W. C., *The Forms of Autobiography: Episodes in the History of a Literary Genre* (New Haven, Conn.: Yale University Press, 1980).

S P R I N K E R, M., 'Fictions of the Self: The End of Autobiography', in J. Olney, ed., *Autobiography: Essays Theoretical and Critical* (Princeton, NJ: Princeton University Press, 1980).

STAROBINSKI, J., 'The Style of Autobiography', in S. Chatman, ed., *Literary Style: A Symposium* (London: Oxford University Press, 1971).

STAROBINSKI, J., *Jean-Jacques Rousseau: La Transparence et l'obstacle, suivi de sept essais sur Rousseau* (Paris: Gallimard, 1971).

STULL, H. I., *The Evolution of the Autobiography from 1770–1850: A Comparative Study and Analysis* (New York: Peter Lang, 1985).

TERESA OF AVILA, *The Life of St Teresa of Avila Including the Relations of Her Spiritual State Written by Herself*, trans. D. Lewis (London: Burns and Oates, 1962).

VANCE, E., 'Augustine's *Confessions* and the Grammar of Selfhood', *Genre*, 6 (1973), 1–28.

—— *Mervelous signals: Poetics and Sign Theory in the Middle Ages* (Lincoln, Nebr.: University of Nebraska Press, 1986).

WARNOCK, M., *Memory* (London: Faber and Faber, 1987).

WEINTRAUB, K. J., 'Autobiography and Historical Consciousness', *Critical Inquiry*, 1 (1975), 821–48.

—— *The Value of the Individual: Self and Circumstance in Autobiography* (Chicago: University of Chicago Press, 1978).

WEST, A. F., *Roman Autobiography* (New York: De Vinne Press, 1901).

WILLIAMS, H., *Rousseau and Romantic Autobiography* (Oxford: Oxford University Press, 1983).

WUTHENOW, R.-R., *Das erinnerte Ich: Europäische Autobiographie und Selbstdarstellung im 18. Jahrhundert* (Munich: Beck, 1974).

ZIMMERMAN, T. C. P., 'Confessions and Autobiography in the Early Renaissance', in A. Molho and J. A. Tedeschi, eds., *Renaissance Studies in Honor of Hans Baron* (Florence: Sansoni, 1971).

Index